D1103156

Hold Tight

[Black Masculinity, Millennials
and the Meaning of Grime]

by Jeffrey Boakye

Influx Press, London

Published by Influx Press

5a Wayland Avenue, London, E8 2HP

www.influxpress.com / @InfluxPress

First published 2017.

Printed and bound in the UK by Clays Ltd., St Ives plc.

ISBN: 978-19103122-5-4

Edited by Kit Caless

Proofreader: Danny Arter

Cover art and design: Dan Evans

For my wife, Sophie, and our first son, Finlay.

Bars

Black music, like always, paved way for the mainstream like hallways. And the verdict, like court days, can be hung like a jury split four ways. Which genre, from the old days, contributes most? Gave the most play? Case in point – Grime's DNA: double helixed long before it was named. It goes back to the clash, back to the get-money streets and the cash. Back to the champagne dance and the flats and the top-floor pirates pulling back wax. Back to the jungle, back to the chat, back to the tape on the stereo stack and we can't overstate the fact that Jamaica's a major part of the narrative track. Brrap.

Early traits were harnessed: Talking the loudest, talking the hardest, talking the fastest, talk from the margins, MC styles flourishing like gardens after a season of seeds were planted.

What came first? What came after? Who what why when how whereafter? What was the question if Grime was the answer? Young black boys with ancient fathers, family trees with distant branches, sisters, olders, mothers, aunts and whole generations all took part in the crafting of something big from the start. Black UK: the diaspora was large. Large as a continent with all the confidence to spread wildfire after a spark.

Brand new but we always knew. Doors kicked open and sauntered through. Who's that became the who's who; who knew what a 2-Step rhythm could do to the market? Bars got parallel parked like cars from MCs far from the charts, if you're asking what made Grime get started, look to the history, look to the past. Look to pavement, from the ground up, where the soundboys of London turned the sound up. Lyrics for lyrics turned the crowd up and UKG just got them wound up. Frustrated, had to go make it. Matrix downloaded the bass kicks. Syncopated, Rinse'll play this even if a champagne rave can't take it.

Now, with a context to bear. A whole new problem for Anthony Blair. Young black people who lived over there in the places containing the least of the share. Not much money and not much care being taken by those who were starting to fear; a newfound voice from a new generation, part deprivation and part cavalier. Brave enough for the violence, louder than silence, too defiant for neat compliance. Stereotypes always need defying; sharing a mic couldn't be more pliant. Grime's not an ASBO soundtrack. Even though there's an ASBO around that, depiction of youth delinquency that they gave to black masculinity in its infancy, that was said to be loud, aggressive beyond aesthetically.

By the time you got to '03, I guess you could say it was always meant to be. Meant to be found, meant to be violent meant to be loud. Meant to be quirky, meant to be different, meant to be hard to define in an instant. What do you call it? What does it sound like? Hard to describe in an audio soundbite. Hard to describe for wide-eyed journalists who had not, could not have heard of this... Genre, culture, scene? Lifestyle for mic-bound teens? And here we're starting to see it emerge from the margins; freed. Seen.

Tracklist

'Amen, Brother' - The Winstons (1969)

'Under Mi Sleng Teng' - Wayne Smith (1985)

'Retreat' - Cutty Ranks (1991)

'How's Life in London' - London Posse (1993)

'Incredible' - M-Beat featuring General Levy (1994)

'Gangsta Kid' - Shy FX featuring Gunsmoke (1994)

'Tri-Fusion' - Dylan Beale (1994)

'Original Nuttah' - Shy FX featuring UK Apache (1994)

'Never Gonna Let You Go' - Tina Moore (1997)

'Moschino' - Glamma Kid (1997)

'Know We' - Pay As U Go Cartel (2000)

'21 Seconds' - So Solid Crew (2001)

'Boom Selection' - Genius Cru (2001)

'Has It Come To This?' - The Streets (2001)

'Pulse X' - Musical Mob (2002)

'Creeper' - Danny Weed (2002)

'Oi!' - More Fire Crew (2002)

'The Heartless Theme' - Heartless Crew (2002)

'Seems 2 Be' - Dizzee Rascal (2003)

'I Can C U' - Crazy Titch (2003)

'I Luv U' - Shystie (2003)

'Functions on the Low' - XTC (2004)

'Wot Do U Call It?' - Wiley (2004)

'Destruction VIP' - Jammer feat. Wiley, Kano, D Double E, Durrty Goodz (2004)

'Pow!' - Lethal B feat. D Double E, Demon, Flow Dan, Forcer, Fumin, Jamaka B, Nappa, Neeko, Ozzie B (2004)

'Do They Know It's Christmas' - Band Aid 20 (2004)

'Orchestra Boroughs' - Mr Wong featuring Crazy Titch, Jme, Flirta D (2004)

'P's and Q's' - Kano (2005)

'Extra Extra' - Devlin (2006)

'Serious' - Jme (2006)

'Talkin' da Hardest' - Giggs (2007)

'Black Boys' - Bashy (2007)

'Rhythm 'n' Gash' - Rebound X (2007)

'Wearing My Rolex' - Wiley (2008)

'Dance Wiv Me' - Dizzee Rascal featuring Calvin Harris and Chrome (2008)

'Too Many Man' - Boy Better Know (2009)

'Next Hype' - Tempa T (2009)

'Disguise' - Boy Better Know (2009)

'Pass Out' - Tinie Tempah (2010)

'Streetfighter Riddim' - D Double E (2010)

'Hello Good Morning Grime Remix' - Diddy Dirty Money featuring Skepta (2010)

'All Over The House' – Skepta (2011)

'Castles' - Skepta (2012)

'ill Manors' - Plan B (2012)

'All Hallows' - CASisDEAD (2013)

'The Cypher' - Ghetts featuring Ghetto and J. Clarke (2013)

'Don't Waste My Time' - Krept and Konan (2013)

'German Whip' - Meridian Dan (2014)

'Shutdown' - Skepta (2015)

'Netflix and Pills' - Nolay (2015)

'Dem Boy Paigon' - J Hus (2015)

'Endz' - Novelist (2015)

'Wickedskengman 4' - Stormzy (2015)

'Coward' – Chip (2015)

'And Dat' - Bonkaz featuring Stormzy (2016)

'10 Missed Calls' - Dread D and Jammz (2016)

'Queen's Speech 4' - Lady Leshurr (2016)

'Thiago Silva' – AJ Tracey and Santan Dave (2016)

'Gunfingers' – P Money featuring Jme and Wiley (2016)

'It's a London Thing' - Jammz featuring Scott Garcia (2016)

'Can't Go Wrong' – Wiley (2017)

Hold Tight

[Black Masculinity, Millennials
and the Meaning of Grime]

by Jeffrey Boakye

Influx Press, London

'Amen, Brother'
The Winstons (1969)

In the month of September, in the year 2006, a man died. The man died on the streets of Atlanta, Georgia, USA. He had very little money and no home. During his life the man did many things, including drumming in various bands. In the year 1969 he drummed on a song with a band called The Winstons. The man spent one hundred and fifty-three seconds drumming throughout this song. For six of these seconds, he was drumming unaccompanied by any other instrument. This is known as a drum break. The song is called 'Amen, Brother'. The drum break in 'Amen, Brother' is known as the 'Amen Break'. The man who drummed the Amen Break is, was, Gregory Sylvester Coleman.

You have heard the Amen Break. You have heard it hundreds, if not thousands of times. You have heard it so often that you do not recognise it as a distinct part of a distinct song. 'Amen, Brother' was recorded and pressed onto vinyl, a material that has been used to mass produce audio recordings in the latter half of the 20th Century. The Amen Break has since been sampled thousands of times, in thousands of songs. Slowed down, it became a staple part of much 'Golden Era' US hip hop of the late '80s and early '90s. Sped up, it formed the backbone of many dance music sub-genres in the UK, most notably Breakbeat, Jungle and Drum and Bass. The Amen Break is deeply entwined in the DNA of modern dance music.

Grime, in its lineage, is inextricably linked to the Amen Break. The conflation of Dancehall/Ragga soundclash culture with Amen-bred breakbeat sparked a revolution in UK dance music that spidered off into Jungle and eventually Grime, via Dubstep, IDM, Breakcore and many others. A suitably long sentence for such a far-reaching sonic evolution.

Any book about Grime has to mention the Amen Break, because it is instrumental to genres of electronic dance music that Grime branches from. So even though you'll struggle to find a Grime track that explicitly features the Amen Break, this book had to start with Gregory Sylvester Coleman. It'd be rude not to, hence my little eulogy three paragraphs ago. And now the beginning's out of the way, we can begin, again.

'Under Mi Sleng Teng'
Wayne Smith (1985)

Some of this is really simple, and some of this is really rather complicated.

Simple:

In 1981, Casio released the model MT-40 electronic keyboard. The MT-40 included, among its very exciting suite of digital features, a 'Rock' preset. The 'Rock' preset comprised a repetitive bass riff of an addictively crunchy digitally synthetic quality.

Simple:

In 1985, three years after its discontinuation, an MT-40 found its way into the possession of a young man called Noel Davey, in Jamaica. Noel Davey was an aspiring musician who couldn't quite afford the Yamaha DX-7, a more advanced digital synthesiser that unfortunately also came with a more advanced price tag.

Complicated:

Noel Davey began a creative partnership with a young reggae vocalist called Wayne Smith. Wayne Smith lived very close to a reggae producer called Lloyd James, also known as Prince Jammy. Prince Jammy had collaborated with Wayne Smith on close to two albums' worth of original material since 1981, at which time Smith was 14 years old.

Simple:

Lloyd James' moniker would soon evolve from Prince Jammy to King Jammy, probably as a result of his prolific work and subsequent accolades within the Reggae scene. It's worth noting that Jammy himself had worked closely with a sound engineer called Osbourne Ruddock, who went by the charming title of King Tubby. King Tubby is largely recognised as a pioneering figure in electronic music production, who may or may not have invented the concept of the remix. In light of what was to come, this may actually be Complicated.

Simple:

The song that Noel Davey and Wayne Smith presented to

King Jammy was built entirely out of the Casio MT-40 'Rock' preset. Lyrically, the central conceit of the song was that marijuana is a preferable drug to cocaine, both of which come with a significant health warning. 'Under Mi Sleng Teng' is a patois expression referring to being under the influence. It followed a mini trend of 'Under Me. . . ' songs including 'Under Mi Sensi' by Barrington Levi. Upon hearing Smith and Davey's work, King Jammy slowed everything down a notch and added some percussion and piano. 'Under Mi Sleng Teng' was born.

Simple:
The song was a hit.

Complicated:
'Under Mi Sleng Teng' had an immediate and devastating impact on Reggae music production. It marked something of a digital revolution in Reggae, shifting production away from live instrumentation to this new, electronic, computerised style. The 'Sleng Teng Riddim', as it would come to be known, unfurled into the very central nervous system of Reggae. Hundreds of artists would go on to use the riddim, evolving a rugged electronic aesthetic that would flourish into modern Dancehall. The keyboard and computer became key components of Reggae production.

The implications on electronic music in general were huge. As the '80s slid further and further into digitised music production, Reggae producers found themselves in a position to make professional riddims using a relatively inexpensive setup. 'Sleng Teng', much like the Amen Break, helped make music production accessible and replicable. It's crazy to think it, but a preset on a mid-range Casio keyboard actually changed the face of modern dance music, forever.

Simple:
The MT-40 'Rock' preset was created by a young woman called Hiroko Okuda, who joined Casio in 1980. The MT-40 was her first project at the company.

Simple:
Okuda studied Musicology at the Kunitachi College of Music in Tokyo. She was a big fan of music.

Simple:
The MT-40 'Rock' preset was inspired by a song.

Complicated:
No-one knows precisely which song Okuda was inspired by. One version of modern musical folklore says it was 'Somethin' Else' by Eddie Cochran (1959). Another says it

was 'Anarchy in the UK' by the Sex Pistols (1976). A third (and this is the one you'll find on Wikipedia) says it was 'Hang On to Yourself' by David Bowie (1971).

Really complicated:
It turns out that Hiroko Okuda was really into Reggae. I mean, enough to have written her thesis about it while studying at Kunitachi.

'I guess there was something reggae-like about the [Sleng Teng] rhythm. I recall being touched by the fact that what I had been listening to every day seemed to show in the product.' – Hiroko Okuda, 'How Casio Accidentally Started Reggae's Digital Revolution', interview with *Engadget*

As James Trew of *Engadget* rightly suggests, this introduces an element of chicken and egg to the whole situation. Did a Reggae sound subliminally infiltrate Okuda's 'Rock' preset, to be later discovered by forward-thinking Reggae producers? Did Reggae give birth to 'Sleng Teng'? Or did 'Sleng Teng' birth a new Reggae?

Simple:
Grime owes a conceptual debt to 'Sleng Teng', not only symbolically (as a genre of music born of democratised, lo-fi

digital production), but also in heritage (as a branch of the electronic reggae that Wayne Smith popularised in the early '80s). By eliminating the need for session musicians and live instrumentation, 'Sleng Teng' introduced a rougher edge to Reggae that would come to characterise it and its later incarnations. Grime, like Jungle, Drum and Bass, Ragga and Dancehall, is a child of 'Sleng Teng', part of a heritage of innovation and experimentation that transformed popular music in the 20th Century.

'Retreat'
Cutty Ranks (1991)

'Retreat' is all about metaphorically killing soundboys with guns, making it a pretty perfect exemplar of soundclash culture. For the record (and if you already know what a soundclash is, please skip ahead to the next paragraph), a soundclash is a kind of audio face-off between competing sound systems, during which music is played at volume in a bid to defeat the opposition, judged primarily on crowd reaction. You'll hear a lot about this sort of thing during the course of this book. Feel free to stop reading and go research the history of the soundclash. Google will provide you with ample results. Other search engines are available.

Out of the many, many gun-focused 'kill a soundbwoy' tracks I could have chosen to include here, it didn't take long for me to zero in on 'Retreat'. Conceptually it sits right in the middle of the metaphor, with Cutty Ranks patiently explaining that he will kill his rivals unless they retreat and surrender, and we get it – it's a figurative threat. But then he starts talking about actual guns and you realise that the riddim is moving on the pulse of a gunshot snare. He starts with an innocuous simile, asking inferior sound systems to pack up their sound like rubbish in a pan, before suddenly switching up to list various modes of firearm (the 16, the 'matic, the M1, the Remington...) before declaring that he will shoot the hand off a boy who tries anything.

The lines are blurred, competitive aggression being pushed as far as possible into the realm of real violence.

It's a recipe that hasn't changed in over two decades. A number of the songs featured in this book feature some element of gun talk and the implicit respect afforded to 'gunman' status continues to permeate the culture, right up until the present day. I have no idea if the current crop of Grimey soundboys are influenced indirectly or not by the Ragga boom of the early '90s but I know for a fact that soundclash culture is a big fish in the primordial soup that birthed Grime. Its on-the-sleeve aggression and murderous bravado is echoed heavily in contemporary MC culture, with patois-laden gun talk par for the course. In all seriousness, it's probably more difficult to find a Grime track that doesn't in some way allude to gun violence. It's a simple equation: Having a gun signals power, being willing to use that gun signals ruthlessness, and power and ruthlessness make for a fairly formidable combination.

At this point, we're in the pre-Grime, pre-Jungle realm of the very early 1990s. As we delve further ahead in years, the intersection of competitive confidence and violence will emerge as a key theme in underground black music. Grime, on a PR level, has suffered from this relationship, with steady accusations of glorifying and promoting violent acts (culminating in the notorious risk-assessment Form 696[1]). A quick rewind to the '90s, via Cutty Ranks and others, might help explain, if not clarify, the position of gun-related violence in a musical context. This is not to justify it, but to unpick the motivation behind – perhaps misunderstood – trigger-happy MCing.

---

1. More about this in the Grime: Demonised section of the appendix in this book.

'How's Life in London'
London Posse (1993)

"I do it in a rap style but in a Yardie accent, and I use my own cockney accent. I won't rap in an American accent or nuthin. It's what's keeping English people back."
- Bionic, the London Posse, early '90s.[1]

Watching Bionic calmly explain the above to Tim Westwood[2] in VHS-quality footage is like watching someone calmly explain the secrets of levitation. Feasible, maybe, but difficult, very.

Bionic and Rodney P, the two lyrical frontliners of the London Posse, are very British MCs. They fully embrace their Britishness and wear it with as much pride as their West Indianness, Londonness and blackness, rolling rhymes in broad cockney accents peppered with the post-Windrush West Indian lingo of London streets. Their flows might echo

US hip hop patterns of the time, but never at the expense of their other, more essential identities. Even now, I find myself doing a little audio Sudoku puzzle to establish exactly what I'm hearing when Bionic and Rodney P start chatting.

I was barely out of primary school when I first heard a London Posse record. It had honestly never occurred to me that rap could be delivered in anything other than an American accent. I'd heard Derek B in the '80s and assumed that was it – rappers from the same country I lived in had to put on a 'rap voice', which meant an American voice. The subsequent problems over authenticity were palpable, even to my pre-adolescent consciousness. UK rap felt mimicky and gimmicky, a shy pastiche of The Real Thing that came from Somewhere Else, Very Far Away. This is something that black Britons have struggled with in the ongoing popularisation of blackness in the mainstream consciousness: the shadow cast by black American success and subsequent pressures to echo African-Americanism.

For all the talk of it being an authentically, indelibly British artefact, Grime has bent to these pressures, as evidenced by the early era of fitted baseball caps, outsize Avirex jackets and Nike Air Force 1s. And in 2017, AJ Tracey, one of Grime's brightest rising stars, went transatlantic for the video 'Luke Cage', proving that the US maintains an authenticating appeal right up to Grime's present. North

America via urban East London.

To be black and British necessitates a conflation of different, often clashing identities. From experience, I can confirm the negative capability necessary to be black and English and Ghanaian and a Londoner and Afro-Caribbean and working-class and middle-class and postcolonial all at the same time. Crafting a persona out of this swirl is almost a conscious act of solipsism. We'll see later, with Glamma Kid's 'Moschino', how artists can choose to promote one identity above all others, but the London Posse did a far more difficult job, far earlier: they showcased all the facets of their personas without dilution, separation or compromise.

This might be the reason why listening to 'How's Life in London' is so electrifying. It sounds fresh and unique and impossibly smooth, steamrolling the peaks of clashing identities with charisma and assertiveness. The video is an exercise in poker-faced posturing, with Bionic, Rodney P and a pack of rudeboys glaring at the camera while scenes of urban strife play out in the background. The (then unlikely) sight of authentic UK rap gangsters is also alluded to in the video's opening, featuring a stiff-upper-lipped voice stating, "Welcome to London" followed by a quick pan to a portrait of the posse, framed in front of Big Ben. They welcome the novelty factor but are nothing less than serious.

"For me coming out with a UK accent, it was against the grain and wasn't accepted. We had to make big pushes for that to be accepted."

- Rodney P, the London Posse, early '90s[3]

Unlike UK hip hop of the late '80s and early '90s, Grime is actually allowed to be British, under little pressure to mimic any other, more dominant scene (apart from the Dancehall patois to which Grime is so heavily indebted). In this, MCs could learn a lot from the London Posse, who actively kicked back against pressures to conform to hip hop stereotypes. They crafted a London-centric aesthetic that was as convincing as it was awkward, proving that black boys in London could be successful on their own terms. They also placed themselves firmly in an international context, dropping references to (deep breath) Japan, Manhattan, Amsterdam, Jamaica, China, Harare, the Philippines, Spain, Norway, Australia and a spattering of London-specific locales. Phew.

With 'How's Life in London', Bionic and Rodney P blew through provincial limitations. Compared to the nervous territoriality of so many current soundboys, the London Posse sported a casual breeziness, globetrotting through verses with a playful back and forth and very British wit. Nowadays we're used to hearing MCs pull UK-specific punchlines but in '93, it was genuinely thrilling to hear things about eating packets of cheese and onion crisps on a *rap* record.

The London Posse took a stand on their identity with no blueprint to follow, making it feasible to be authentically what you are without adulteration. Grime MCs, pay your respect to originators of a stance.

---

1. London Posse 'mini documentary' by Joel Stagg, YouTube, watched by me in June 2016.

2. This is the first time Tim Westwood will get a name-check in this book. The next time will be in 2009. He deserves more than two footnotes, but there you go.

3. See first footnote: same again.

'Incredible'
M-Beat featuring General Levy (1994)

'Incredible' blew up in 1994, when its re-released, remixed version started getting major mainstream radio play and hit number eight in the Top 10 (back when the Top 10 meant quite a lot more than it means now). The significance of this cannot be overstated.

'Incredible' came into being at the cusp of a Jungle wave that had been building momentum in the underground for a number of years. Jungle, up until 1993/94, had been a dark sub-genre of electronic dance music borne of Dancehall and Amen Break beats. 'Dark' being the operative word. Like many underground genres, it was characterised by a brooding malevolence that gave it an anti-mainstream appeal.

An easy assumption to make is that 'Incredible', and its stellar success, represents that moment when an underground sound crosses over to the mainstream. It's essentially a pop song. It's danceable, it's fun, it replaces any sinister undertones with carnival exuberance, and it starts with the exclamation "Yo!", which is impossible to say without momentarily turning into a six-year-old sliding around on the kitchen floor.

Case in point: the BBC 1Xtra Sixty Minutes Live studio session of August 2014. Watch what happens to Jammer, Fekky, Jme, Dizzee Rascal, Lethal Bizzle, Tempa T, Footsie et al when MistaJam throws the 'Incredible' intro on. They turn right back into the wide-eyed pre-adolescent kids they were in 1994, and General Levy, spitting those classic bars, turns into a dreadlocked Father Christmas made real. It's a euphoric moment and encapsulates the essential joy that 'Incredible' brings – much more than simple nostalgia.

Ironically, the most incredible thing about 'Incredible' is its credibility. For a song that operates perfectly well in a pop context it is incredibly, impossibly authentic. When Levy calls for the attention of the junglist massive, there is no doubt over his right to claim kin with the scene. This has much to do with his soundboy heritage, having come up through the Dancehall soundsystem culture of the late '80s and early '90s. His patois is genuine and his "Booyaka!" unaffected, lending the whole song a weight that keeps it grounded in spite of its accessibility. Even the most devoted

'90s Ragga fan and earliest Jungle devotee couldn't argue that General Levy wasn't a real soundboy[1], complete with a vocal trademark (the icky icky hiccough flow) in line with early '90s Ragga style.

Then there's the production. 'Incredible', initially intended to be an instrumental, was designed as a Jungle track. It isn't pastiche or homage; it's the real thing, with the rolling basslines and rave chops that would fit into any 1994 Jungle set, no questions asked. Compare it to hits of the pop-Reggae renaissance from the likes of Snow, Bitty McClean, Peter Andre etc, which sound like just about good enough facsimiles of something authentic, and 'Incredible' stands proud as authentic in its own right.

Grime, consciously or not, operates within this pop/ underground dichotomy. It's a genre that is undoubtedly connected to the streets but catering wholeheartedly to the clubs. It's dance music, built out of grooves and audio hooks wholly intended to hype crowds. Grime is grimy, but it's not particularly grim. It must be remembered that even the most roadman MC comes from a lineage of soundboys whose primary function is to start parties.

Like Jungle, Grime is dance music that is relatable due its sonic energy, often edgy in content but always embraceable in execution. 'Incredible' and General Levy's ebullient lyrical windmilling was, and will always be, a shining example of the underground emerging into the light.

---

1. As a cautionary aside, 'Incredible' was so successful that it more or less derailed General Levy's entire career. He was quoted as saying "I run Jungle" in an interview with *The Face* magazine, a comment that resulted in a collective cold-shouldering from key players in the scene. Moral of the story? Don't create hype that you will subsequently find impossible to not believe in. And don't do interviews when things go better than you expected.

'Gangsta Kid'
Shy FX & Gunsmoke
(1994)

[Insert nuanced essay on the intersection of urban social decay and fictionalised crime, exploring the psychological appeal of violence alongside Grime's chicken-and-egg relationship with aggression. Aborted introductions below.]

Attempt 1

Don't laugh, but when I first heard 'Gangsta Kid' (on tape, courtesy of my very cool cousin Kwabena), I thought the opening was real. Please don't ask how I thought a shooting in London had been captured in stereo quality audio.

Attempt 2

Fantasy violence is grounded in a very real social context.

Attempt 3

Jungle music is part of a tradition of tightrope-walking musical genres. It's simultaneously intimidating and joyful, bursting with an energy that bleeds into aggression via Gatling gun Amen manipulations.

Attempt 4

Some stats:

185 since 2005.

17 in 2015.

128 stabbed.

32 shot.

Attempt 5

Due to a combination of background, temperament, nature, nurture and ultimately chance, I've avoided the worst aspects of violent crime, but as a young black male growing up in South London, the realities of violence were never far away.

Attempt 6

It's ironic that some genres of music can act as an escape from violence whilst simultaneously promoting violent acts. The debate over music's link to crime and criminality is nothing new, a figure eight of cause and effect. It's chicken and egg.

Attempt 7

There's an understandable allure to gangster mythology. Anti-establishment folk heroes who live outside of society's laws. Easy to romanticise. My psyche was forming in the early '90s, parallel to the flourishing of Gangsta Rap stateside. It honestly took me the best part of my adolescence to appreciate that Gangsta Rappers aren't actually real gangsters. Which is embarrassing, because that's like admitting you thought that Scorsese movies were documentaries.

Attempt 8

Violence is exciting. And it's empowering. Because it gives you status. And it spits in the face of decorum. And decorum, as we all know, is intensely boring, hence why so much entertainment has a violent streak – because of the thrill it offers, enabling us to peer into the well of savagery hidden behind society's veneer.

Attempt 9

Real life violence is not entertaining.

Anyway, conclusion:

'Gangsta Kid' is an earlyish example of the relationship between violence and underground black music in the UK, a legacy that Grime has carried somewhat awkwardly into the 21st Century. It's energetic and sinister in a kind of silly way, using violence to provoke excitement. The violent lyrics we often hear in Grime achieve a similar goal, but let's face it, Grime is heavily hampered by its context, by realism. Often treated as reportage more than art, it falls victim to the same preconceptions and misconceptions as Gangsta Rap – a highly stylised artform that gets measured by its verisimilitude.

It's unsurprising, then, that Grime has become ensnared in the gangsta spell in light of the irresistible thrill and supposed authenticity offered by violence, fantasised or otherwise.

'Tri-Fusion'
Dylan Beale (1994)

Up until about eight minutes ago, I was banking on the fact that the 'Streetfighter Riddim' chapter (page 186) would convince you of the fundamental significance of computer gaming in Grime culture at large. How naïve. Because, as of this paragraph, it turns out that Grime might actually have been invented by a computer game in the first place. Sort of.

Wolverine: Adamantium Rage, was a 16-bit beat 'em up released on the Super Nintendo Entertainment System and Sega Mega Drive. If you were any good at the game you might have made it to the second level boss, at which point you would have heard a 16-bit soundtrack called 'Tri-Fusion', featuring orchestral stabs, glitched-out percussive syncopations and a moody topline synth. Yes, it's Grime, and it predates 'Pulse X' (the official unofficial 'first ever Grime track') by eight years.

This is a big deal. The whole premise of this book is that Grime evolved over many years, a subculture that unfurled into the mainstream consciousness via a series of milestone moments. *Shakes head*. Not the case. Because the entire genre might have been realised in one track, in one go.

And it might not have been a fluke:

'I was heavily influenced by Reggae, hip hop, Jungle and then eventually Techno and Hardcore. It was basically all North London music, because that's where I was living.'
-Dylan Beale, interview with Paul Gibbins, SBTV, July 2016

This means that the world's 'first ever Grime track' was indeed birthed from all those genres that we know to have fed into Grime's DNA. Beale continues to explain that the 'mind-bogglingly small' amount of sample space he had to work with lent the track a rough, raw sound – the same sound that would come to typify Grime in its early days of DIY-digital.

The real significance of *Wolverine: Adamantium Rage* lay in the fact that it has been discovered at all. To recognise means to re-cognise, meaning to re-understand, meaning to understand something in a new light. There is an appetite for Grime that might be creating its recognition in popular culture, in turn suggesting a heightened Millennial relevance. It looks like the spirit of Grime was alive long before the name was adopted.

'Original Nuttah'
Shy FX feat. UK Apache
(1995)

I was about 16 when Ali G first landed on terrestrial television with a slot as 'voice of da yoof' on Channel 4's *The 11 O'Clock Show*. The character was ridiculous and instantly controversial. People couldn't work out if Sacha Baron Cohen was a white man drawing comedy at the expense of overblown black stereotypes, or an off-white comedian poking fun at people who were wholly ignorant of black culture, through a knowing, hyper-exaggerated parody of urban youth. Ali G was a cacophonous blend of black stereotypes, arguably as grotesque in execution as black and white minstrels, but tempered with a level of insight that made him seem authentic-ish. The exaggerated West Indian patois was ridiculous, but accurate enough to pass off as real to unknowing victims. The FUBU-inspired '90s hip hop outfits were pure costume, but acceptably black enough to be met with credulity from those who didn't realise that black people don't always look like extras in Puff Daddy videos.

When I first saw Ali G, I was right in the middle of my teenage dalliances in alternative comedy. So like a lot of people, I picked up on the satire straight away. I saw a comedian with just enough not-white in him to get away with presenting a persona of blackness to unsuspecting victims. He reminded me of all those not-black kids who wholesale adopted aspects of black culture in urban and suburban contexts, with varying degrees of success. The name itself, 'Ali G', alludes to an Asian or perhaps Muslim heritage, much of the comedy being drawn from the concept of an Asian kid morphing his identity into some semblance of black cool, and getting it hopelessly, hilariously wrong.

There are two reasons why I wasn't particularly freaked out by Ali G. The first reason is that I was fully aware of how the conflation of cultures that constitute 'blackness' in the UK (Afro-Americanism meets postcolonial diaspora via West Indian roots and culture and urban street smarts) is a fertile ground for misunderstanding, and therefore comedy. The second reason is the existence of UK Apache.

UK Apache is undoubtedly the main reason that 'Original Nuttah' survives as a UK dance classic. The song itself, produced by Shy FX, is a perfectly poised example of Jungle, that genre that bridged Ragga and Breakbeat with such explosive energy in the early 1990s. Its low-wail siren and extended intro, before huge Amen drop, is a blueprint to Jungle perfection. But it's Apache's vocals, originally freestyles performed over 'Gangsta Kid', that set the whole thing on fire. He's electric, pulling you in with a chaotic introduction of self in which you can actually hear competing identities jostling for position, before an effortlessly addictive Reggae/Bhangra melodic phrasing that should never, ever be replicated in type.

Then, after the London and Kingston shoutouts, the Amen drums kick in, the bass wobbles into overdrive and you get that volley of lyrical punches about how much of a proper nuttah Apache is. Twenty-one years later and his boasts retain as much weight as ever. His energy is infectious and indelible, making an initially underground hit into a timeless overhand smash.

But the relevance of 'Original Nuttah' goes far beyond its legacy as an iconic Jungle hit. In terms of race and identity, it actually might be one of the most important songs of a generation.

When I first heard 'Original Nuttah', I was old enough to understand that there was some kind of racial context in the mix. I was busy familiarising myself with black music of all genres, well aware that youth culture in general was being heavily tinged by a specific kind of blackness. UK Apache, I thought, was an example of the cross-cultural racial melting pot; an Indian (I assumed) MC operating within the realm of West Indian blackness (specifically through Ragga culture). To me, he legitimised non-black blackness. He made me realise that identity was a shifting, idiosyncratic reality that had more to do with biography than geography. He represented a perfect storm of conflicting identities, an identity crisis made virtuous, the exact same construction of self that typifies second and third generation people of colour.

'Many people thought I was Jamaican Indian... I used to socialise with real Jamaicans.'
-UK Apache, interview with Uncle Drummer, 2015

'I was imitating being a Jamaican – I'd dress like a Jamaican, walk like a Jamaican, talk like a Jamaican, but I wasn't Jamaican; I was a Jafaican. . .'
-UK Apache, *VICE*, 2016

But watching UK Apache in the 'Original Nuttah' video now, with his super-animated posturing and caricature-level street cred, you realise just how close he is to ridicule. If he was any less legit in style, execution, performance and acquaintances, he'd be a farce. He'd be Ali G. But the quality and the authenticity of his music dismisses all risk of derision. In the '90s, beatmakers such as Shy FX were the architects of some of the most exciting music to emerge out of these great British Isles, but it was MCs like UK Apache who were establishing the more visible cultural guidelines.

The legacy of 'Original Nuttah' is twofold. First, the persona of the MC as a hyper, unstable, dangerous nutcase bristling with raw, uncontrollable energy. UK Apache was explicit in this, presenting himself as wild and freewheeling, characteristics that UK-born MCs continue to spin well into Grime's present. Second, and more importantly, the notion that music can be a bedrock upon which one can find or craft an identity. Artistic expression supersedes racial, biographical and cultural barriers while simultaneously recognising those very same parameters; something that is way too easy to ignore when the artist seems to fit the expected criteria. For a non-black MC, in 1995, to deliver an iconic moment in a very black sub-genre of electronic dance music is, I think, a big deal. I would argue that Grime MCs (many of whom are young black males of second and third generation Afro-Caribbean descent) are not simply recognising their black identity but are actively crafting it, empowering themselves through a musical-cultural heritage. Grime demands to be taken seriously and it takes its heritage seriously, as proven by the deep respect paid to West Indian culture in the very seams of the Grime scene. Perhaps, then, 'Original Nuttah' is an early example of what we might call *cultural empowerment*, with UK Apache a noteworthy example of the successfully self-crafted persona.

Grime offers a clarity of identity for a generation of black youths who aren't what their parents were, whose role models can be found in the static of pre-Internet white label vinyl. And there's a little bit of the Original Nuttah in every MC who takes a step into soundclash culture.

'Never Gonna Let You Go'
(Kelly G Bump-n-Go Mix)
Tina Moore (1997)

Jungle sped through the mid '90s at 180 beats per minute, giving a generation of ravers exactly what they were looking for: fast, energetic dance music.

The problem with things that go very fast is that they tend to be a bit scary, a bit alienating, and sometimes a bit dangerous. Like motorbikes, or roller-coasters, or wasps. Jungle was no exception, drawing huge appeal from the junglist massive, but pushing many other ravers off the dancefloor in search of something, well, a bit slower.

This appetite for slower, less terrifying dance music was met by something from the United States called Garage. Garage, a sub-genre of House, was an electronic dance music typified by gospelly piano riffs, soulful lead vocals, a solid 'four on the floor' kick drum and, crucially, a bpm of 130. Fast enough to be fast, but slow enough to satisfy all those dance fans who didn't want to notch it up to 180 in the Jungle rooms.

Now, one of the best things about going slow is that you get more control. It's the difference between driving through an obstacle course at 15mph and driving through an obstacle course at 115mph. Enter Todd Edwards (also known as Todd 'The God'[1] Edwards), a House and Garage producer who drove his sounds very carefully indeed. By which I mean he took Garage and started tinkering with it in all sorts of interesting ways. Todd Edwards' production trademarks include adding cut and spliced vocal samples, rendered virtually unrecognisable and diced into audio snippets that actually replace the sampling of instruments. You've heard this sound a caps lock LOT throughout the '90s and early Noughties, but we'll get to that in a few paragraphs. For the moment, the important thing to stress is that Edwards introduced a glitchy kind of aesthetic to electronic music that would soon branch off into the DNA of those UK sub-genres of which Grime is one instance.

As the '90s rolled on, UK dancefloors continued to shuffle to the 130bpm of House and Garage, not to mention the hypnotic, pupil-dilating pulse of Trance, originally on loan from Germany and hovering between 120-150bpm. But, as tends to happen when things slow down, there emerged a renewed appetite for things to speed up again. UK DJs began playing Garage cuts pitched up from 130bpm to something closer to the 180bpms of Jungle, hovering around the 140bpm mark. Enter Speed Garage. Suddenly, thanks to pioneering pitch shifters such as DJ EZ, UK DJs were spending their Sundays[2] playing sped-up Garage to weekend ravers who wanted it smooth and fast. We scrabbled around for a name for this phenomenon and UK Garage seemed to do the trick.

The onset of UK Garage is hugely significant in the lineage of Grime, insofar as it refuelled MC culture. Legendary Jungle/Drum and Bass MCs Skibadee and Harry Shotta[3] had already made an artform out of intricate lyricism over frenetic bpms (and would continue to do so well into the Noughties), while MC Det had more or less perfected that skippy, post-Ragga soundclash toast flow. What UK Garage offered was a new, mainstream-ready platform for MCs to showcase themselves on, via instrumentals that seemed tailor-made for a non-hardcore rave experience.

The birth of UK Garage is Very Important Indeed in Grime's timeline, but not nearly as monumental as the germination of 2-Step, the branch of UK Garage that would inject a bouncy restlessness to the audio palette of electronic music. 2-Step was like taking the seatbelt off. It did away with the predictability and safety of a 4/4 drum rhythm and started getting playful with it. Kick drums were getting chopped out of the beat and replaced with oddly positioned snares. Meanwhile extra percussive hits were being thrown in at unusual intervals. Syncopation was leading the dance, meaning that off became the new on. 2-Step was funky and offbeat and bubbly and unpredictable and, ultimately, became a new audio playground.

The Kelly G[4] Bump-n-Go remix of Tina Moore's 'Never Gonna Let You Go' is widely acknowledged as the first ever 2-Step record, hence the 656 words I have just taken to introduce it. The song was an undeniable hit, peaking in 1997 at number 7 in the UK charts and leading a resurgence of crossover Garage that would include the likes of Craig David, Shanks & Bigfoot, Artful Dodger, Oxide & Neutrino, Heartless Crew and So Solid Crew before evolving into the petri dish in which Grime would cultivate. 'Never Gonna Let You Go', with its elusive drum pattern and hi-hat palpitations, was a subtle but definite sidestep away from UK Garage towards the ADHD jitteriness of Grime. In short, a new pulse had been established via a funky remix that would reverberate deep into the sound of urban music in the UK.

---

1. This nickname has something to do with his legendary status in the House cosmosphere. Or the fact that he's a Christian. Or neither. Maybe it's

just because 'God' rhymes so well with 'Todd'. Who knows?

2. Promoters at the time tended to reserve Friday and Saturday nights for more popular, crowd-pleasing genres of Dance, meaning you had to step out on a Sunday night if you wanted a Speed Garage fix. True story.

3. I would argue that Skibadee is to Grime what Rakim is to hip hop, the originator of a flow that serves as a template for subsequent MCs. Harry Shotta is quite simply a monstrously talented MC.

4. Kelly G: prolific music producer, remixer, arranger, erstwhile vocalist and easily confusable with jazzy saxophonist Kenny G. Kelly G definitely didn't invent the concept of syncopation in modern music, but he definitely did popularise syncopated post-Garage rhythms with this song. Kenny G, as we all know, popularised the sexy sax.

'Moschino'
Glamma Kid (1997)

Grime is the grandchild of the Windrush generation.

Spend any time listening to Grime and you'll hear heavy influences of West Indian, specifically Jamaican, culture. Grime's idiolect is riddled with patois, so much so that terms such as 'blud', 'wagwan', 'mandem', 'send', 'bare', 'skank', 'wasteman', 'roadman' and so on have entered its consciousness at a fundamental level. Songs are readily released with 'Riddim' in the title, following a long-standing Reggae tradition, whilst the notion of 'clashing' (as in the Reggae, Ragga, or Dancehall soundsystem face-off mentioned earlier) is a core aspect of Grime MC culture.

The impact of Jamaican culture on black Britain is indelible. The West Indian immigrants who travelled to post-war Britain in the late 1940s congregated in urban parts of the country alongside postcolonial African immigrants, forging new Afro-Caribbean communities. Following the 1948 British Nationality Act, which gave British citizenship to members of the Commonwealth, the UK became a home away from home for a generation of Africans and West Indians. It would prove to be the Jamaican diaspora in particular that would contribute to a very visible black British culture.

I grew up in Brixton in the early 1980s. As the child of Ghanaian migrants (my parents were part of the late '70s influx) you would be forgiven for assuming I had a very West African upbringing. I kind of did, at home, but the reality is that the West Indian influence was pervasive and unavoidable. By the time I was in primary school I was au fait with many aspects of Jamaican culture. Walking the streets of Brixton was education enough. Hearing the slang, the patois, the rhythms of speech, seeing rudeboys bopping street with that unmistakably Yardie[1] lean, eating the patties… and of course, listening to the music.

With two older sisters I had a direct line into youth culture of the late '80s. I was too young to go out to the clubs, but I was old enough to play the tapes and records at home. And living within five miles of London's then-premier black music radio station, Choice 96.9 FM, I always had a close connection to the airwaves.

The reason Jamaican culture was so ubiquitous among

black people of all heritages at this time was the same reason black culture is so pervasive today: because it's cool – and cool is contagious. What makes Jamaican culture cool is open to debate; the laid back attitude, the casual confidence, the outlaw status[2] that comes with a badman/rudegyal attitude, perhaps a combination. Whatever it is, black music (spearheaded in London by Jamaican rhythms and riddims) had, has and probably will always have an appeal that draws youth. Nowadays, it might be Grime. In '80s London, some of the blackest music to hand was Caribbean.

Between 1991 and 1996 (I can't believe it was only a five-year stretch), a show called *The Real McCoy* aired on BBC Television. *The Real McCoy* was a comedy sketch show featuring an exclusively Afro-Caribbean and Asian cast (at a time when anyone not white was deemed 'black'). I was a huge fan. My sisters and I would watch an episode, record it on VHS, and watch it again. It became a cultural reference point, full of pastiche, through which I re-evaluated my own ideas of Britishness.

In the latter stages of the programme's lifespan, there was a series of sketches about a Reggae superhero called 'Conscious Youth' and his arch nemesis, 'Ragga Star' (stay with me). The premise was that the wholesome, socially conscious Reggae of Conscious Youth (pronounced yout, no 'h'), was being challenged by the aggressive ignorance of Ragga Star, portrayed as a growling Frankenstein's Monster of Dancehall. Anyway, the series of skits ended with Conscious Youth triumphantly destroying Ragga Star via the means of socially aware Reggae music. Now this was all very sweet, but it was also erroneous. Because in real life, Ragga Star was winning.

Ragga, with all its aggression, sexuality, indecipherable patois and riddim-riding energy, was irresistible. Alongside black music exports from the US (hip hop, New Jack Swing, RnB) and homegrown dance music, it took hold in the '90s and infiltrated youth culture. There was definitely a place for traditional Reggae, but Ragga, or Dancehall (which would evolve into Bashment), definitely had the edge. The Reggae Hits compilation series embodied this duality. Each instalment was split into soft, smooth Reggae from the likes of Beres Hammond alongside some hardcore Ragga riddims, laced with soundclash lyrics from the likes of Cutty Ranks, Mad Cobra and Shabba Ranks. I loved it. And I'm pretty certain Glamma Kid did too.

When Glamma Kid dropped 'Moschino' in 1997, it was a hit. It's a straight-up Ragga song about the latest must-have designer brand. (In '97, rudeboys in London really were wearing 'crazy Mosh' jeans and jackets. I jumped on the bandwagon in my own little way by getting a pair of Moschino glasses with abacus-style MOSCHINO letters on the left arm. Hold tight Clear Vision opticians on Coldharbour Lane). The song sounded authentic and Glamma Kid sounded authentically Jamaican, with everything from the heavy patois and high-pitched whine-style delivery. Which is all very interesting, because Glamma Kid was a 22-year-old Londoner from Hackney.

Like a lot of Londoners, Glamma Kid has strong Afro-Caribbean roots, but 'Moschino' saw him leading with an identity that was partly crafted, partly affected. When I first heard 'Moschino' I assumed I was listening to a Beenie Man or a Red Rat, not someone who I could get to on the Victoria Line and a couple of buses.

And it worked. A year after the release of 'Moschino', Glamma Kid released his debut album, *Kidology*, and picked up a MOBO Award for Best Reggae Act (beating, among others, one Mr Levi 'Reggae Reggae' Roots. True story – Google it). The album featured a fairly impressive roster of producers and collaborations, including Timbaland, Flipmode Squad and the Ruff Ryders from across the pond, and Shola Ama from closer to home. Writing for *The Guardian* in 2000, Paul Lester questions Glamma Kid's conviction, authenticity and consistency of vision, stating:

'This baby-faced young Londoner fails to convince as a bona-fide, sexually-charged Yardie. In spite of his

Caribbean roots (his father is from Jamaica) and nasal baritone, he has neither the experience nor the authority of a Beenie Man or a Bounty Killer, and there's something of the eager pup about him, snapping at the heels of his idols.'

Maybe that's fair enough. But 16 years later, with 20/20 hindsight, we can allow our perspectives to go wider. I don't know if he was the first to do it so successfully, but Glamma Kid represents a generation of young British born Afro-Caribbeans who were carving their own identities (hold tight John Agard) from the roots of their heritage, and serving it up for mainstream consumption. Glamma Kid tied his identity to his Jamaican-ness, as opposed to his Londonness, or Britishness, or Hackneyness, exercising his rights to self-definition.

Grime shares something of this mentality, with MC after MC after MC choosing to identify themselves as from the streets. Listen to a random selection of Grime tracks and you would be forgiven for thinking that the average Grime MC was born into the following exciting life pattern:

Urban decay
Broken home
Failed at school

Selling drugs to people (successfully)

Shanking people (successfully)

Hated on

Local hero

Shooting people (successfully)

Being a sick MC

Fame and fortune

Linking girls (successfully)

The reality is that Grime's hyper-stylised street-ness is one aspect of urban culture that has been magnified to represent the whole. MCs are basing their authenticity in the edgiest persona they can find (a common trait across all genres of youth music). The conundrum this raises over authenticity and identity is not easily solved. Grime does indeed suffer from an identity crisis, bold enough to shout its aggression but too insecure to let the image drop. On the road to success it doesn't seem to matter if you aren't entirely the thing you say you are, as long as the image you project has a tangible context. Especially if the image you project has a tangible context. In the 1990s, Glamma Kid chose to be a Yardie. In the 2010s, Grime kids are choosing to be roadmen, perhaps proving how little has changed in the popularisation of marginalised cultures.

1. Please note: when I say 'Yardie' I'm referring to the affectionate, colloquial label that Jamaicans sometimes use to refer to other Jamicans, not the underground gang. As a non-Jamaican myself, I apologise if I've overstepped the mark. Feel free to cross out the offending word with a pen.

2. I think this might be the most important footnote in the book. Profanity is prohibited by law in Jamaica. In 2011, Nicki Minaj was fined the equivalent of £7 for swearing on stage at the Montego Bay Reggae Sumfest. In the same year, Drake was issued a warning for (allegedly) calling out "bloodclaat" while on stage at BritJam. This means that the bad language so often evidenced in Dancehall lyrics gives MCs an outlaw status beyond just being badly behaved.

'Know We'
Pay As U Go Cartel (2000)

Out of the two big Pay As U Go songs you might have been expecting to see in these pages, 'Know We' is recognisably grimier than 2001's 'Champagne Dance'. 'Champagne Dance' might have reached number 13 in the charts and propelled the Cartel to the Top of the Pops stage, but 'Know We' has got the reload-baiting patois hook, the less than glossy production finish and, most excitingly, a Street Fighter reference, when Major Ace promises to bun you "like Ken". It also proves conclusively that Wiley is a time travel overlord, able to quantum leap into any crew of the late 20th/early 21st Century and consistently rhyme on a single syllable for more than two lines at a time.

Early soundclashes between Pay As U Go and Heartless Crew have sparked a bit of a debate over who is responsible for the evolution of Grime out of the embers of UK Garage.

Wiley has gone on record saying that Heartless were among the first to '[spit] sick bars on garage'[1], despite doing exactly this himself in 2000 in Pay As U Go. The 2001 Sidewinder Pay As U Go/Heartless face off is a particularly historic moment, during which Wiley interrupts proceedings to announce "lyrics for lyrics, calm!" (a moment subsequently immortalised by Skepta in the song 'Lyrics'), before quantum leaping into 2015 to magnanimously pronounce Heartless as 'the originators' on Twitter.

It's difficult not to put Pay As U Go into the 'originators' box when you look at the Cartel roster, not least of all Wiley himself, but also including Flow Dan (chisel-faced Yardie flow) and DJ Target (producer and future Radio 1Xtra host), both of whom would go on to take up positions in Roll Deep, as well as pioneering Rinse FM legends Slimzee and Geeneus, alongside God's Gift[2], Maxwell D, Major Ace and Breeze.

Add it all up and Pay As U Go is huge cog in the history of Grime, with an iconic legacy. If there were mountain ranges in East London, the Pay As U Go line-up alone would be worthy of a Mount Rushmore tribute. As it stands, widespread recognition from Grime's pioneers, and this chapter, will have to suffice. Respect, paid.

1. Twitter, May 2015

2. Whose immortally potent verse on Dizzee Rascal's 'Hold Ya Mouf' remains the only song in the history of music to replace rhyming couplets with the sound of a clocked shotgun.

'21 Seconds'
So Solid Crew (2001)

In 2016 Grime was daring to dream.

Mainstream interest was peaking, books were being published, MCs were setting their sights on cross-Atlantic shores, US hip hop giants were co-signing left, right and centre, Drake had a BBK tattoo. . . The scene was starting to look less at itself and its kitchen sink past, and more at the infinite roads of possibility ahead. There's a confidence and deliberate polish to contemporary Grime. Skepta and Kano went head to head for Album of the Year at the Mercury Awards. Skepta even won it. Grime MCs are starting to believe.

It wasn't always this way. Early Grime is typified by a street level authenticity and gritty realism that is widely accepted as a fundamental part of the culture. Yes, Grime can be whimsical and tracks are often reflective, but for the most part it's a genre of anti-establishment energy, grounded in the brittle contexts of 'real life'.

I would have loved to have been in the ideas storming meeting for the '21 Seconds' video. I can see it now: label execs and artistic directors sitting around a table of Krispy Kremes, chewing through a list of potential locales.

'A club. Bottles of Moët, girls dancing, trilbies indoors.'
'Maybe. How about a car, driving through London. At night?'
'Yeah, a TT.'
'Two TTs, on the way to the club.'
'With a limo.'
'A stretch limo!'
'Or... wait, hear me out... how about a post-apocalyptic end of days open-air catwalk in the 5th or 6th circle of hell with helicopter SWAT team arrivals and Lisa Maffia pausing time to rupture the space-time continuum and step through portals and all-black-everything leather outfits in a permanent electrical storm, with Kaish in white contacts. How about that?'

I have no idea who said that last part. Maybe Megaman. But that's irrelevant. The point is that So Solid Crew were enormously, outrageously ambitious in scope, vision, execution and success, a fact perfectly encapsulated in the video to their 2001 number one single, '21 Seconds'. The impact of '21 Seconds' is undeniable. It was an instant chart hit that threw a South London-based Garage crew into the national consciousness. And it did so with a flamboyance and theatricality akin to the Bad Boy-led, Hype Williams-directed shiny suit era of US hip hop. At the turn of the century, So Solid Crew were main-staging it at the Brits, battling with the likes of Blue, 5ive and Sophie Ellis-Bextor for chart dominance, and generating serious column inches in the mainstream music press. When I started Uni in September 2000, So Solid Crew posters were on sale at Freshers' Fair. It's safe to say that they had taken 2-Step Garage out of South London and fired it clean into the stratosphere.

One of my two major regrets in life is trading a cassette tape of Delight FM So Solid freestyles for a tape of Shanks & Bigfoot and Sweet Female Attitude. Don't get me wrong, I love and 'Sweet Like Chocolate' and 'Flowers', but I wince at the thought that I might never hear those ess oh ess oh ell eye dee pirate radio flows again. So Solid came up through underground airwaves in a subculture that would go on to intrigue and scare the mainstream, an oft-repeated tradition in popular music (Jazz, Punk, hip hop...) that would be seen again in the mid-Noughties emergence of Grime.

Grime, in its chart-baiting exuberance and genuine urban edge, can be placed firmly in a post-Garage lineage. In this, So Solid's legacy is palpable, with '21 Seconds' a stellar example of the underground breaching the mainstream without apology, fear or compromise. The members of So Solid Crew were far removed from their pop star contemporaries, but they became undeniable figures within pop culture. And this all happened in spite of (rather than due to) the darker, criminal elements of their pasts and personas, including jail time, convictions for assault and gun crime. It must be stressed just how quickly and easily So Solid became a scapegoat for urban crime in the UK. Yes, there are references to criminality in '21 Seconds', (such as the ease with which Megaman can carry two gats) and other songs are littered with violent references, but '21 Seconds' is essentially a posse cut more concerned with personality showcase than street confession. It's a million miles away from the hyper-lyrical multisyllabic wordplay of so much modern Grime, closer in tone to the flow heavy, freewheeling, charisma-led chatting of '90s MCs; another important factor contributing to the song's likeability.

While we're on the topic of likeability, hold tight Kaish on turning however many words of double-time spitting into a recognisable, quotable hook. A feat equalled by, of course, 'Breakfast at Tiffany's' by Deep Blue Something, the chorus to which I, you and everyone you know, definitely know all the words.

Whether or not pop history will recognise So Solid Crew as 'important' is irrelevant in light of the group's already legendary status within Grime. You just have to hear the relish with which Ghetts likens himself to Megaman in 2016's 'You Dun Know Already'. Or Skepta's respectful homage of a 2-Step flow in 2012's 'We Begin Things', featuring Megaman. Or Chip's Father Christmas moment upon meeting Skat D. Or my wife's ongoing infatuation with Ashley 'Asher D' Walters. Or any number of the timeless, timeless '21 Seconds' quotables. Skat D drops a bar that alone deserves a plaque in the Natural History Museum as one of the World's Eight Wonders. When sales from this book have come through, I'm fully going to hire a team of mathematicians to work out the Golden Ratios at work in that bar. I know the Fibonacci Sequence is in there somewhere.

So Solid were trailblazers who inspired a generation. The mad thing is that they are yet to be matched in audacity by the generation they inspired. I would argue that while '21 Seconds' predates Grime, it provides a blueprint that Grime is yet to fully realise: embrace your roots, keep it dark, shoot for the stars, bring your personas to life and invite the mainstream to come running behind you.

'Boom Selection'
Genius Cru (2001)

Whenever I hear 'Boom Selection' I feel like I'm right in the middle of the party. Like, 11.37pm, just after the bottles are popped and everyone's found the dancefloor at the same time, just after you've undone another button on your shirt but just before you're mopping your brow with a paper napkin/your sleeve/someone else's face (delete as appropriate). It's a proper, bouncing, party tune, and everything you might expect from a song with 'boom' in the title[1].

This kind of makes perfect sense, seeing that, historically, 'Boom Selection' is right in the middle of the party. Released in early 2001, it arrived in the midst of a UK Garage wave that had been gathering momentum since 1999, bringing all manner of artists into the limelight and effectively transforming the pop landscape. In 2001, Garage was riding high: glossy, club lit, and inviting the country to dance to a new, syncopated beat.

'Boom Selection' is a perfect representation of everything that Grime would start to reject little more than a year or two later. The champagne raving, Evisu-clad decadence of UK Garage was to prove an ill fit to the jittery energy and po-faced posturing that Grime would bring to the table. Depending on how you look at it, the hook from Kano's 'Flow of the Year' (2014) could either be a call for alcohol at the party, or an assertion that raving absolutely won't happen unless a big, bumbaclart riddim is on the menu, suggesting that Grime's principal concern is not to soundtrack hedonism.

'Boom Selection' is the last stop on UKG's sashay down the red carpet before it took a left turn into the alleys and backstreets of Grime. Sonically, you can just about hear Grime knocking quietly through the song's syncopated kicks and menacing bass. But as the singalong chorus fades (and as we'll see in the next few chapters to come), successive years will mark a point of no return for the direction of urban music in the UK.

---

1. Other songs with 'Boom' in the title include 'Boom Boom Boom!' by the Outhere Brothers, 'Boom Shake the Room' by the Fresh Prince and DJ

Jazzy Jeff, 'Boom Boom Pow' by The Black Eyed Peas, 'Boom Shakalaka' by Alchemist Project, 'Boom Biddy Bye Bye' by Cypress Hill and, of course, 'Boom Boom Boom Boom!!' (two exclamation marks) by the Vengaboys. Most of these songs are not designed for any level of analysis, so I've already gone way too far with this footnote.

'Has It Come To This?'
The Streets (2001)

There's an elephant in this book, and it's quietly stamping through the background of these pages with the following question tattooed on the side of its fat, lumbering body:

Is grime is damaging to the community it stems from?

As a lyrical genre, Grime is characterised by an energy that boils over beyond soundclash bravado into violent aggression. Many (not all, but many) of the lyrics you will see referenced in this book outline violence, stylised or otherwise, perpetrated by young black men against other young black men. The camaraderie, collaboration, craft, criticality and creativity inherent in Grime is all too easily overshadowed by this unhealthy tendency towards black male violence.

In this, the genre does a lot to reinforce some of the least helpful stereotypes often levelled at young black men: that we are violent, hyper-heterosexual, misogynistic, reckless, anti-establishment, unacademic, unduly ostentatious and consumed with the pursuit of wealth. Of course, these are traits that are often prescribed to maleness in general (more on that shortly) but the complications are multiplied when applied to black masculinity in particular. In his 1991 book 'Understanding Black Adolescent Male Violence', Amos N. Wilson writes of young black men being provoked into a 'reactionary masculinity' that is ultimately detrimental to their own wellbeing:

'These males, often misguidedly and ignorantly assuming that they are successfully defying white male authority and dominance, defying "the system", expressing their independence and "masculine prerogatives", expressing their "manhood", have been misled or misdirected into violently attacking and corrosively undermining the peace, stability, and the very viability of the Afrikan [sic] American community.'

Arguably, Grime is typified by this kind of reactionary masculinity, built on bravado and deep-rooted notions of masculinity in society at large. Cue elephant, casually trampling through the undergrowth. The assumption for men (of all colours) is that vulnerability = weakness, which is very untrue because vulnerability means being able to be harmed, while weakness means not being strong enough to withstand things that can cause harm. Everyone is vulnerable, but men are not allowed to be. Men have to be tough. Men can never be weak.

For black men, added complications lie in the concept of 'double consciousness', a term coined by W.E.B. Du Bois[1] over a century ago, whereby the black male is 'always looking at one's self through the eyes of others'. Black men are socially invisible, often unseen and unheard in mainstream channels of society, while simultaneously hyper-visible, as easily noticed as a mark on a blank sheet, and thus open to high levels of scrutiny. Being black comes with a whole list of expectations and preconceptions, many of which are tied to age-old stereotypes rooted in the 'white gaze'[2]. In the eyes of the dominant, white mainstream, 'black' equates to all sorts of traits, including but not limited to athleticism, hypersexuality, threat, violence and anti-intellectualism.

In this context, there is a perverse logic to the masculine posturing we have come to expect from black, urban music. Young black men entering the public sphere readily use masculinity as a shield to their vulnerability, reflecting an exaggerated black masculinity back to the white gaze and to the male gaze in general. It's a survival strategy and it works. Throw a dust sheet over your insecurities – put your hands over your ears, shut your eyes and start screaming. Vulnerability – gone.

***

On paper, Mike Skinner was an absolute no-hoper. A no-go, dead in the water, car crash fail of an MC. First off, he was the wrong colour. As in white. Which made him all too visible and subject to scrutiny against the very black backdrop of UK Garage. Next, he was from the wrong place. As in not-London. Which was all the more highlighted by his awkward Brummie pronunciation and cockney tinged flow. Then, he wasn't a particularly exciting lyricist, at least in the crowd-hyping reload tradition of lyrical excitement. His flow was awkward and out of the pocket, his voice light on bass and low on rasp. On the mic, he sounded suspiciously like someone called, well, Mike. And finally, he was somehow smaller than life. His lyrical content was mundane and ordinary and realistic in a sobering, stop and think kind of way, a muted counterpoint to the exaggerated club-lit personas that were emerging from the UK Garage scene of the early 2000s.

And yet with 'Has It Come To This?', the lead single from his 2001 debut *Original Pirate Material*, he found a hit that drew critical and popular acclaim alike. I think this has much to do with vulnerability, which hopefully begins to explain this chapter's introduction.

'Has It Come To This?' is a quiet but defiant celebration of the mundane. The opening lines lift the listener into a position of absolute mastery over a realm of absolute averageness, consisting of lazy, class B drug use, computer game distraction and semi-stoned screen time. After this invitation to make yerself at home, Skinner goes on to assert that this ain't a club track, which is an active rejection of UK Garage bottle-popping excess. He continues to actually question his own credibility, asking us if we think he's ghetto and explaining that we (the adolescent everyman) walk on a tightrope of street credibility. All the while, he seems acutely aware of the risk of becoming victim to the streets, sidelining himself as a watcher of the show. There is scant bravado in lines that refer to bravery in the face of defeat met with a deep introspection and on-the-sleeve self-awareness.

It's deeply, deeply vulnerable and I would argue that this is the key source of his success. Mike Skinner's appeal lay in his dead-stare confrontation with his own vulnerability, as an MC, as an artist, as a person. 'Has It Come To This?' makes a virtue of all those things that would detract from Skinner's credibility: his whiteness, his non-Londonness, his lack of polish as a lyricist, his mundane, middle-class-disguised-as-working-class existence, his disinclination towards violence, his introspective musings, his muted braggadocio. Skinner is the very opposite of the reactionary masculinity I spoke of earlier, in a field that, by 2001, was becoming characterised by male invulnerability. It's weird, but he flipped every expectation of urban masculinity just before Grime would define the rules of urban masculinity for the next 15 years.

Colour plays an important role here. It's easy for us to accept Mike Skinner's vulnerability because we aren't conditioned to see whiteness as invulnerable. His brooding, nervous brand of street wisdom is an easy sell. He can perform vulnerability and lead with weakness. Compare that to the line-up of black artists who have equally introspective songs in their back catalogues, but come to prominence in their most aggressive, toughest guises, under implicit pressure to be the active aggressor rather than passive thinker. And here comes another elephant lumbering through the room:

'Mike Skinner was the first to prove that a British rapper could speak directly to a nationwide constituency in a voice entirely his own.'
-critic Ben Thompson, quoted in *The Guardian*, 2011

'As UK garage takes on more and more of the lifestyle accessories of the US hip hop scene, Mike Skinner, the

21-year-old behind The Streets represents a brilliant break with cliché. . . And as such, he's one of the most original British pop voices for years.'

-John Robinson, *NME*, 2005

'If you're ever asked what it was like being young at the start of the 21st Century you could do a lot worse than dig this album out of your collection provided, of course, you've taken it out of your CD player. Genius.'

-Christian Hopwood, *BBC Music*, 2002

'Mike Skinner, a.k.a. The Streets, could be the most gifted rapper London has ever produced. . . Skinner nails the quiet desperation of the white working-class like a pub-hooligan Marshall Mathers, with all of Slim Shady's good humor [sic] and none of his insanity.'

-Jon Caramanica, *Spin*, 2001

'What I've been successful at is characters and stories and drama. . . That's always been what's got me through – I know I can tell a good story.'

-Mike Skinner, interviewed by *The Word*, quoted in *In The City* by Paul du Noyer

Being white and poor and 'normal' (in the white gaze) made

it incredibly easy for the mainstream to accept Mike Skinner as the voice of authentic Britain, especially within the context of black UK music. It doesn't matter if the persona he speaks through is authentically him or not, because it is a persona that is easily identifiable as young and British, with no racial distractions to confuse matters. He was a safe option, telling a story that the mainstream was ready and willing to believe in. It wouldn't be until 2003 that the mainstream would be ready, or at least invited, to accept the loud desperation of black adolescence via Dizzee Rascal's equally acclaimed debut, *Boy in da Corner*.

In 2001, when 'urban' music was beginning to evolve into flawed masculinity, 'Has It Come To This?' was a very pertinent question to ask, to which Mike Skinner offered an alternative, couched in storytelling, personality, and an ironic confidence drawn from the well of vulnerability.

***

Whether or not the mainstream is even close to accepting the realities of fully grown black masculinity is debatable. Skepta may be getting close, nominated for an Ivor Novello[3] and winning the Mercury Prize 2016, but this is arguably within the context of a blackness that has been played out for so long that it is understandable, no longer threatening, and actually quite palatable. In this sense, Skepta's success is something of a pyrrhic win for black masculinity. It's a triumphant emergence from the margins, yes, but it simultaneously confirms existing hierarchies in its affirmation of the aggressive, dangerous, black 'other'. Where Skepta's moment in the sun celebrates preconceived, potentially limiting notions of black maleness, Mike Skinner enjoyed a swift mainstream acceptance that extolled the idiosyncratic virtues of being Mike Skinner.

It's not controversial to state that the archetypal Grime MC's vulnerabilities play second fiddle to a roadman stereotype. And it's equally fair to say that this stereotype cannot possibly represent his totality of self. Many Grime artists explore aspects of vulnerability (if you look hard enough), but few, if any, have achieved popular success via this route. The closest we ever got might be the Mitchell Brothers, who fused a lairy wideboy aesthetic to everyman tales of casual discrimination and social marginalisation, including not being taken seriously in expensive West End department stores ('Harvey Nicks') and being stopped and searched by the police ('Routine Check'). Perhaps ironically, the Mitchell Brothers were signed to none other than Mike Skinner's very own record label, The Beats. The relatively short lifespan of their career (only two Mitchell Brothers albums were released, between 2005 and 2007, compared to The Streets' six albums between 2002 and 2011) might be proof of a sobering fact – that black vulnerability just doesn't have the same legs as its white counterpart.

---

1. *The Souls of Black Folk* by W.E.B. Du Bois, published in 1903. Philosophical gems regarding race can be found therein.

2. I've come across this phrase in various places during my intellectual travels, but this one is credited to *Look, A White!* by George Yancy.

3. Other notable Ivor Novello nominees include Tinie Tempah, Dizzee Rascal (winner in 2011 for the Inspiration Award), and Roots Manuva in 2016 for Best Contemporary Song. The Streets picked up two nominations in 2005.

'Pulse X'
Musical Mob (2002)

This might be as close to the birth of the sound of Grime as we're going to get. Internet has it that 'Pulse X' was moulded from the bits and buttons of a PlayStation (it was actually made on a programme called Rebirth, but there you go), with an irresistible combination of bulbous bass synths and abrasive handclaps that skate out of the realm of Garage into something else entirely, something new. And when it's dropped at the rave, it goes off every time, with a rawness that can't age, won't age.

The beauty of 'Pulse X' lay in that 8-bar flip between bouncy, 2-Step hi-hats and echoing bass stabs, dungeon hollow and ricocheting with syncopated clap snares.[1] It's an MC's playground, offering space and routes for lyrical pirouettes and punches alike. In context, with the 20/20 hindsight that I'm relying on for this book to make any sense at all, this is important. Up until 2002, MCs who wanted to spit bars and only spit bars had to make do with Garage instrumentals, Drum and Bass, or go down the hip hop route. There wasn't a natural space for these MCs because existing genres of dance music were serving other purposes – they weren't about the MC as centre-stage artiste. MCs were thirsty for the sound that 'Pulse X' offered, as demonstrated by its huge white label success after early dubplate spins from the Heartless Crew in the early Noughties. The arrival of instrumentals like 'Pulse X' and 'Creeper' opened the doors to a shiny new MC playground in which the scene, early and unnamed, would evolve into Grime.

Produced by Youngstar, who would famously go on to produce 'Stand Up Tall' on Dizzee Rascal's second album, 'Pulse X' deservedly wins a place in the Grime hall of fame as a foundational track in the genre's embryonic stages. Minimalist, simplistic. A game changer if ever there was one.

***

2002: Year Zero

2002 can be taken as Year Zero for Grime, which makes it very tempting to deconstruct and seek out all sorts of socio-historic, political and economic significances. In fact, the past week or so has involved me reading all sorts of sources about Tony Blair and his second term in government as Prime Minister. I've been trying to work out if New Labour's approach to anti-social behaviour might have fed into the context for Grime's germination. I've combed through Ministry of Justice statistical notices and found that 2002 was the first year that ASBOs were issued following conviction[2], which might put Grime into context as the sound of the ASBO generation, especially when you consider that ASBO-related convictions peaked at almost 3,000 in 2005 – Grime's heyday.

I've been trying to work out whether or not the death of the Queen Mother, coinciding with the Queen's Golden Jubilee, has anything to do with anything. I very nearly derailed myself by writing a paragraph about Leicester City FC opening its new stadium in 2002, culminating in 2016's fairytale Premier League win (which symbolically parallels Grime's journey from Bambi-legged sub-culture to dominant sound of modern youth, if you over-analyse it). I even wrote a (now deleted) section on Grime as the real sound of New Labour, capturing in audio the mood of marginalised urban youth, who categorically didn't believe that 'Things Can Only Get Better'[3]. Then I weighed up the importance of BBC's launch of 6Music as an accessible source of alternative World music in 2002, against the launch of BBC 1Xtra as an accessible source of black music, in the same year. Then I decided that all that was too much to weave into an appreciation of 'Pulse X', so I put three stars and wrote everything you've just read above.

As we get closer to the present day, the significance of 2002 will continue to sharpen into focus. Keep reading.

---

1. 2016 saw the return of the mid-song beat flip in Grime via 'Dem Tings Dere' (Riddim Commission featuring D Double E) and the Murlo remix of 'Naila' (AJ Tracey). Both songs might make you swerve into a bollard if caught off guard, that's how funky they are.

2. This footnote is dedicated to the fact/urban legend/pub quiz factoid that one of the earliest Anti-Social Behavioural Orders was issued to pirate radio DJ and Grime forebear Slimzee of Rinse FM, prohibiting him from accessing any roof of any building over four floors high without permission.

3. This was the title of that D-Ream song used by New Labour to soundtrack the optimism of a shift into Labour government after 18 years of Tory rule. It was not a great song in 1997. It is not a great song now. It will not be a great song the next time you read this.

'Creeper'
Danny Weed (2002)

As the perfect counterpoint to the sparse 8-bar reductions of 'Pulse X', you get 'Creeper' – just as important in the emergence of a Grime sound but significantly different in style.

'Creeper' is busy, bouncy and restless, with syncopated ADHD percussion just about kept in check by a slowly evolving pulse of synthy strings. This is a huge part of the Grime recipe, released in that pivotal year when the ingredients started to come together. Another game changer that proved to be MC catnip, inspiring classic freestyle sessions from the likes of Wiley and Dizzee.

Danny Weed sheepishly admits that as producer, he 'really wasn't technically that good'[1], but that's a huge part of 'Creeper's charm – the fact that it grew organically out of the need to make beats for MCs to rhyme on. As part of the initial Roll Deep line-up, Danny Weed was, is, part of the architecture of Grime, feeding off what was lacking as much as from what was available:

'When you've got nothing, I suppose that did inspire us, we were around that energy, we were from council estates, and that's what naturally came out. So when things start to go well, and life's a little bit more glossy, you don't naturally make that music I suppose.'
-Danny Weed, *i-D*, 2015

Much of 'Creeper's appeal comes from its DIY charm, reflecting the context from which it was born. The glossy, optimistic sheen of the late '90s had properly worn off by '02. Garage didn't reflect the high rise realities of so many young people in London, so the music would, of course, have to shift in tone and style. 'Creeper' is one of a handful of instrumentals from this period that captures this lurch towards grittiness. It sounds crude and handmade, yet aspirationally inventive, the audio equivalent of a boy racer's modified hatchback. In 2002, Blairite Britain was far from the utopia of left-wing optimism presented to voters in 1997, wrestling with itself over anti-social behaviour and the causes of anti-social behaviour. Blair's New Deal tried to reconcile these tensions, 'explicitly [seeking] to provide new opportunities in return for new responsibilities.'[2] In an important sense, Grime's pioneers were early victims of this ideological conflict, expected to behave in a socially responsible manner whilst living in contexts that invited 'anti-social' behaviour. This, perhaps, is what characterised Grime as an anti-establishment artform from the off, music for kids who have got nothing in the first place.

Grime purists would readily highlight 'Creeper' as the definitive sound of authentic Grime. Listening to it in 2016, the argument stands. Its genetic code can still be heard in some of the most recent examples of the genre, confirming its position as a load-bearing branch in the Grime family tree.

---

1. *i-D Magazine*, 2015

2. Tony Blair, 'My Vision for Britain', *The Guardian*, 2002

'Oi!'
More Fire Crew (2002)

With its stripped-back Korg Triton production, UK-specific hook and high energy, danceable aggression, 'Oi!' is an obvious pick in the rundown of songs that seeded Grime. But its significance to the genre goes beyond ear deep.

First, there's the energy. The title of 'Oi!' is 'Oi', with an exclamation mark. 'Oi' with an exclamation mark is something you might shout in greeting, or reprimand. It's impolite, and borderline offensive. And it's British. And unrepentantly working class. It's also the name of sub-genre of Punk intended to highlight and promote Punk's working class origins. Compared to the late-Garage gloss of songs from So Solid Crew, Pay As You Go Cartel and Heartless Crew, 'Oi!' is abrasive. But just like a cheeky "oi!", it's eminently approachable, helped along by bubbling 2-Step flows and a playful back and forth between the three More Fire MCs.

Next, there's the paranoia. The song's intro comprises a fantasy sequence of anonymous haters hating on all three members of More Fire Crew. The rest of the song serves as a high-octane introduction to each member, each declaring themselves before stating their collective identity at the end. Part way through, we hear a flat exchange between the Crew musing over how hated they are, before announcing themselves as the newest trios of MCs. Then you get the big finish ending, with the whole Crew triumphantly chanting the hook together.

I raise all this because it's a strangely self-conscious conceit for a song that is ostensibly about bravado. In announcing themselves as the most "brand new" trio of MCs around, it's interesting that Lethal Bizzle, Ozzie B and Neeko start with self-denigration. Grime, in its competitive spirit and murky, urban context, is understandably suspicious. You just have to consider the endless reference to haters. For young black males (Grime's dominant demographic), London's streets are a paranoid place. You might get seen. You might get watched. You might get robbed. You might get attacked. You might become a victim. So instead you become an aggressor, as a barrier to the risks. You use hatred and suspicion as validation of your credibility. In 2002, 'Oi!' was a particularly bright example of this kind of paranoid energy, proving that it was possible to turn anxiety and insecurity into chart success. A year later, Dizzee Rascal would demonstrate this frantic paranoia throughout *Boy in da Corner*.

The legacy of 'Oi!' is most obviously evident in the 2016 Section Boyz remix which, as it happens, is disappointing and nowhere near as vibrant as the original. So let's not dwell on that one. I would argue that 'Oi!' has a more important legacy in the work of Grime artists who successfully marry inward-looking self-consciousness with pop appeal. Skepta's 'underdog psychosis' explorations are a prime example, ranging from the moody ruminations of songs such as 'Reflecting' (2009) and 'Castles' (2012) to the energetic, Grime-pop examination of self, 'That's Not Me' (2014).

For me, this is where Grime starts to get particularly interesting, when you realise you can dance in the venn diagram of insecurity and bravado. In 2002, Grime's Year Zero, Lethal Bizzle, Ozzie and Neeko startled us by shouting 'Oi!', and we're still jumping 14 years later.

'The Heartless Theme'
(aka The Superglue Riddim)
Heartless Crew (2002)

Sometimes you're having a polite conversation about evolution and the person you're talking to reveals that they're slightly insane. It's that point when they say that evolution can't be real because we still have all the animals we evolved from. You then realise that you might be insane too, when, for a split second, you see the logic. Then you remember that you aren't insane, shake the thought out of your head, and remind yourself never to talk about evolution with strangers at the buffet table.

Heartless Crew's 'The Heartless Theme' is a bit like one of those missing link animals. Part glossy nonsense, part credible street anthem, it's a bridge between What Came Before and What Would Come After. The sparse production makes it sound almost post 2-Step, coupled with an incessant topline whistle that's a far cry from the lushness of Garage. Then, after a minute or so of ear-squint toastings via a staticky megaphone, the song pounces into action with proper bars for proper ravers, interrupted by a 'melodic' do-it-yourself chant-along chorus that I'm not going to dwell on here.

2002 marks a pivotal moment in the history of Grime. It's the year that Wiley established the Roll Deep Crew, while BBC launched Radio 1Xtra; the year that two schoolboys started producing bedroom PC instrumentals that would become Ruff Sqwad classics; the year that Musical Mob stripped Garage down to its grimiest foundations in 'Pulse X', offering an audio blueprint to the genre. It's the year that DJ Slimzee hit record on Rinse FM and delivered the Sidewinder studio mix, featuring a still-talking-to-each-other Dizzee Rascal and Wiley.

Undoubtedly, 'The Heartless Theme' was bubbling away in the primordial audio stew from which Grime would emerge, and (chorus aside) it can and will continue to hold its own in any 140bpm playlist. In this, it survives as one of the key rivets of 2002, a crucial year in the development of the genre. Respect, paid, once again.

'Seems 2 Be'
Dizzee Rascal (2003)

The reason that *Boy in da Corner* represents such an insanely important moment in the history of Grime is that it was never actually supposed to represent an insanely important moment in the history of Grime. I don't know Dizzee Rascal personally, but I don't imagine he designed his debut to be the blueprint to a genre. My Internet research throws forward contradictory results in this debate. In one interview with Channel 4[1], Dizzee actively shuns the idea that he was making quote unquote Grime, stating that he, 'just wanted to make songs to make the raves go mad'. He continues:

'I didn't see it as Grime, and when people said, oh yeah, yeah you make Grime, I didn't like that. I didn't know what to call it.'

Jeffrey Boakye

Then you get a Pitchfork interview where he seems to accept the assertion that he 'made *Boy in da Corner* pretty much knowing that it would be the first Grime record.'[2] Either way, whether the album was the deliberate arrival of an underground movement or not, it was always going to be the audio thumbprint of Dylan Mills; idiosyncratic, unique and far from indicative.

Yes, *Boy in da Corner* is of a scene, of a time. Dizzee Rascal chops through well-trodden ideas, tropes and aesthetics, with vignettes of urban decay met with high-energy soundclash aggression, doing what was being done by his peers. But beyond that, it's not a Grime album, or an Eski album, or a UK Rap album, or a hip hop album, or an electro album. It's a Dizzee Rascal album. Sonically, *Boy in da Corner* is the sound of possibility. The 8-bit electro-fusions of 'Stop Dat', 'I Luv U' and 'Seems 2 Be' are juxtaposed with bare bones sample work in 'Fix Up, Look Sharp' and the rocky, Grunge-tinged riffs of 'Jus' a Rascal'. Then you have the Eski-bop bounciness of '2 Far', as a little post-2-Step reminder. It's neither a genre-hopping series of crossover attempts or a po-faced parade of identikit Grime – it's experimentation, expression and musical freeflow. (Worth noting that Dizzee cites the early Crunk sounds of Three 6 Mafia as a key influence of his production style, putting him up there as an forerunner of the Trap sound that has become so ubiquitous in UK music of late.)

Lyrically, *Boy in da Corner* is way much more than soundboy bravado. Of course, Dizzee does his fair share of hater-baiting and self-aggrandisement, but there's so much more going on here: defiant social commentary on teenage relationships ('I Luv U'), old-school morality tales about female promiscuity ('Jezebel'), dry-eyed laments to days gone by ('Sittin' Here'). And Dizzee touches on all these subjects in a mercurial, shifting flow that switches up track by track, in seemingly endless invention; from the foot-stomping couplets of 'Fix Up, Look Sharp' to the near-incomprehensible double-time patter of 'Jus' a Rascal' and everything in between.

Before we get to why 'Seems 2 Be' is a standout in an album replete with gems, here's an alphabetical list of moods that the song comprises:

Antagonistic

Apprehensive

Aspirational

Boastful

Cathartic

Danceable

Descriptive

Energetic

Erratic

Grim

Honest

Innovative

Menacing

Nostalgic

Paranoid

Playful

Reflective

Serious

Triumphant

Vulnerable

Wise

Wistful

Witty

Youthful

'Seems 2 Be' is an easy pick for One Of The Most Important Songs On *Boy in da Corner* because it encapsulates every tonal shade of Grime in one track, before Grime had fully realised itself as a genre. It is a scream of focused discontent, triumphantly paranoid, taut with the irresponsibility and boundless energy of youth. As an historic artefact (along with 'Stop Dat' and 'I Luv You'), 'Seems 2 Be' captures the raw spirit of Sidewinder club nights and early Grime rave energy. As a crafted song, it does the important job of giving voice to a generation hampered by love and war and hate and life, inviting us to dance along to the threatening realities of harsh life.

Read that last sentence again and ask yourself, what better way is there to describe Grime?

The critical acclaim of *Boy in da Corner* is well documented. It is a remarkable album that threw Dizzee Rascal into stratospheric realms of critical and commercial success. More than that, it laid foundations for the potential of Grime. Whether or not it is a deliberate blueprint for the genre is, I think, irrelevant, because it captures lightning in a bottle, with 'Seems 2 Be' shining as a near perfect moment of illumination.

---

1. 'Music Nation', Channel 4, November 2014

2. Pitchfork interview with Mark Pytlik, June 2005

'I Can C U'
Crazy Titch (2003)

Irresponsible Things You Might Do

When You Become a Grime MC:

1) Give yourself a weird-sounding nickname. Because having a name that sounds like a 12-year-old made it up when you're not 12 anymore might make it hard for people to take you all that seriously. And it ties you to a street persona that might make be difficult to shake. But if you do it well, you leave yourself with a cool-sounding persona for all time.

2) Make really catchy songs about random acts of aggression. Which might accidentally legitimise casual violence and/ or suggest that your authenticity is measured by your capability for violence. This is particularly problematic if

you are a young black male, who everyone already assumes is violent and anti-social.

3) Endorse misogyny as a by-product of asserting your masculinity when you accidentally on purpose start objectifying women as a commodity to be won like a trophy or fixed like a problem.

4) Hopelessly confuse your actual personality with a supposedly credible persona and talk about crimes you don't commit in real life[1]. (You might be forgiven for this one, if you admit that you are playing out a fantasy of romanticised criminality, like a child pretending to be a baddie in a game of Cops and Robbers. Or you might talk about crimes that you actually have committed in real life. This might be confession, or bravado, or both. Or you might start committing crimes that you haven't yet committed, and then start making music about it.)

5) Replace whole words with phonetically identical single letters in the titles of your song.

6) Make music videos in which you pose and posture as some kind of invincible hardcase, when you are in fact a musician and entertainer.

Carl Dobson, aka Crazy Titch, is guilty of the first five.

For anyone naïve enough to equate authenticity with criminality, Crazy Titch is the realest MC in the scene. He's so real that he's currently serving a 30-year stretch for involvement in the murder of a music producer, over a supposed diss track, in 2006. He's a legitimate street criminal, with a rap sheet going back to Young Offenders. He got his two GCSEs (English, D; Maths, C) while incarcerated[2]. He went to prison for robbing a post office. He's the product of a broken society who chose a life of crime. He's the face of Grime's true griminess. And like so many artists in the scene, his lyrics are swollen with threats of physical violence, grievous bodily harm and sexual aggression.

But he's also an MC. He's fun, playful and energetic, and his 2003 release 'I Can C U' stands as an irresistibly catchy Grime classic. He doesn't sound like a murderer. The song doesn't sound murderous. It's fun, in the Eskibeat vein. You can sing along to it. No surprises that his 2004 follow-up came with the title 'Sing Along', with a video set in some kind of backstage BRIT School audition outtake. It's all a bit mad, but it works. The 'I Can C U' video, set in a series of pretty uninspiring locations, turns the dilapidated backstreets, arches, walkways and footbridges of East London into a free-for-all open air rave venue. In daylight.

It's worth noting that this was one of the first ever Grime videos, period, and definitely the first from an unsigned act, which a) makes Titch a pioneer in the scene and, b) means that he is not guilty of point number 6 at the start of this essay.

In the early Noughties, Crazy Titch established himself as the archetypal angry hype man of Grime, sparking a legacy that has been continued by the likes of Jme[3] and Tempa T. The difference (as we'll see when we get to 2006's 'Serious' and 2009's 'Next Hype') is that Jme and Tempa T craft a whiplash energy and cartoon violence that is aggressive, but not particularly malevolent. Titch's biography makes it difficult to view him in the same light. The altercation that led to his 30-year stretch reads like a wince-inducing lament to juvenile delinquency. I mean, how many Grime MCs talk about getting a gun and ending the life/career/verse of some anonymous rival? But Crazy Titch was crazy enough to play it out in real life. Over some pretty innocuous diss bars, I might add, levelled not at himself but his brother, Dwayne Mahorn aka Durrty Goodz. And the rundown of what he actually did makes for sobering reading. (Real life criminal acts that involve shooting people in the back and limbs tend to be more disturbing than exhilarating.)

Carl Dobson was 23 years old when he was sentenced to life imprisonment, effectively ending his career at a point when he was poised for acclaim and stardom. In the parallel universe in which he hadn't set in motion the series of events that led to his incarceration, Crazy Titch might have opened the 2012 Olympics, or sat on The X Factor panel, or released a Mercury-nominated album.

The art imitating life imitating art debate that surrounds his life and music is a möbius strip that can never fully explain just how infuriating the demise of Titch's career is, not just as a personal tragedy but as a reflection of the societal conflicts embedded in Grime's DNA. It's infuriating that I've found it impossible to write this chapter without referencing Crazy Titch's criminal status because I don't want to etch-a-sketch erase his identity as an artist and entertainer. He is living proof of the fact that violence is easy but unrewarding, something he talks about with candour and insight. His narrative is directly inverse to that of a lot of Grime artists who play up their supposed criminality within their music (in a bid to promote a street-toughened persona), but essentially live the crime-free life of a professional musician. Titch did it the other way around.

Crazy Titch's life sentence feels like a pronounced moment of loss in Grime's narrative. We will never know what he might have achieved if he hadn't spiralled down, or the heights to which his talents could have ascended. But as it stands, his legacy remains intact and his influence on the scene absolute, which is powerful testament to the impact of his early movements in Grime's earliest days.

---

1. A quick poem: Crime and Grime are two words that rhyme. Often put together, a lot of the time. Authenticity from street credibility, which in turn is linked to criminal activity. An MC has got to be capable of robbery, physical violence and class A shottery. Which, ironically, creates a snobbery: You can't be real if you're not a proper G.

2. According to the ever-trustworthy journalists from early-21st Century *VICE Magazine*.

3. Keen-eared readers will recognise Jme's, "say my name" homage to Crazy Titch ('Man Don't Care', 2015). He also shouts out Titch in the same song, hailing him as an old-school rudeboy.

'I Luv U'
Shystie (2003)

As a song, Shystie's version of 'I Luv U' is a little bit necessary and a big bit relevant.

The necessary thing about 'I Luv U' is that it is a 'reply' to Dizzee Rascal's 'I Luv U' – which is a song that does for gender relations what bellyflops do for calm, still waters. It's a tense, paranoid, dystopian love song in which Dizzee Rascal advises against making declarations of love to young women who entrap young men into long-term relationships by having sex with them and maybe getting pregnant.

Splash.

Even though the original 'I Luv U' features a female perspective in half of the chorus, a full-blown riposte was always going to be welcome, which Shystie happily provided.

The relevant thing about Shystie's 'I Luv U' is that it is a landmark moment for Grime's soundclash energy being applied to gender politics. Shystie is well known for her appetite for diss tracks and dubplate drama[1], having gone toe to toe with Lady Fury back in '08 and Azealia Banks back in 2013, after collaborating with her on 'Control It' and finding out that she was a nightmare to work with (allegedly). As she explains in a 2014 interview with Complex:

'I'm from a scene where, if you do get disrespected, you put it on a dubplate and you put it out.'

Which is exactly what 'I Luv U' is all about, just that rather than targeting Dizzee Rascal specifically, she levels her vitriol at macho attitudes and misogyny in general.

It may have taken us until 2004 to meet one, but we can now confirm that the female Grime MC is not a mythical creature. She is very real indeed and, purely by dint of existence, faces three very real challenges. Listed below:

Empowering Yourself In A Scene Characterised By Machismo.

Very difficult, because it necessitates a high level of sustained aggression just to balance the wobbly seesaw that is 21st century gender politics, in which girls are still supposed to be 'the fairer sex'. Shystie tackles this head on in 2016's 'Dem Way Deh', in which she says repeatedly that, when it comes to MCing, she is not just good 'for a girl'.

Existing As A Minority Within a Minority.

As a black, British, working-class cultural artefact, Grime exists in society's margin. Women are a minority within this margin, making them especially visible and open to scrutiny/criticism.

Being An Automatic Delegate For All Your Female Peers.
Linked to above. When your identity becomes so tied to your gender that your every move is treated as representative of your peers.

Shystie embodies all three. Signed to Polydor in 2004, she was the first female Grime MC to land at a major label, emerging into the limelight in parallel to Grime's emergence from the underground. As an artist, she was everything you might expect from a female Grime star – feisty yet feminine and fearlessly belligerent and. . . oh shit, I'm suddenly sounding like an eager-eyed label executive.

In 2004, there must have been a major label steeplechase looking for the First Lady of Grime, a poster girl to go up alongside all those Channel U poster boys. Hackney-born

Shystie was an obvious contender, with the right sound from the right place and the right look at the right time, with a career sprung from tensions inherent in the scene.

---

1. *Dubplate Drama* was also the title of the mid-Noughties, interactive Channel 4 series starring Shystie as a record deal-seeking musician.

'Functions on the Low'
XTC (2004)

(Or Ruff Sqwad vs XTC vs Stormzy vs the Internet vs Nostalgia vs the Grime Renaissance)

There are three big mistakes you can make with 'Functions on the Low' (from here on in to be called 'Functions' to save characters). The first one is thinking that it in some way belongs to Stormzy because it's the instrumental used for his famous song about shutting up, entitled 'Shut Up'.

About 26 million people have probably made this mistake. I got this number by roughly chopping 52 million in half. 52 million is the number of YouTube views 'Shut Up' has gained to date, at the time of writing. I assume that roughly half of these views are from New Grime Fans who have never heard of 'Functions' or XTC until Stormzy said 'Shut Up' a lot over the loop. I fully appreciate that this is not an exact science. I am not a scientist. In a way, these people are very wrong and very right at the same time, because no, Stormzy did not produce 'Functions', but yes, he did bring it to the forefront of 2016 by releasing a very successful YouTube 'freestyle'[1] using the instrumental. There are now millions of people in the world who are unable to hear the opening strains of 'Functions' without instantly picturing Stormzy in a red Adidas tracksuit, surrounded by his mates on a crisp autumn afternoon.

The second big mistake is thinking that 'Functions on the Low'[2] is something to do with Ruff Sqwad. Which, again, is kind of true but kind of completely wrong at the same time. 'Functions' was released on white label in 2004, around the same time that Ruff Sqwad were active and putting out music. Internet has it that the song was wrongly uploaded to Limewire[3] with its production credited to Ruff Sqwad, which has left a lot of people in a state of confusion right up until the crafting of this sentence. Because the song never had an official release, it's understandable that people would assume the mp3 tag to be correct.

Despite the wrongness of attributing 'Functions' to Ruff Sqwad, you can see where the mistake came from on a musical level. 'Functions' has all the hallmarks of a Ruff Sqwad track, starting with lo-fi, Fruity Loops construction met with an innocence and almost wistful charm. Its quiet,

Oriental phrasings evoke a setting far removed from the brick and concrete of 21st Century East London, offering something whimsical and romantic. Drips of dew melting into lily pads while rising sun awakes the forest. Something like that. Incidentally, this might be the secret to the success of 'Shut Up', in that Stormzy laces his aggression and bravado over a quiet, poised, reflective instrumental. It creates a delicious contrast and alludes to Stormzy's depth as an artist, even when he's just telling people to shut their mouths. Anyway, the point is that many Ruff Sqwad classics share something of this reflective poignancy, which might explain why that kid on Limewire jumped to the conclusion that 'Functions' must have been a Ruff Sqwad production. This might also have something to do with the fact that XTC actually does have Ruff Sqwad affiliations. (If you YouTube hop long enough, you'll find footage of XTC lacing flows over a Rapid instrumental on a Risky Roadz video from '06.)

'Man try say he's been on grime since day
Tell my man shutup
Mention Stormzy everyday
Oi rudeboi shutup
Big up you 2015 grimeheads from Sussex tho'

-ashwin o, YouTube

The third and final big mistake is to think that 'Functions' is more or less important than it really is, because of its relationship with Grime's quote unquote 'renaissance'. The quote above is a top comment on one of the videos for 'Functions' on YouTube. The reason it's a top comment is because it captures the tension between Grime's underdog past and its prosperous present. Grime is drawing new attention from new fans, but the culture has a heritage that reaches back into history. Stormzy's flip of 'Functions' simultaneously confirms this heritage while creating a new context for it. You can absolutely enjoy Grime 2016 without any appreciation of Grime 2004 but there is a level of appreciation that you miss if you don't have the knowledge. It's the difference between the single reflection offered by one solitary mirror, and the infinities created by two mirrors facing each other in opposition. Deep.

***

If I had my way and was In Charge Of Everything, I would make it so that 'Functions' would play quietly out of the pages of this book when you first open it. It's the perfect soundtrack to musings on Grime's past and present. It's got a stillness that invites reflection, a haunting beauty that whispers. In the space of one paragraph, Dan Hancox called it 'heartbreaking', 'breathtaking', 'a masterpiece', and 'quite simply one of the greatest tracks in the history of British electronic music'[4], which is more praise than most art gets from most people, and you can see where he's coming from. It doesn't matter that 'Functions' is pretty much the only thing XTC really put out there that stuck[5], or that the last we heard he had a few Soundcloud tracks and a mixtape of unreleased material on the cards (2014). In 2004, he laid an important paving stone in Grime's history and it's proven smooth enough and robust enough to withstand the heavy footfall it readily deserves.

---

1. I put 'freestyle' in inverted commas because there is almost no consensus over what constitutes a freestyle these days. I always understood it to be an off the top of the head, made up series of rhymes that make sense in real time. Others believe a freestyle is any rhyme over any beat that isn't a fully realised song with a fully realised concept. There are hours of debate over this on the Internet. That's for another book, for another time.

2. I know I said I would call it 'Functions', but sometimes in writing you have to break all your promises for the sake of meter and rhythm. Well done for noticing though.

3. For the 26m people who thought this was a Stormzy song, Limewire is a file-sharing service from the Olde Internete, which people used to upload music to share with the world for free. Kind of like YouTube but without

visuals or a grammatically incorrect comments section, and a much longer wait time between clicking on something and actually experiencing it.

4. *The Guardian*, 2012 (and yes, *The Guardian* is the only newspaper that seems to have any interest in Grime. Because it's so liberal and right on, I mean, Left on). Hold tight Hattie Collins by the way, a real life, proper journalist who really and properly covers Grime.

5. That said, the 'Misty Cold' instrumental will probably emerge as a Grime classic if Stormzy ever decides to reintroduce it to new fans.

'Wot Do U Call It?'
Wiley (2004)

In a parallel universe not too far from our own, a statue of Richard Kylea Cowie stands in Mile End Park, East London. The statue is frequently visited by hipsters on pilgrimage from other parts of London. They stand and take selfies with the statue, whilst playing songs written and recorded by Richard Cowie on their iPhones[1]. Members of the local community often walk past the statue without paying much attention, because it has become part of the area's mis en scene. Once a year, on Richard Cowie's birthday, crowds of people gather to join in communal renditions of some of the previously mentioned songs. Small children walking past the statue sometimes let their heads turn in curiosity as they ask their parents, 'Who's that statue of?' The unveiling of the statue, in the mid 20-teens, made front-page local news and garnered some interest from national press.

Richard Kylea Cowie is the lesser-used name of the East London-based MC and producer known as Wiley[2]. The parallel universe described above very nearly became our actual, real universe when a Change.org petition to have a statute of Wiley erected in East London drew 5,002 supporters. The petition, initiated by Julie Adenuga (related of course, to Joseph 'Skepta' and Jamie 'Jme' Adenuga), is now closed, meaning that there may never be a statue of Wiley in East London. This is in spite of the fact that there are very good reasons why Wiley should be immortalised in this rather grand manner.

One of the biggest successes of Grime as a genre is that it actually has a name to go by. Grime is a legitimate musical genre, with related artists, Spotify playlists, devoted fans and a whole set of cultural norms. In 2004, this was not the case. The music we now know as Grime was emerging from the fires of 2-Step/Garage, fuelled by lo-fi electronic production and a generation of MCs who absolutely, energetically, furiously wanted to spit bars. The RnB-infused hooks of mainstream Garage were being jettisoned in favour of frantic lyricism and blippy electronica, all at the scream if you wanna go faster pace of 140bpm.

Wiley is one of the key architects of this sound. His dalliances in post-Garage, post-Jungle 2-Step resulted in the birth of a whole new genre dubbed 'Eskibeat', spearheaded by the 'Eskimo' instrumental in 2002. 'Eskimo' is prototype Grime for the ages. It sounds like what happens when a robot accidentally ingests mind-bending drugs. It sounds like the bastard love child of neon-flavoured Hubba Bubba and a PlayStation. In 2002, it sounded like the future, and in 2016, the tin foil hasn't crinkled. 'Eskimo' is a foundational piece of the Grime puzzle[3] which in turn makes Wiley one of Grime's founding fathers, and as he says in 2016's 'Bring Them All/Holy Grime', he's already made a scene. I really wished more people had signed that petition.

The Eskibeat sound gave birth to a handful of ice-cap themed classics including 'Ice Pole' (2002) and 'Igloo' (2003) released on white label by Wiley Kat Records (Wiley's independent record label). These tracks shared a more or less identical audio palette; vibrant, fizzling and ever so slightly abrasive. Wiley had successfully crafted a sound but it wasn't really until 2004 that he fully constructed the concept.

The central conceit of 'Wot Do U Call It?', released by XL Recordings in 2004, is that a new sound is emerging that people can't quite define. The sound is 'urban' and reminiscent of Garage and 2-Step, but it's definitely not Garage and it's definitely not 2-Step. And that's the whole song; Wiley frantically telling you that what you are hearing is new and exciting and definitely not what you think it is. This is important because it confronts the quest for legitimacy that a subculture eventually must face. To this extent, 'Wot Do You Call It?' can be read as a manifesto or mission statement – declarative, proud and slightly paranoid – a rhetorical question that kind of requires a real answer at the same time. What is this music?

I would argue that alongside DJ Slimzee (legendary Rinse FM pirate radio DJ, *Boy in da Corner* collaborator, recipient of one of the country's first ASBOs) and Jammer (Roll Deep member, Boy Better Know member, Neckle Camp member, NASTY Crew member, founder of Lord of the Mics, basement clash hoster, dreadlock waver), Wiley is one of Grime's true founding fathers. He's opened doors for aspiring MCs in the scene for as long as a scene can be said to have existed, and not just as part of his Roll Deep collective. In an important sense, Wiley has been Grime's greatest philanthropist, nurturing young talent and laying the foundations for their music industry exploits. A 2016 *Not For The Radio* interview sees Wiley compare his role in Grime to that of organising a 'youth club', calling himself a 'helper figure'. In the same interview he explains the 'burden' of carrying a scene through its infancy up through adolescence, a martyr's task, perhaps, when you consider how mainstream stardom has largely evaded Wiley while some of his protégés have reached truly Dizzee[4] heights of success.

It's worth dwelling on Wiley's generosity. His 'godfather' status is due as much to his paternalism as it is to his musical influence. Danny Weed describes the feverish altruism with which Wiley splurged £15,000 on Iceberg clothing after sealing his first album deal. The stash of clothes soon became a lending wardrobe for kids on the scene, stored at Danny's house for those special occasions when you absolutely need a £450 Iceberg jumper.[5]

Whether you accept the picture of noble sacrifice or not, there is a benevolence to Wiley that is hard to deny, which might explain why thousands of people signed a petition to immortalise him in the streets of East London. His actions have been of benefit to a culture, be it through promoting the Grime scene, crafting the sound of a culture, or simply releasing as much music as he can. In 2010 he made 203 tracks of original music available for free download after parting company with his manager. That could be, like, 20 albums. For free. An act of frustration, undoubtedly, but way more than a publicity stunt. So when he says: 'I looked at a whole scene, instead of one person,' you kind of have to nod in agreement, especially when you see the paternal pride with which he talks about the MCs who succeeded him and the MCs he clashed with in the past. Watch the interview – you'll see what I mean.

'Wot Do U Call It?' marks a moment of self-promotion

and self-realisation for Wiley that transcends the individual and begins to raise a culture. He asked us to go one way if we didn't like it and another if we did. A generation complied.

---

1. Most trendy people use Apple Inc products. Fact.

2. The only song in the history of ever that features Wiley's real name is 'Standard' by Jme, in which he lists a bunch of BBK's real names, because, I would imagine, he knows them like that and you don't.

3. Like, a corner piece, or even a corner piece already connected to one of the straight edges with a recognisable bit of the picture on it.

4. Pun intended.

5. *i-D*, July 2005. It might just sound like a funny anecdote, but underlying the eccentricity is a community focus that lingers around Wiley's persona and image.

'Destruction VIP'
Jammer
feat. Wiley, Kano, D Double E, Durrty Goodz (2004)

The opening track to Jammer's inaugural Lord of the Mics compilation sounds like a triumphant arrival. But ironically, for the first song on the first LOTM, it also sounds a lot like an encore. It's a chariot race lap of honour, replete with a symphony of glorious horns and bugle trills. The battle has been won and the war is over. The generals are celebrating over the bodies of slain enemies, announcing themselves as kings, and I'll stop this analogy now before I end up re-writing Lord of the Rings instead.

Jammer lines up a who's-who of brand name MCs to lace the track he crafted, none of whose sheen and credibility has faded in the twelve years since 'Destruction' was released, despite wildly differing narrative arcs: Wiley, Grime's easily identifiable 'godfather'[1]; alongside the poster boy turned veteran Kano; alongside the everlasting MCs' emcee, D Double E; alongside the one who almost didn't make it (with a brother convicted for murder and a year on trial for the same case), Durrty Goodz. Then you get Jammer himself, the nodding dreadlock, irrepressible and ever-present, an absolute devotee of a culture he helped realise. His Leytonstone-based basement studio (known as 'The Basement' or 'The Dungeon', aka his mum's house) has become something close to a Grime Mecca, drawing mythical status from the roster of MCs who have passed through over the years. It's an iconic backdrop for Grime's early years, covered in low-lit graffiti, a youth club slash cathedral for MCs willing to carry out the pilgrimage.

'Everybody's come through here… If you wasn't coming to the basement, you wasn't relevant. You're not part of what's going on.'
-Jammer, GRM Daily

This is absolutely true. The birth of the *Lord of the Mics* DVD series itself came from Jammer inviting Kano to clash Wiley on camera, in situ, in the basement, on the stairs. The result is some seriously iconic footage at a seriously low video resolution, with a text-to-win mobile number that I'm pretty sure won't be active on any network any more.[2]

I've heard Jammer describe himself as 'a businessman'. Actually, what he specifically says in the NFTR interview I'm referring to is:

'I'm a businessman. I'm there. To make. The light. On the situation.'

And all those Christopher Walken pauses are entirely necessary to convey how awkward that sounds as Jammer gesticulates hopelessly from the dark recesses of a black rain jacket. The fact remains that Jammer has made Grime his business for the best part of the 21st Century so far but it's hard to work out if his mission is financial or evangelical. If his own stats are to be believed, he's sold 25,000 CDs 'off his own back'[3], so maybe it's both.

He may be too fanboyish to satisfy the role of scheming entrepreneur, but Jammer also seems too much of a scheming entrepreneur to be the purely altruistic culture spokesperson[4]. 'Destruction VIP', therefore, is not simply a celebration of the Grime MC. It's also a savvy business move, declaring itself with a confidence made absolutely audible in Jammer's incessant shouting over the mixdown, like a market trader selling hot goods that are probably fake, but he'd rather you thought they were stolen. The song undeniably deserves classic status but it also marks a very early instance of the commercialisation of a nascent genre. Which, of course, makes it an all the more important artefact in Grime's infant years.

---

1. For the record, Wiley has to get Best Verse on this one for his addictively repetitive "don't know you" flow, which jettisons rhyme and wordplay in favour of listing all the aspects of struggle that Wiley knows well, and you don't. No surprise that MCs can't stop channelling these bars all the way into 2016: ie Jme's verse on Tinchy Stryder's 'Allow Me'; Chipmunk and Stormzy trading "don't know yous" on 'Hear Dis'.

2. I'm pretty sure Novelist channels this aesthetic in the video to 'Endz', unless of course his street team really expects people to text +447860 025 707 for more info. I wouldn't know, I haven't tried, and my phone broke after I dropped it at the garden centre. True story.

3. *The Guardian*, 2010. Six years later, who knows how many CDs he's shifted. Not many, if the CD really is as dead as Tempa T and Jme said it is.

4. That said, you can't doubt Jammer's altruism in the scene. The number of MCs he's showcased or brought to the fore via LOTM and other projects can't fit into this footnote.

Pow! (Forward)
Lethal B
feat. D Double E, Demon, Flow Dan, Forcer, Fumin, Jamaka B, Nappa, Neeko, Ozzie B (2004)

Like 'Destruction', 'Pow!', Lethal B's invincible 2004 posse cut, proves that Grime was never really about lyrical moshpit competitive conflict. MCs have always been in active collaboration, putting pirate radio cypher energy into fully crafted songs. Jammer set the tone on his first Lord of the Mics offering, making it clear that hungry MCs could occupy the same space at the same time. A few tracks later, you get 'Pow!', a song comprised primarily of adrenaline and exclamation marks.

'Pow!' speaks of a moment in earlyish Grime when the genre was kicking down doors, announcing itself in the charts with unrelenting, unrepentant aggression. Tonally, it's reminiscent of 2002's 'Oi!', complete with the monosyllabic hook and virtually identical chorus. Detonating into the charts at number 11 in late 2004, 'Pow!' came with its own health warning, drawing controversy with its subliminal gun talk and supposedly terrifying ability to cause spontaneous violence at nightclubs. Much has been said of the riotous fury swimming in the veins of the Forward Riddim, not least by the song's progenitor, Lethal B, who had this to say about the song, regarding one Mr David Cameron:

'Don't dismiss us... We've got more power than you have on the youth. You're a millionaire guy in a suit, your life is good – you can't relate. These kids can relate to people like myself, Wiley, Dizzee, Tinie Tempah, Tinchy: we're from the council estates, we lived in these places where they live, we know what it's like. We're the real prime ministers of this country.'

-*The Guardian*, 2011

It's easy to over-romanticise 'Pow!' as some kind of generational war cry, rallying against The System in delirious, adolescent energy. There's a mythology surrounding the song and its banned-from-the-airwaves notoriety that invites this. Not to mention the fact that it was actually, genuinely banned from a number of clubs due to these alleged spontaneous combustions of violence that would erupt on dancefloors whenever it dropped. If you believe some of the press from the time, 'Pow!' wasn't so much a song as a weapon of mass destruction. I would argue, however, that its true legacy can be found in its reincarnations, namely the fact that it keeps on drawing MCs into studio collaboration. We had the original 'Pow!' In 2004, then we had the sequel, ('Forward Riddim 2') in 2005, this time featuring the Fire Camp, including Kano and Flirta D, before the heavyweight 'Pow! 2011', featuring Jme, Wiley, Face, Ghetts, P Money and Kano. I'm fully expecting 'Pow! 2020' to land in a few years' time. Let me know how that pans out.

'Do They Know It's Christmas' Band Aid 20 (2004)

Yep, they do know it's Christmas, because 'they' are fully sentient human beings who can grasp the concept of seasonal religious holidays. Nope, Africa is not a world of dread and fear – it happens to be a continent consisting of 54 distinct countries with a tapestry of rich cultural histories, in which, believe it or not, there are sources of fresh water other than the bitter sting of tears. And how difficult would it be to industrialise the production of tear-water anyway? And no, it probably won't snow in Africa this Christmas but it probably won't snow in Walthamstow either, and I'm pretty certain I can survive this tragedy without resorting to bitter sting tear-crying, probably because I'm African. I'm also pretty certain that something actually does grow in at least one of the 54 countries of which Africa consists, and I've been in a few Ghanaian rainstorms on the few occasions

I've visited, but I was younger at the time so maybe it wasn't rain. Maybe it was all those adults crying down bitter tears when they realised it wasn't snowing. Anyway, a few facts:

1. The Band Aid charity supergroup project has been repeated three times since its 1984 inception: 1989, 2004 and 2014. This means that we[1] have been asking if Africans know it's Christmas for over 30 years.

2. Band Aid 20 marked the first time that lyrics were added to 'Do They Know It's Christmas'. The lyrics in question were Dizzee Rascal's contribution to the song.

3. Dizzee Rascal is a very well-known Grime MC.

4. Dizzee Rascal takes ownership of 30 words in the Band Aid 20 'Do They Know It's Christmas', 16 of which ask if we would survive Yuletide if we were deprived. The remaining 14 ask us to stop feeling guilty and give a little help to the helpless.

5. The next highest total of words is Dido, with 21.

6. Dizzee Rascal once referred to himself as an African from E3[2].

7.   Dizzee Rascal has never shed bitter tears over a lack of snowfall. But he does have flows as cold as the city of Moscow[3].

Writing for the BBC in 2004, Darryl Chamberlain described Dizzee's rapping on this song as 'embarrassing'. Jeremiah Abbott, from Hackney in East London, commented on the same article saying 'the Dizzee verse is essential in every way'. Depending on how you look at it, they might both be right.

---

1. 'We' is quite possibly the most dangerous word in the world, in that it creates an us and them out of the collective human We.

2. 'Bluku Bluku!' - D Double E featuring Dizzee Rascal. E3 is a postcode in the middle of East London. Africa is a land mass in the middle of the planet Earth.

3. Moscow is the capital city in a country called Russia, which is often cold and enjoys heavy snowfall. There are parts of Russia that, like many parts of the world, actually do fill me with dread and fear. E3 is not one of them.

'Orchestra Boroughs'
Mr Wong
feat. Crazy Titch, Jme, Flirta D
(2004)

Just so you know, I'll spend a lot of time in this book discussing race, with particular focus on that handrubbingly debatable black/white dichotomy. Grime sits comfortably in the world of binary opposition: black to the mainstream's white, poor to the mainstream's rich, aggressive to the mainstream's passive... In a word, Grime might best be described as 'other', and nowhere is the otherness debate more piqued than in terms of race.

But Mr Wong embodies a gloriously quirky curveball that proves how idiosyncratic Grime was in its earliest phases, by effectively using racial identity as a gimmick.

Before we get into it, it must be said that 'Orchestra Boroughs' is a near perfect example of the hyperactive energy that characterised Grime before Grime was honed into a marketable commodity. It's big and silly and rough round the edges and fun, showcasing personalities that are so big that they come across as caricatures. Flirta D, the malfunctioning human sound machine, Jme, the one who WILL beat you up, and Mr Wong, the. . . Chinese MC. Here, Mr Wong leans into his unusualness by turning his Chinese identity into a unique selling point, crafting a whole verse around the punchline "Chinese boy". I'm pretty certain that, at one point, he declares himself as a Chinese person being a white person trying to be a black person. This is ample evidence of the fact that Mr Wong is either a genius or insane, as is the fact that his 2016 comeback album was entitled, wait for it, *The Yellow Michael Jackson*.

'Whoz Dat Boy?' (2007) is further evidence of the identity shenanigans that Mr Wong was up to back in the day. The video starts with images of China on a map and East Asian symbol crashes, before Wong starts gurning and gesticulating theatrically on the streets of London. It's played for laughs while being simultaneously aggressive, which more or less sums up Grime's early shtick.

'Orchestra Boroughs' is a solid example of what Grime looks and sounds like, from the crunchy digitised synths to the repetitive hook verses to the overblown machismo. It's fundamental griminess puts Mr Wong into a category of Grime legends complete with slippery mythology and years-long absence from the scene. But far more important is the fact that it proves how identity shenanigans were always an integral part of Grime. Most Grime MCs look the part of a Grime MC (ie: black, urban, male), but Grime was always about playing up to an archetype. Mr Wong, in being so ostensibly different, automatically and necessarily highlights the level of identity play going on in this, existing as an exception to the rule that Grime is perpetuated by a majority of urban black boys, or a minority of angry working-class white boys (or an even smaller minority of angry girls).

One might argue that every Grime MC is living a persona that is at least partly theatrical, something that was so much more explicit in the early era than now. The size of your persona was genuinely a measure of an MC's worth as an emcee (as demonstrated by the hypermasculine posturing of Jme, alongside Crazy Titch's exaggerated aggression, followed by Flirta D's irrepressible sound effect vocal explosions), which explains the outright quirkiness of MCs up until the mid 2000s (after which things started to feel a bit more serious).

It's easy to summarise Mr Wong as a Grime footnote who offered a bit of light relief in the scene's early years, but the interplay of light and dark in Grime is worthy of further inspection. Grime represents a curious intersection of hypermasculinity and quirky weirdness, the latter gradually giving way to the former as the scene developed in the early 2000s. But despite this cool lava shift towards absolute seriousness, you don't have to look far to see the legacy of comedy and banter in Grime's central nervous system. Lethal B is a particularly resonant example, adding an 'izzle' to his initial and carving out a lane as a muscular party starter, with wobbly tunes about dancing like Uncle Fester and aggressively silly adlibs. DENCH. Then you get the likes of Tempa T and Jme, and to an extent Dizzee Rascal, self-styled jokers who fuse aggression and tomfoolery in pretty much equal measure. Not to mention the comic genius of Big Narstie, who has somehow crafted a persona built of hilarity and badman posturing in equal measure.[1] Elsewhere, the punchlines, punning and heavy wordplay of even the most serious lyricists (see Ghetts, Devlin or Giggs) reminds us of Grime's propensity for the humorous, for the indirect, for the quirky.

As dark and moody as it frequently gets, Grime has always retained a lightness of touch born of quirkiness[2]. This makes sense considering how easy it is to satirise Grime. It's so outsized, overblown and swollen with attitude that it sometimes feel like a pastiche of itself anyway, a subtle nuance that many Grime artists have played with from day one. The 'angry black man' archetype is so intense that it's risible, hence the fact that we can find instant humour in a

'Chinese boy' doing Grime in the first place. So Hold Tight Mr Wong and Hold Tight 'Orchestra Boroughs', an early reminder that serious silliness will always have a place in Grime's consciousness.

---

1. My one wish for this book is for Big Narstie to read it, translate it back to me in his own words, and then for me to write down what he says, verbatim, before publishing it again. That would be mad.

2. I expand on these ideas in the Grime: Stylised section of the appendix.

'Ps and Qs'
Kano (2005)

In 2004, those cocaine-snorting label executives trying to take Jme's integrity for a couple of bags were not discovering Grime. They had already discovered it. And they were looking for the Next Big Thing. Dizzee Rascal had secured his place at the music industry top table with his critically acclaimed debut *Boy in da Corner*, and it was obvious that Grime was a commodity with a future. From a commercial point of view, the scene had made its arrival and now needed a boy off the corner to push into the limelight, a poster boy, if you will.

Kano, the N.A.S.T.Y crew MC from Grime's spiritual home of East London, was already looking like that boy. My wife will tell you how good looking he is. With soulful doe eyes, sweet-boy cheekbones and a face that was, in his own words, 'made for the telly'[1], he seemed an easy pick for the future face of commercial Grime. He told us we might see his face in a magazine, or in a fur coat in *Face* magazine, and we absolutely did. I think. Google searches are coming up with nothing but I'm pretty sure that *The Face* magazine did indeed feature a fresh-faced, fur-clad Kane Robinson splashed all over its front cover at some point. Then there was that *RWD* cover, the one with a brooding K.A. decked out all Tony Montana alongside the declaration: '2005 belongs to Kano'. In '05, Kano was arriving – in style. He wasn't commercial, but he definitely had hit lines.

A few months later saw the release of Kano's debut album *Home Sweet Home*, and it was everything you would expect of a rising Grime star with commercial appeal's major label debut. In a word: infuriating. *Home Sweet Home* was thin on the bat-to-the-face aggression that made Grime so exciting at the time and heavy on chart-baiting crossover efforts aimed at a non-Rinse FM listening demographic.

When Kano rhetorically asked how he could stay underground, he was externalising the central dilemma that runs through his first album. He seemed all too perfect a candidate to cross from Grime's primordial soup into mainstream success, but the journey itself would leave him too far removed from his underground status. The softened edges of *Home Sweet Home* created a discord that some critics found 'wretched'[2], 'uncertain'[3] and 'unbearable'[4]. And then, in and amongst all the confusion, highs and lows, you get 'Ps and Qs'.

I remember reading somewhere that 'Ps and Qs' almost didn't make it, having been penned before the album was officially put together, which, in context, kind of makes sense. As far as *Home Sweet Home* goes, 'Ps and Qs' is something of an anomaly. It doesn't satisfy any tick box major label criteria and is brilliant as a result. It wasn't a deliberate bid to be a Grime anthem like 'Boys Love Girls' was (incidentally the second ever song Kano produced himself). It wasn't a crossover attempt. It wasn't a bubbling raver like 'Reload'. It was a slightly paranoid, autobiographical announcement of self; a summary of Kano's experiences as an almost infamous, famous underground star. In terms of content, Kano slides around a recognisable palette of topics: low-level criminal activity, local fame, further-reaching fame, breaking the mainstream, wearing fur coats, *et cetera*. Everything one would expect from a hungry MC.

Let's not forget that in 2005 Kano was more battle MC than Grime artiste. You just have to listen to his merciless dismemberment of Flirta D on Deja Vu over Footsie's 'Prang Man' instrumental[5]; radio-show diss bars forever captured by Jammer on the first *Lord of the Mics*. 'Ps and Qs' is definitely pugilistic, due in part to producer Davinche's deliciously dramatic rolling synth. But it's also smooth. The snares aren't harsh and the bassline is a few steps away from menacing.

And, it's undeniably charming.

His bragging is almost parochial, starting with locality, bulging out to vague claims of 'overseas' fame, then retracting quietly back to the UK. Kano's bravado comes with a charm borne of humility. He knows where he's from; a Great British MC who makes great, British songs. 'This Is England', the St George's Cross-waving ode to England from Kano's 2016 album *Made in the Manor*, stands as testament to this, proof that Kano takes as much pride in his provenance as he does in his prowess.

Kano is still crafting. His flow is imperious and nimble, full of unpulled punches and subtle brushstrokes alike. He's never compromised the artistry of his lyricism and has always put the work in, making it impossible to dismiss him as anything less than influential. The numbers might suggest otherwise, but Kano is easily one of the all-time greats, who continues to grow in stature.

In an important sense, the tensions within *Home Sweet Home* echoed a much wider tension within '05 Grime. How could the genre evolve into mainstream legitimacy without compromising the essence that gave it mainstream appeal in the first place? It's no surprise that little more than a decade later, Grime is in a position where a 'renaissance' can be said to be happening. It's a genre anguished by a desire for acceptance that is (ironically) most free at its most abrasive. 'Ps and Qs', in all its poise, is a perfect sonic snapshot of approachable Grime, from an artist with charisma, skill and substance enough to weather the storm. And for all its internal conflict, it stands up as an uncompromised example of commercially viable Grime, for all time.

---

1. In March 2016 (two days before my birthday), Ben Beaumont-Thomas (writing for *The Guardian*), described Kano (in a moment of perfect poetic poise) as 'Impala-eyed', before labelling him (accurately) as 'the UK's prettiest MC'.

2. Alexis Petridis, *The Guardian* – ouch.

3. Alexis Petridis, *The Guardian* – fair enough.

4. Alexis Petridis, *The Guardian* – ouch, again.

5. 'Prang Man' sounds like a firework having a fight with an electric guitar. It's brilliant, and confirms Footsie's genius as a producer. I will reference it as much as I can in the writing of this book, without hesitation or apology.

'Extra Extra'
Devlin (2006)

Here are a few of the things that Devlin said about Wiley in his 2006 diss track 'Extra Extra', released in the midst of an ongoing beef (that may or may not have started because Wiley accused Ghetts' mother of having dry toes):

You have sex with underage girls.

You have an uncontrollable cocaine addiction.

You are fake.

Your career is on the decline.

You are a mediocre MC.

You are old.

You have released albums that nobody buys.

You want to have penetrative anal sex with 'kids'.

You perform acts of fellatio in and around the district of Romford.

These are all pretty incendiary accusations to throw at someone. But despite having said these things about Wiley, and recorded them, and encouraged strangers to listen to these recordings on various public channels, Wiley very generously said he rates Devlin and labelled him a Grime treasure in 2016's 'Bring Them All/Holy Grime'.

Devlin was barely 17 when he recorded 'Extra Extra', stepping into the ring in solidarity with The Movement, a clique of Grime MCs consisting of Ghetts, Wretch 32, Devlin, Scorcher, Mercston and Lightning. 'Extra' is super harsh and super militant, landing punches with serious intent. Devlin puts his Dagenham drawl to devastating use, aiming to dismantle Wiley in a merciless display of lyrical pugilism.

Devlin's enduring respect in Grime is rooted in his fierce authenticity. He is unapologetically white, by which I mean he does nothing to distract from his identity as a white Briton. His flow has none of the West Indian flavour you might expect to have sprinkled into the cadence of a Grime MC, typified instead by elongated, cockneyed vowels and jaw-jutting glottal stops. He's also unapologetically ordinary, by which I mean he presents himself with an almost dour understatement. Where so many Grime MCs do everything possible to build themselves superheroic, extraordinary personas, Devlin's confidence stems from his scowling realism. His name, Devlin, isn't an alter-ego or self-empowering act of neologism; it's simply his last name. Devlin. James Devlin.[1] And he's unapologetically low-key. His biography is almost Dickensian in tone, snaking to success through a series of rags to riches obstacles, via the dole and the council estate. This might explain the frustration that seems to lie in wait behind his scowling lyricism; he's had a life of downs before the ups, and cannot shake the pessimism. All very evident in songs such as 'Community Outcast' (detailing the downbeat existence of a poverty-stricken single mother) and 'Life's Fucked Up', which, as alluded to by the title, suggests that life is indeed fucked up.

'Anyway, I just find it easier to address darker subjects.'
-Devlin, interviewed for *The Observer*, 2013

Fair enough.

Devlin embodies Grime's serious side, part of the reason that his 'Extra Extra' diss bars are so devastating. They come from that place of cold, hard reality that Devlin seems so comfortable in. But the flip side to Devlin's perma-frown is a lyrical energy that is hard to match in the scene. Far from simply being the archetypal 'crazy white boy'[2], he has a controlled intensity that demands respect, saying serious things in a serious way, with serious intent. In 'Extra Extra' we see a level of aggression that could have backfired if it wasn't so fearless. Devlin throwing disses at Wiley in '06 is like if Eminem fired shots at Dre in '98. A sharp intake of breath would have been required. Ten years later, we can all breathe easy – Devlin knew exactly what he was doing and continues to do it well.

---

1. It helps that Devlin is a very cool sounding name.

2. More on this topic in the essay Black mates and white niggas: On whiteness into Grime, written by me, later in this book.

'Serious'
Jme (2006)

When he made 'Serious' way back in 2006, Jme couldn't forget Sam told him it was a hit. He had to have bare meetings with pricks: Labels, A&Rs, radio playlists, managers... all looking at him like a dick. They weren't rating him, but guys they were rating, now, ain't shit. But Jme's still about. In fact, he's more than about right now. Sold-out tour, smashing it out, about twenty features, smashing 'em out. See him in a six cylinder, three litre, two turbo, ragsin it out. So don't tell him that Grime shouldn't be the music that man's putting out.

Jme embodies the solution to one of Grime's biggest problems: its own identity crisis. Jme is like Grime's antidote to its own neurosis. Jme might be about as real as it gets, because he uses Grime to embrace the very elements of his identity that Grime would otherwise shun. The enigmatic moniker 'Jme' is two vowels away from the very real name 'Jamie'. Jme isn't Jamie's alter-ego: Jamie is simply Jme. He's a contradiction in terms, which makes him fascinating.

As an artist, Jme is full of heart-warming contradictions. His lyrics are full of violent aggression (punching noses, breaking jaws, slapping top lips, singeing moustaches, poking out eyeballs with a bamboo skewer...), but coming from that impish frame, it comes off more like playground taunting than terrifying malevolence. His energy is hyperactive. Even when he threatens to suffocate a man with about two Gs ('Man Don't Care', 2015), it's a playful, almost endearing cartoon violence, any intended malice lost in the ADHD nerdism that Jme spins so well.

Then there's his street/not-so-street dichotomy, perfectly summarised by a line in 'Man Don't Care' questioning how someone with a university degree can be doing what he does on the mic. In a scene where academic success has very little bearing on your credibility, this is a very pertinent question. Equally, in a country where black boys have a historically difficult relationship with formal education, the question stands: Why would a university-educated young man turn MCing into his Plan A? There's a moment in the 'Man Don't Care' video where Jme takes a prop university degree and sets it alight in a blazing rejection of societal expectations and mainstream definitions of success. He then proceeds to use this to set fire to the microphone that he has chosen to define him, before rapping a few bars into the flames. It's a powerful conflation of ideals that ultimately empowers him. He can do what he wants, how he wants, with or without the acceptance of mainstream society. Grime, in its idiosyncratic tunnel vision and ADHD energy levels, is much the same; a symbol of empowered disaffection. And as Kano so succinctly put it in the *Beats and Bars* mixtape, penning bars can offer a legitimate alternative to penning a UCAS application form.

Then there's the whole cool/nerd thing. As a professional producer, performer and Grime MC, Jme probably has one of the most street-credible occupations in the country. His affiliations with other cool people run deep in the scene (Google his features list) and he's a core member of the Boy Better Know family. At the same time, he lives and breathes nerdism. He collects Pokémon cards (and trades Charizards on Twitter for copies of his album). He obsesses over technology, stating heartfelt preferences for iPhone over Blackberry, Xbox over PlayStation. He dropped a Harry Potter reference. He's performed in a full-body replica Iron Man costume. He boasts about putting stones in a Casio watch. And he's eminently sensible. No alcohol (in a rave, he'll get a lemonade and ice), no smoking (cigarette smoker, that's not he), no credit (he will never live life beyond his means) and no meat (apologies to all aquariums but he rolls with a couple pescatarians, vegans and vegetarians).

In 2006, 'Serious' was the perfect introduction to Jme's stereotype-bending persona and the song still stands as a direct challenge to Grime's obsession with hypermasculinity. When Jme calls out the entire scene, questioning (in his trademark, no-nonsense couplets) the link between social deprivation and aggression, he establishes the song's central conceit, that MCs who seek authenticity through street credentials alone are actively holding the culture back. This was a particularly progressive sentiment in 2006, when Grime was still a burgeoning genre. With 'Serious', Jme not only pre-empted Grime's self destruction but demonstrated an alternative mindset for a Grime MC: plain speaking and authoritative without pandering to roadman stereotypes. The introduction to 'Punch In The Face' from his 2008 album *Famous?* says it all, in which all you fake gangsters out there are called out on acting like you've never felt pain, had family, fallen in love or watched television.

In all of this, Jme is Grime's first (and only?) true Everyman. Part of the reason for his enduring appeal is that he reflects the very real experiences of his fanbase. *Famous?* contains all manner of down-to-earth reference points; burning CDs for your mates before going out, having gaming consoles in your room, getting the train to university, not having much money in your pocket, not selling drugs for a living, NOT being famous... the list goes on. Jme outlines ordinary experiences for ordinary people, forcing us to re-evaluate accepted notions of 'realness' in urban culture. When he invites everyone to be Jme, he is underlining the universality of his perspective. And he does so without resorting to introspective, low-key navel gazing or moody, shuffling beats, keeping the music upbeat, the beats bubbly. As he states in the 'Serious' chorus; have fun, dance to the music, don't take yourself so seriously.

Jme's universal appeal is not limited to fans. His (extensive) list of features is testament to the respect he has won from his industry peers. Furthermore, it's no coincidence that Grime's godfather, Wiley, and Grime's prodigal son, Tinie Tempah, have both signalled Jme out as one of the scene's realest, from polar ends of the Grime spectrum. In his unwavering devotion to Grime and watertight Everyman appeal, Jme has positioned himself as one of the scene's unshakeable pillars. As he says in 2015's 'Same Thing', he can't make a comeback because he never went anywhere in the first place, an enigmatic and cryptic assertion that you can make absolute progress by staying absolutely still.

'Talking da Hardest'
Giggs (2007)

There's a line in 'Talking da Hardest' where Giggs asks a rhetorical question about being "quiet".

It always gets me thinking. Because, in many ways, Giggs is an unmistakable introvert. His persona is understated and low key. His voice soft and low. His alias 'Hollowman' literally refers to invisibility, an allusion (I assume) to the 2000 Kevin Bacon sci-fi thriller about an invisible man who lets his condition erode his morality. There's a background quality to Giggs that gives him a subtlety we don't always see in Grime stars.

Case in point, his 2011 BBC performance of 'Look What The Cat Dragged In' at the Reading Festival. Or, more specifically, his post-performance interview. Muted, slightly awkward, almost shy, you can see the introvert. At that point, Giggs was still promoting his debut album *Let 'em Ave*

It, on the way towards generating mainstream success. Five years later, Giggs has more or less established himself as one of Grime's elder statesmen, with a weighty back catalogue of mixtapes and features, but when he was a burgeoning industry talent there was a palpable insecurity that shone a light on his quietness.

In a world that celebrates the extrovert (reality TV anyone?) and often views the introvert with suspicion, the real question here is whether or not introversion is a problem for the Grime MC. At one end of the spectrum you have your Tempa Ts; overblown caricatures of extrovert, reactionary masculinity. Most Grime veers into this lane, the genre largely typified by violent content and anti-social self-empowerment. At the other end of the spectrum you might find your Devlins and Mic Righteouses; introspective social analysts angsting over their own neuroses. Most artists dip into various points of this spectrum at various points in their careers, with catalogues that fluctuate between punch-in-the-head audio aggression and inward-looking psychological inspection.

What makes 'Talking da Hardest' particularly worthy of examination is the tension it holds between both states. It feels like a moment of extroversion from a confessed introvert. As a declaration of arrival ('Talking da Hardest' was the tune that put Giggs on the map, a pre-Trap anthem that set the tone for what some people call 'Road Rap'), it is unquestionably bold, packed with all the super-masculine tropes we have come to expect from Grime: sexual proficiency, social power, wealth, criminal success and aggression. But it does so with a quiet rather than loud confidence.

In this, it must be stated that music making of any kind is an introverted process. Forget the stage show. Sitting down to write and record songs involves introspection, patience, craft and care. All artists share something of the introvert – they have to. Perhaps, then, Giggs is just another example of, rather than exception to the rule. Grime is brash and loud and anti-social, but in an important sense Grime MCs are Romantic figures, in the English Literature sense of the word. Far from just hyping up crowds with rhyming couplets, the modern MC is reflective, searching, nuanced and analytical, exploring ideas and moods through the lens of their lives, experiences and desires.

In this sense, 'Talking da Hardest' can be read as a definitive example of the triumphant introvert, or the introvert unleashed. Giggs shuns his quietude and pushes his persona through the whisper barrier into husky audibility. And he does so with a freewheeling exuberance that is genuinely elating. Go hit play and try to not get caught up in his relentless volley of internal rhymes. Flow-wise, Giggs gets it right in the pocket on this one, surfing the beat with gladiatorial confidence. He's gone on record as saying that he thought his voice was too deep to be accepted in the MC fraternity, but the unusually low timbre of his voice cruises seamlessly through the stuttering drums, punctuated with the (now trademark) adlibs "Ummmm!" and "Jheeze!", satisfying little explosions of energy that burst through the cool at exactly the right time.

To return to the title for a second, it's easy to believe that for Giggs, talking really IS the hardest. The weight of his experiences (selling drugs, evading the law, facing the risks of urban violence, two years imprisonment for firearms offences) give him street authenticity but also act as a burden. He has gravitas but he's not bragging, simply explaining his past as opposed to glorifying his street credentials. The workmanlike manner in which he describes his drug-dealing past comes across as factual and understated, with a coolness that goes in the opposite direction of hype.

No punchlines. No wordplay. Just cold hard statements of the reality of things, if your life involves selling illegal substances at a profit. The lowest of profiles. As he states in an interview with journalist Paul Morley: 'Everyone says it's negative what I'm talking about, but it's just everyday life to me, and everyone else... It's not really negative; just what's happening.'[1]

It's a wonderful contradiction that Giggs embodies – the soft-edged understatement of a street-hardened introvert. For me, this is why 'Talking da Hardest' will survive as a canonical track, an example of Grime being honest and vulnerable without compromising any of the toughness that the genre demands.

---

1. Youtube. Giggs interview with *Guardian* journalist Paul Morley, uploaded by Overground Online, 2010.

'Black Boys'
Bashy (2007)

I may have grown up on an estate in Brixton (hold tight Myatts Field) but I'm not road. I grew up a black boy in a predominantly black area and now, I'm a black man. Statistics say I could be dead or in jail but I've always been positive.

I've made a few movements towards success, not least of all teaching in London for the best part of a decade, during which time I've taught many black boys. Some of whom I hope I've encouraged to make their own positive movements. Some of whom fell out of formal education prematurely in line with frustratingly common trends. And now I have a son who will no doubt be labelled a 'black boy' as he grows up. All of which makes my tolerance for 'black boys' incredibly high, while firmly flicking my cynicism switch to the 'off' position.

The way that Bashy introduces 'Black Boys' with such a plosive emphasis on bigging up black boys sets a tone of urgency bordering on agitation, as though he's desperate to shout about an issue that has been sidelined for way too long.

"Look -"

He launches into the first verse like a manifesto, spitting his big up to black boys with all the authority of someone explaining something to someone before they lose their patience. It takes little more than a bar for him to define a UK-centric, black-British success. Bashy shouts out rich black men, like Puff 'Diddy' Daddy and Nelly, who represent the aspirational 'baller' success stories that we have inherited from US culture, via hip hop. Bashy is quick to clarify his position with the assertion that he was even happier when he saw Dizzee Rascal pick up a Mercury, because he's a black boy who is similar to him. Suddenly, the lens has shifted from a general picture of black success to something closer to home, personal and recent. Grime, in its earliest moments, was demonstrating a whole new potential for black adolescent empowerment.

This is what Bashy zeroes in on for the bulk of verse one, carefully listing a who's-who of cultural architects and pioneers within the scene of which he's part: Dizzee Rascal Kano, Lethal B, Wiley, Megaman and So Solid

But the beauty of 'Black Boys' is in its scope. Bashy allows his perspectives to go far beyond the immediacy of his context as a Grime MC, crafting a sprawling ode to all corners of positive blackness. He invites us to recognise MCs as just another strand of black talent[1], in the same bracket as female soul singers, male soul singers, business entrepreneurs, top-flight footballers, actors, comedians, politicians, athletes, newsreaders, and, poignantly, fathers (specifically his own father). There is no other song in this book that puts so wide a frame on black success[2], and this is important when you think about the limited scope through which Grime is often viewed.

It's a point of tension that Grime conforms so readily to certain black stereotypes, and this is something that Bashy tackles head on. In this respect, 'Black Boys' is a relatively rare instance of 'conscious' Grime that prioritises social critique over soundclash party-starting. When Bashy admits to almost crying over 'Cry' by Swiss (the So Solid member well-known for being in the 'conscious box'), he's referencing a tradition of critical, enlightened UK lyricism. Career-wise, he's far from a quote unquote conscious rapper, but there's an earnest clarity to 'Black Boys' that makes it a defining moment in his story (and the most famous song in his catalogue).

So far, 2007 has been represented by 'Talking da Hardest', the explosive birth of grimy road rap from an unassuming industry outsider. 'Black Boys' gives us another 2007 angle entirely. From the moment you hear the wistful strains of that Five Stairsteps sample flip, you know what you're in for: an open-eyed, open-hearted, open-letter to black masculinity – and it delivers exactly this. Ashley Thomas isn't trying to prove a persona or confirm his credibility here; he's outlining a tribute to himself and his peers, an explicit acknowledgement of positivity in the black community.

---

1. Rodney P we've already seen in the London Posse chapter. Blak Twang makes his first *Hold Tight* appearance in this footnote, which is kind of embarrassing, because Tony Rotton is officially an influential British MC.

2. Ashley Thomas' career is equally diverse, having famously gone from bus driver to MC to actor to brand entrepreneur to actor again to whatever happens to pique his interest at any given time.

'Rhythm 'n' Gash'
Rebound X (2007)

I'll let Twitter[1] handle this one:

Rhythm and Gash is the best tune ever made

@joeweall

If rhythm and gash doesn't get u gassed

then I dunno what will

@EmmaDockseyx

If I die can someone make sure Rhythm and Gash

gets played at my funeral

@Benanarama

Rhythm and Gash on bbc news lol

@kyrang

Probably heard rhythm and gash more
than any other record at Glastonbury
@brian_o

Mix any song with rhythm and gash
then suddenly you're a dj
@frvsvr

Rhythm and Gash will forever be brought out
@dillonmaisuria

It isn't a grime set without Rhythm and Gash
@Chris_Idialu

Why can I not escape rhythm and gash?
@seaward99

Stop playing rhythm and gash. Please.
@mcooperwrites

Rhythm and Gash should be banned
@JoshBonello

This is what happens when a song is too perfect.

1. 'The Rise of Rhythm 'n' Gash (According to Social Media)' by Joseph Patterson for Complex UK, 2015. Credit where it's due: an excellent article online about the enduring appeal of 'Rhythm 'n' Gash', in which Joseph Patterson explores the song's 2015 rise in popularity and pulls a few tweets off the timeline. In the spirit of ongoing research, I thought I'd have a look at the 2016 response.

'Wearing My Rolex'
Wiley (2008)

The mid-Noughties saw a continued push towards electro-dance in the Grime-Pop continuum, as the commercial viability of Grime MCs became more apparent in the mainstream.

With 'Wearing My Rolex', Wiley peaked at number 2 in the UK charts in May 2008. Two months later, Dizzee Rascal would secure a number 1 slot with 'Dance Wiv Me', the Calvin Harris-produced track released independently on Dizzee's Dirtee Stank label. Arguably, 'Wearing My Rolex' is yet another exhibit in the case of Wiley paving the way in Grime, albeit accidentally. This particular foray into the mainstream remains one of his most commercially successful moments, but it wasn't particularly calculated, it wasn't released independently and it didn't spark a legacy upon which he would build a stable career in Pop. Tales of

Wiley's spikiness and unpredictability within the industry have reached almost mythical levels (he famously failed to appear in the video for 'Rolex' due to any combination of: a strop, a spot on his face, a recent scar following a knife attack, fear of the video being 'white people's vision'[1], a phobia of foxes, or a complete and irredeemable breakdown in communication with Kim Gehrig, the video's director, depending on which version of events you decide to believe) but his status as Grime's godfather solidifies with every sentence written about him.

The crossover success of 'Wearing My Rolex' lay not in its promotion of Grime so much as its stripping back of Grime's ebullient lyricism into a serviceable dance hook. See, Wiley can spit; he's got bars upon bars, he's not afraid of rhyming 'knows it' with 'knows it', and his extensive back catalogue is a running tap of skippy flows. In 'Rolex', however, his lyricism is reduced to something far more accessible: a memorable clutch of bars that are danceable and chantable, laced over a solid four-on-the-floor beat and a nifty sample of a lesser-known 1991 House tune (hold tight DSK).

It's a formula that I'm surprised hasn't been repeated since, but that may be because it's actually quite difficult to locate the pocket that 'Rolex' so neatly slots into. It's an impeccably balanced dance-along featuring enough Wiley to push it through the anonymity barrier, without sounding like a bait crossover attempt. 'Heatwave', Wiley's pop offering from his 2012 album *The Ascent*, didn't quite get the alchemy right (too charty, not enough clubby) and hasn't survived as a classic as a result. Wiley was one of the first to make Grime, leave it, try something else, and come back to it. 'Rolex' remains the shiniest artefact of this diversion.

---

1. This could probably justify a whole separate essay. The video, backed by record label Asylum, was a deliberate crossover bid. This meant that it circumvented all the usual Grime tropes, opting instead for an altogether sexier conceit: Wiley being hunted by models in fox outfits and being systematically robbed of his personal effects until left standing in his underwear. In a tradition of electro-dance videos that routinely feature sexy female models in scanty fancy dress, this is innocuous enough, but the positioning of Wiley as a the brunt of a visual punchline does raise an eyebrow. It's a deliberate softening of the Grime MC that works by dismantling a stereotype, yes, but it dances that line between softening and mockery. If Wiley really did accuse the video of being 'white people's vision' (as suggested by a supposed video shoot insider on the blog somesuchstories.tumblr.com), it might be because he was sensitive to underlying identity politics.

'Dance Wiv Me'
Dizzee Rascal

feat. Calvin Harris and Chrome (2008)

It's 2003. You are a 13-year-old girl and you are madly in love with Justin Timberlake. It's the best day of your life because you have just been given front row tickets to see him perform live. You squeal with delight.

You are at the arena, clutching your digital camera and sobbing with anticipation. The lights spin through the dark and the crowd is euphoric. A booming voice announces the first support act.

Wait...

Now imagine you are Dizzee Rascal. You have just stepped out on stage in the UK leg of the Justified World Tour. You peer into the screaming thousands and see a sea of faces, predominantly teenage, predominantly girls. Launching into an energetic rendition of 'Fix Up, Look Sharp', you realise that you haven't quite got the songs to engage with a mainstream pop audience. Yet.

It's 2007. Now you are Calvin Harris. You have had a top 10 hit in the UK charts with a song called 'Acceptable in the 80s'. You are enjoying yourself at the BBC Radio 1 Big Weekend in Preston where you meet, among other people, Dizzee Rascal. He is really enthusiastic. You exchange numbers. Later, you spend a lot of time meticulously producing the backing track to a dance song that will eventually become 'Dance Wiv Me', recording your vocals separately to Dizzee's, which you exchange remotely.

Keep imagining you are Calvin Harris. You have been nominated for prestigious awards on both sides of the Atlantic. You hold the record for the largest number of top 10 singles taken from a single studio album. According to Forbes, you have been the world's highest-paid DJ for three consecutive years (2013-15 inclusive). You have performed to one of the largest ever audiences in the history of the Coachella Festival. You model for Emporio Armani. *The Sunday Times* Rich List has you down as being worth £96m in 2016, ranking you as the 27th richest music millionaire in the UK. 'Dance Wiv Me' was your first UK number 1.

It's 2008. You are the boss of XL Recordings, the record label that Dizzee Rascal used to be on. You recall a conversation with Dizzee after he presented you with 'Dance Wiv Me'. You remember not being convinced that this divergence into dance-pop was the best next step for his career[1]. Imagine your face when you discover that 'Dance Wiv Me' has topped the charts at number 1, having been released independently on Dizzee Rascal's own label, Dirtee Stank. It is his first independent release after parting company with XL, and the first independent UK number one in 14 years.

It's 2016. You are Jeffrey Boakye. You are in the latter stages of finishing *Hold Tight: Black Masculinity, Millennials and the Meaning of Grime*. You have been debating the Grime-Pop continuum for a number of weeks now. When you discover that 'Dance Wiv Me' was the first in a string of four number one singles from Dizzee Rascal's fourth album, *Tongue n' Cheek*, you realise that it has an automatic pass into the annals of Grime history. You write this chapter.

---

1. An oft-quoted conversation, referenced in 2009 by *The Daily Telegraph*.

Frisco's verse in
'Too Many Man'
Boy Better Know (2009)

Do not get it twisted. Put the carnival stormtrooping synths
to one side for a second, ignore the crayon-subtle attempts
at genre-bridging (hold tight Skepta: we now know how
to make a tune for the mainstream, radio, roadman and
stage show at the same time), sharpen the focus on your
microscopes, and you'll see that 'Too Many Man' is about
one thing and one thing only: Frisco.

From the moment he comes through like, what is it on?,
to the moment he slews any man, slews any any man, Frisco
makes absolutely sure that his absence would have left the
song one man short, which would have been disastrous
because they would have to have called it 'Not Enough
Man', which is ridiculous. Frisco's verse is so good that
it makes 'Too Many Man' relevant in whatever year you
happen to be reading this. He cuts into the beat with shark-

fin clarity, radaring in on nothing in particular and calmly continuing to ride the surf of that clap clap rhythm with a string of simile-free, metaphor-free quotables.

2009 was the year Frisco left an indelible thumbprint on Grime with a verse that stands pillar-strong in his career. And if you pay close attention to verse two of 'Funny' (produced by Chase & Status in 2013 and surviving as the only Grime song in existence to feature a SpongeBob SquarePants sample), he's still forgetting the hype; if it is on then it's on. An eternal badman salute to Big Fris for taking the hero leg in BBK's most famous posse cut and turning it into an everlasting lap of honour.

The rest of
'Too Many Man'
Boy Better Know (2009)

Purely because I don't want any awkward moments when
Frisco shows this book to his friends.

Yep.

'Next Hype'
Tempa T (2009)

'Son,' I'll say with a grave look in my eye. 'If you don't tidy your room and eat all your vegetables, he'll sneak into your room in the night while you're sleeping...'

'Who will sneak into my room, daddy?'

'Tempa. Tempa T.'

My son will gasp and pull his duvet up to his eyes in fear.

'That's right. And Tempa T will flip your mattress and search for the cash. And kick your HDTV off the stand. And he'll even take all of your CDs.'

'Not my CDs!'

'And you won't get ANY of them back.'

Then I'll creep out of his room and whisper 'Tempz!' in the middle of the night, to freak him out.

On Halloween, I'll get an Incredible Hulk costume from the kids' section at Sainsbury's and spray-paint it West

African brown. Then I'll make a high-top out of cardboard, sellotape it to my son's head and send him to school as Tempa T. And I'll teach him to say things like "boy off the ting" and "WOOOYY".

Years later, he'll persuade his uni mates to dress up in matching Tempa T outfits and ironically go out on a next hype. They'll go to the local park and chase down a man flying a kite. The police will be called and my son will spend a very non-ironic night in a prison cell.

On his wedding day, my son's Best Man will relay this anecdote to the cheers and grins of an assorted collection of close family and friends. This will mark the first and last time that 'Next Hype' will make it on to a wedding playlist.

***

In 2009, Tempa T turned the angry, unstable, permanently aggressive, ridiculous, furious hype-man into an official Grime archetype and in doing so, he made it tacitly OK to be violent and silly at the same time. A caricature of aggression, he announced his arrival on the scene with 'Next Hype', growling his way through a series of ridiculous threats and promises of bodily violence, sugar coated with an undeniable playfulness.

Yes, 'Next Hype' is violent, but unlike so much Grime

before and so much Grime since, it invokes a level of exaggeration that almost tips into sarcasm. Tempa T showed us that Grime didn't have to limit itself to kitchen sink grittiness, offering an outrageous, overblown and ultimately funny slant on the anger and aggression that society so often associates with black boys. The video reinforces this, where even the most plausible acts of violence are lampooned into snippets of pantomime. The ridiculousness of chasing a man down for flying a kite in the park is juxtaposed with the very real prospect of a group of weapon-wielding boys chasing another group of boys at night, but we are invited to smile through both scenarios like a Tom and Jerry sequence. Also, the addition of Tim 'pre-ironic UK godfather of rap' Westwood sets a comedic tone from the off, in the one-time-only role of Tempz's line manager at Pars R Us.[1]

But, all that said, it's not purely silly. Arguably, the energy that fuels 'Next Hype' is drawn from the same well of protest and political agitation, with anti-social behaviour a close cousin to anti-establishment behaviour. As Tempa T explains:

'It's not about the [lyrical] content, it's about the energy and aura... The persona I portray gives a voice to those who use it as a way of expression.'
-*The Guardian*, February 2011

Despite a limited back catalogue, Tempa T remains a relevant figure in the scene, having carved his own lane as Grime's go-to noisemaker. It's hard to imagine Lethal Bizzle's testosterone-fuelled ode to the insanity workout, 'Rari WorkOut', without Tempz's musclebound presence. And it was a serious no-brainer to get him shouting about lions, gorillas and bears on the all-star remix of Solo 45's 'Feed Em To The Lions'.[2]

Ultimately, 'Next Hype' earns its place on the list because it somehow signifies a scream and sigh of relief at the same time. Like professional wrestling, or Death Metal, or any other genre that turns dangerous things into entertainment, it takes a few of the teeth out of belligerence without sacrificing the energy behind the bite, offering a relatively safe space to vent anger and frustration. However, this kind of anger-based dance music just might be inviting anger as well as channelling it. Sonically, 'Next Hype' stands as a moment of roid rage but ideologically, it might have more focus than that metaphor suggests, releasing Grime from the pressure to inflict pain with its punches whilst simultaneously encouraging us to step into the ring.

---

1. I'm guessing Pars R Us would be where one would go if one felt the need

to be brought down a peg or two by being insulted, or dissed, by a paid professional. I don't imagine this business model would be particularly successful in the real world, outside of Tempa T's imagination. On an unrelated note, it's really easy to dismiss Tim Westwood as a figure of derision, because of his ridiculous affectations and, well, whiteness. But the reality is that Westwood is a crucial, crucial figure in the establishment of hip hop in the UK. He fought for the cause in those years when the cause wasn't being supported, opening doors for a lot of artists, UK and otherwise. Respect where respect is due. That's why he's the manager. Note: Westwood would go on to reprise a similar role in the video to Roll Deep's 'Shake a Leg'. Note: Westwood also picked up the Legacy Award at the 2016 Rated Awards, in recognition of his long and celebrated career in black music.

2. Classic Tempz. He more or less just shouts about animals in the jungle for 16 bars, not really even bothering to push it that far into metaphor territory.

'Disguise'
Boy Better Know (2009)

Because this must be the world's first and only Public Service Announcement on the risks of accidentally bedding a transvestite, delivered via a Grime-inspired Transformers sample flip, and that really is an amazing thing.

That said, here's an essay I could write about 'Disguise' and the evolution of lad culture in Grime.

The Essay I Could Write About 'Disguise' and The Evolution of Lad Culture in Grime:

I would start by stating how 'Disguise' has a distinct lads-on-tour flavour, sounding a lot like a banter debrief session after a wild weekend in Amsterdam. Then I could talk about how the catchphrase "mandem in disguise" summarises the overall tone of the song: cheeky and silly in equal measure.

There's a lot I could go on to say about the rise of laddism among Millennials, where having a laugh/acting like an idiot is the modus operandi and punchlines are the currency of choice. Then I'd discuss how Grime has definitely taken on an element of lad culture in tone, audience and content, embracing banter as much as hard-jawed street credibility. 'Disguise' is a prime example, with Skepta, Jme and Jammer trading bars about mistaking men dressed as women, for women.

Next, I'd riff on the rise of Grime as a Festival soundtrack, sliding out of the shadows of pirate radio onto the sunny stages of summer festivals, where lads and ladies can large it before term starts.

Moving on, I could talk about how juvenile and puerile lads are, and how they exist in an immature state of adolescence. It's the mentality that makes boys say 'euuurghh!' all the time. I know that it's not supposed to be that deep, but I could continue to suggest 'Disguise' is very much a juvenile response to transvestism in the 21st century, characterised by a kind of shocked excitement. If I went further, I could even lift the lid on latent homophobia in modern masculinity, explaining how there might be fear and fascination behind the banter.

And all this from a song that bases its central conceit in the similarity between the words 'transvestite' and 'Transformers'.

'Pass Out'
Tinie Tempah (2010)

**Top Five Moments I Have Been Called Tinie Tempah,
In Reverse Order:**

Leaving Canonbury Station and two girls almost bumping into me before double-taking and saying, 'Raah. He looks like Tinie Tempah innit?'

Entering Peterborough services and hearing some guy shouting, 'Tinie Tempah!', to which I replied, 'For fuck's sake.'

At a wedding in Hull where a fellow guest insisted on getting a photo taken with me in the belief that I actually really was Tinie Tempah.

Upon arriving at work in the mid 2000s and a colleague declaring, 'I thought I saw you in *The Guardian* today, but I think it was Tinie Tempah.'

And in 1st place:

Returning to my flat in Highbury Stadium Square, after a mis-timed trip to the shops, to be confronted with an army of Leeds fans being police-escorted along Avenell Road towards the Emirates Stadium for an Arsenal home match. Without enough time to get to the foyer before meeting them head on, I get spotted, alone, and a chant of 'Tin-ie! Tin-ie' goes up. I shuffle along nervously in my skinny jeans and square frames.

All of this is just a long-winded way of saying that Tinie Tempah is now ingrained in the UK's collective consciousness. He's as recognisable a celebrity as you can get; he's high-fived the future king, mid-BAFTA performance; he's sat on talk show sofas and hobnobbed with Hollywood stars; he's hosted *Never Mind the Buzzcocks*; he's become Mr *GQ*, Mr London Fashion Week, Mr Red Carpet; he's a festival headliner. He probably has a yacht. Does he have a yacht? I bet he has a yacht. Somebody Google 'Tinie Tempah yacht'[1.]

With the release of 'Pass Out', Tinie Tempah was fired into the mainstream on a trajectory that has yet to decline. He might get an OBE one day. He might even fuck about and record the first rap Bond song. He might end up marrying Princess Eugenie and sneak into the royal family that way. With Patrick, you get the impression that Anything's Possible, because 'Pass Out' shot for the stars, and bullseyed in spectacular fashion.

It did not take long for 'Pass Out' to go from a radio maybe to eight-figure YouTube views and wedding playlist mainstay. It sold over 90,000 copies in its first week and entered the charts at number one. The reason being, it's a great pop song. It defies convention, clocking in at a way-too-long 4 minutes 28 seconds (3:57 radio edit), building to a dancefloor-igniting Drum and Bass crescendo (hold tight the Amen Break). It's got Ragga-tinged guitar licks and 8-bit synth fluctuations tangling in symphony. It's commercial to the nth. It's full of nonsensical pop quotables about running for buses and having to call on your mum's sister to accommodate your wardrobe, and it even manages to survive some seriously timestamped reference points (The Hills? G Shock watches? Concorde?)[2]. And it's unmistakably British, because everyone knows Prince Charles and almost everyone can identify with not having been to Scunthorpe.

Now, while you might struggle to find 'Pass Out' on any

'credible' Grime playlist, the facts cannot be denied. Tinie Tempah is a Grime MC. Sort of. Well, insofar as he came up in the exact same Channel U pathways that birthed the current crop of Grime artists. His 2006 'Wifey Riddim' is a much-loved and loved-up affair at 140bpm (which, btw, could almost be Dizzee Rascal if you ear-squint hard enough) that a) showcased his mic skills and b) put him on the map. Then there's the soap operatic 'Tears' from around the same time, which is only really worth mentioning for that moment in the video where Tinie enters a party, grinning, carrying two bags of ice, to a legit hero's welcome. Anyway, if you continue to YouTube hop for long enough you might stumble across the video to 'Doin Me' where a very fresh-faced Tinie plays supporting MC to Bruza. If you don't know, Bruza was, in the early Noughties, a very legitimate contender for A Grime MC That Might Make It. He had a unique, East End growl style of delivery, he was front-covering *RWD Magazine* on occasion, and he could get a crowd shouting "Get me!" with relatively little difficulty. Bruza frontlined the Aftershock camp of MCs that Tinie was affiliated which included Krucial, DDark and Mz Bratt. But Bruza didn't crossover like Tinie Tempah did. Because Bruza never made a 'Pass Out'.

'Pass Out' represents the absolute zenith of Grime's potential to go mainstream. Tinie has done the thing that so many Grime MCs have attempted to do – break out of the underground and stay out. Since 'Pass Out' we've seen a handful of sun-drenched chart-breaking hits and he's never had to do a back to basics move to reconfirm his authenticity. His collaborations list is extensive and diverse, ranging from fledgling pop divas and US rap B-listers to Grime up-and-comers, and everything in between. You've got to respect that fact that he's got summer bangers for mums to sing along to in the Iceland carpark, and songs like 'Lucky Cunt', which actually features the phrase "Lucky Cunt" in the chorus. Eclectic.

In all, Tinie Tempah's position is clear as a successful UK rap export. While he might not have left a blueprint for exactly how to do it, and while many have tried to go mainstream (with various 'do not try this at home' degrees of success), he's definitely left us the best example of a genuine, timeless crossover hit, which sounds exactly like 'Pass Out'.

---

1. I just Googled it. It didn't reveal if Tinie Tempah has a yacht or not, but it revealed that he was invited to a private party on Rihanna's yacht in 2012. That's the kind of life that Tinie Tempah leads, it would appear. I am currently not on a yacht. But I have been invited to go drinking on a canal boat in Camden. Not by Rihanna. I declined the offer.

2. Before you accuse me of casting aspersions on Tinie Tempah's ability to achieve profundity, I'll go on record as saying that he has delivered one of most profound lines in Grime history via his 2014 Fire in the Booth freestyle, in which he drops a poignant line about Stephen Lawrence. If you time stretch that line and read between the static, you'll get a whole essay on racism and the empowerment of black communities in the late 20th Century, through abrasions with society at various levels.

'Streetfighter Riddim'
D Double E (2010)

I've been thinking about this opening section since I opened it and I've finally decided: it's nigh-on impossible for me to fully express the monumental significance of D Double E in Grime culture. Even the most cursory of Google searches will reveal that D Double has been at the heart of the scene for as long as a scene can be said to have existed. As part of the original N.A.S.T.Y Crew, he established himself as a legitimate founding father and continues to prove his stripes in solo projects and alongside Footsie as part of the Newham Generals[1]. His respect within the scene is unquestionable and unparalleled, and as the scene approaches something of an adolescence, he has emerged as a figure of absolute authority. An ongoing string of collaborations serves as proof of his industry status. His affiliations are watertight and his persona has evolved without compromise. His voice is unmistakable, his adlibs irresistible[2], his reloads infinite. And most significantly, he just doesn't release any bad songs, turning your car journey or iPod session into live club experience, one track at a time. Oh my gosh. Budu-bap-bap. It's D Double.

So, we've established that D Double E is an important figure, but what makes 'Streetfighter Riddim' an important song? First, a flashback, and apologises in advance if I patronise any '90s babies who may be reading.

It's hard to believe that not that long ago, kids would huddle in kebab shops and mini-cab offices to play on arcade machines. For 50p a go (or an old chunky 10p covered in tin foil[3]) you could enter the arena and pit your skills against whoever in a range of classic beat-em-ups. And none come more classic than *Street Fighter 2*, the game that dragon-punched its way into the consciousness of an entire generation.

Street Fighter 2 isn't just a game; it's a culture. If you're of a certain vintage, you definitely have a preference for Ryu over Ken, can pull off a flying kick, low punch, dragon punch combo, and probably have joystick-flick muscle memory programmed into your wrists. Playing the game was gladiatorial, complete with hecklers. You had to have skills to even step up to the plate, otherwise the humiliation would be instant and complete. At one point in history, part of the rudeboy skillset included being a don at *Street Fighter*. Winner stays on.

In this context, it is wholly unsurprising that computer gaming and Grime share something of the same Venn diagram. The vast majority of Grime artists enjoying 21st Century success were raised, in part, on a diet of arcade classics and 16-bit console gaming. You just have to listen to the electronic blips that are a key part of the Grime sound to see this in action. It's no coincidence that MC battle events with names like 'Beatfighter 2' (Don't Flop) are being hosted and promoted as recently as February 2016, while Charlie Sloth has successfully turned the 'Perfect' sample into his own radio bomb drop. 'Streetfighter Riddim', in its direct referencing of arcade skills as a reflection of general badboy status, is the Grime/gaming perfect storm.

The beauty of 'Streetfighter Riddim' starts with a basic premise. Think about it – a Grime song about being adept at a computer game. That's so real it's almost unreal. D Double E takes the energy and competitive aggression of Grime and places it in the context of a game about fighting, through which he then explores the usual tropes in a satisfying pile up of similes: bravado, lyrical skill, status, reputation and winning. As far as extended metaphors go, you won't find better, laced over a neat sample flip of the wonderfully blippy Capcom soundtrack. (Hold tight Swerve on production[4].

And while we're here, hold tight Dizzee Rascal on the sample flip of Chun-Li's theme in 2004's 'Streetfighter'.)

While none of this is particularly novel (Flirta D was making ADHD computer game noises as a staple part of his lyrical repertoire in 2004), 'Streetfighter Riddim' captures the nostalgia of gaming and energy of Grime with an honesty and purity that nudges towards the timeless. In an era where MCs are increasingly compelled to prove their worth via tall tales of supposed roadman activity, it's a rare privilege for a song that leads with real life and death issues – how good you are at making one set of pixels beat up another set of pixels. "Perfect."

Honourable Mentions:

'Cheque One-two' - Sunship (1998)
How this hasn't had an official Grime remix yet is beyond me. Addictive 2-Step beeps and blips in the pre-Grime primordial stew.

'Foolish' - Flirta D (2004)
No one before or since has so comprehensively incorporated video game soundbites into their flow. Production also sounds like a Mega Drive start screen.

'Streetfighter' - Dizzee Rascal (2004)

Early Grime toastings over a flip of Chun-Li's theme.

'Baraka' - Jme (2008)

Also known as the 'Mortal Kombat Riddim'.

'Who Are You?' - Chipmunk (2008)

In which we are informed that Chip also grew up on *Dragonball Z* and *Street Fighter*.

'Chillin' Wiv Da Man Dem' - Dizzee Rascal (2009)

Where Raskit makes a hook out of passing the pad.

'Look Out' - Skepta featuring Giggs (2009)

Who promise to run up and take all the gold coins like Mario and Luigi. BLING.

'Castles' - Skepta (2011)

Remember, it's real life, no computer game. Yes Skepta, we're living in the *Streets of Rage*. Typically reflective musings from Skepta via a Mega Drive reference.

'Let's Play a Game' - Eyez and Dubzy (2014)

Juxtaposing a moody Trap-tinged beat with everyman visuals of two friends going head-to-head on FIFA, and resulting in a pitch-perfect representation of the competitive spirit of MCing.

'Game' - Jme (2015)

Jme flips hardcore nerdism into badboy status with unquestionable authority. The third verse is all about how he will destroy you on Xbox Live. Extra points for the Charizard Pokémon reference.

'Lock Arff' - Section Boyz (2015)

"Phone kill like E. Honda". Please @ me if you know what the hell Knine is talking about.

'The Very Best' - Jme (2015)

A song about longevity in the Grime scene and Pokémon.

'Been the Man' - Tinie Tempah featuring Stormzy, Jme, Ms Banks (2015)

Where Jme says he's the final boss.

'One Take Freestyle' - Stormzy (2016)

Summarising the relationship between gaming and rapping in one neat metaphor about the rap game and winners staying on.

skit - Skepta (from 2016's Konnichiwa)

An entire skit devoted to *Call of Duty* multiplayer online shit
-talking.

Fire in the Booth - Kano (2016)

A Dhalsim reference for anyone who remembers and or
cares.

'Panasonic' - P Money (2016)

Where he builds an entire song concept out of Guile's special
move. Which was always annoyingly hard to pull off. The move,
I mean: hold back for two seconds then forward and punch.

'Whippin Excursion' - Giggs (2016)

A lot of men concern themselves with looking good (Ken
is notoriously vain) and looking after their 'Barbies'. Giggs
does neither, acting in the rather more feral manner of a
shocking lime green jungle creature. "Blanka" also doubles
up as 'blank her', confirming the cool callousness towards
women.

---

1. Answer: 'Prang Man', produced by Footsie. Question: What does a set of
steak knives in a pinball machine sound like?

2. When a character gets KO'd in *Street Fighter*, their dying wail is echoed in slow motion as they settle in the pixelated dust. D Double's 'echo machine' adlib is a rendition of this. I'm embarrassed to report that this has only just dawned on me, as of this week.

3. Other ways of getting free goes include sandwiching a one penny piece to an old 5p piece with chewing gum (the machines thought this was a pound coin), or using an oven clicker to spark up credits on the coin slots. I don't know which desperate, penniless player first discovered that any of this worked, but it did, and I thank them.

4. Back in my DJ days, I very nearly bought an import copy of a *Street Fighter* 2-themed Break record full of all the original gravelly Capcom samples. I'd like to think that had I done so, I would have produced something close to Streetfighter Riddim, but the reality is I would have looped a funk break and replaced the horn stabs with hadoukens. Ah well.

'Hello Good Morning Grime Remix'
Diddy Dirty Money
feat. Skepta (2010)

The Grime co-sign is a tricky thing. So much so that every time I sit down to write about it I end up pulling the wrong end of the shoelace and creating a knot that I have to unpick with clumsy fingers. This paragraph alone has taken me over two weeks to craft, and I'm still not getting it right. The problem is that tastemakers from across the pond are sitting up and taking notice at the exact moment when their validation means less than ever before, which creates a Möbius strip of debate that I get lost in, every time. It's happening again.

Grime 2016 is more than capable of advocating for itself, as proven by the latest generation of MCs reared on a Grime diet. There's a carefree confidence to modern Grime stemming from the fact that MCs only have themselves to impress, putting out local music with a global reach. The latest crop of Grime poster boys are making international waves with music that, ten years ago, might have only made local ripples.

When Sean Puffy Puff Daddy P Diddy Diddy Combs put out an open call for a UK MC to remix 'Hello Good Morning' (the lead single off his Diddy Dirty Money project debut), it felt like the ultimate co-sign for UK Grime. It felt like one of the hip hop tsars had reached a lazy arm across the pond and nodded his approval, like a Roman emperor pulling a grimace and offering a smirky thumbs up. And we responded. You might remember a little hashtag meltdown over which MC should take up the challenge, before Skepta was selected and did his flip.

The song had already seen one official remix featuring T.I., Rick Ross and Nicki Minaj, as well as a 'Team UK remix' featuring chart-hanging Grime poppers Tinchy Stryder and Tinie Tempah, but Skepta's efforts would tip it into a new direction. His remix had an altogether grimier sound that nudged away from pure pop, with frantic synths and a tweakedbpm, not to mention some pretty raw lyrics about liking tea but not liking crumpets.

It's worth noting at this point that Diddy is not a rapper, or a musician, or an artist, or a philanthropist, or a promoter of culture, or a fan of emerging genres of music from London, England. He is a business mogul, a moneymaking personification of the multinational business model, and a former back-up dancer, with the ability to find funky 8-bar loops in popular records of yesteryear and loop them into hits during the mid-'90s. His career has been a study in product diversification, of which music is just the most visible branch. In this context, the 'Hello Good Morning' Grime remix is a mere blip in his career's shark-slow heartbeat, part of a promotional push for his Diddy Dirty Money rebrand. This, more than anything, might explain why the song hasn't really endured as an important chapter, or page, or footnote, or punctuation point in the Grime canon. I mean, one of its YouTube videos only has 922,000 views.[1]

If Grime was the plucky hero of a Zelda-like quest, 'Hello Good Morning' would represent the deceiving king who promises wild riches but delivers only desperate hope. Grime would be momentarily lured off its noble path, before realising the truth and turning its back on the king's empty promises. Then it would sail off into the horizon to fulfil its destiny. In a black tracksuit.

Nowhere is this more apparent than in the opening verse of 'Ace Hood Flow' (2014), in which Skepta defiantly rejects the arm he embraced four years earlier, by asserting himself as a musical powerhouse and pouring scorn on British MCs trying to emulate a US sound.

A few years later and Skepta, representing the maturation of Grime, is levelling the US hip hop/UK Grime seesaw. The truth of the matter is that Drake signing with BBK does more for Drake's credibility than it does theirs. Kanye's 'All Day' call-out (Skepta got the call to get a stage full of MCs ready) confirms rather than creates Grime's credibility. Pharrell is indeed talking Numbers with Skepta, but *Konnichiwa* really wouldn't have suffered from his absence. And Diddy isn't even in the conversation. Evolution.

---

1. The levels of irony enclosed in this statement are so convoluted that I have no idea if I'm being facetious or not. This is what the Internet has done to intelligent debate.

'All Over The House'
Skepta (2011)

As a song, 'All Over The House' is a pretty innocuous affair: an electro slow jam about two people making love[1], all over the house. The accompanying video, however, is another matter altogether: an X-rated, fully pornographic moment in career Russian Roulette that momentarily put Skepta in the same genre bracket as low-budget UK porn. And when it landed, it was very nearly All Over for his future in music.

Skepta has tried more keys to mainstream success than any artist I can think of. 'All Over The House' represents the Let's Try A Porno Soundtrack key, banking on the old adage that sex sells. On this level, it was a complete success, igniting controversy and interest in equal measure. The video streamed on worldstarhiphop.com, thus exposing Skepta to a huge US audience and arguably paving the way for future stateside successes.

For Grime, 'All Over the House' is a first and last: the first time a Grime artist has dabbled in pornography to build music industry notoriety, and the last time anyone will get away with doing that before scooping a Mercury Prize five years later. Fact.

1. I say 'making love' because nothing is more romantic than comparing sexual intercourse to a CD tray going in and out.

'Castles'
Skepta (2012)

The opening line to 'Castles' should be plastered all over the Teacher Development Agency website landing page. By which I mean that whenever someone decides they want to be a teacher, they should be forced to read how Skepta's teacher told him he was a sideman, after which he told her to remember him, and now she's contacting him via email asking if he can talk to the kids at assembly.

It's a perfect summation of the fraught relationship between black male youth and formal education. It's a provocation and lament that asks serious questions about how black boys become marginalised and how desperately they need positive role models, aching with bitterness, anger and frustration. In two lines, Skepta paints the saddest picture of black success, channelling the vulnerable child and the calloused adult all at the same time.[1]

The rest of the song follows in this vein – introspective and knocking quietly on the door of insight. After reflecting on failing at school, Skepta chews over being distrusted by shop security guards and potentially ending up a 'statistic' due to his racial profile, all the while frowning at the media for making him view himself with suspicion and thinking he's looking at his enemy when he looks at his own people. Then he empathises with the 2011 London rioters (I haven't yet told Boris Johnson he's lucky Skepta made it rapping), ponders the futility of urban gun crime via a punchline about how everybody in the hood wants to spray a 16, and admonishes himself over the stupidity of casual drug use.

Skepta's recent spate of crowd-pleasing Grime anthems might be drawing fresh recognition from his student loan roadman fan contingent, but he's undoubtedly at his best when he's wrestling with issues of identity. 'Castles' is a prime example, in which he places his success within the widest possible social context. And the conclusion is clear: any sense of triumph is shackled by social stereotyping and historic tensions, which of course reflects the position of Grime in the popular consciousness.

The insecurity that Skepta wears so openly in 'Castles' is infrequently seen in Grime, though, perhaps, shared by the scene at a deeper level. The masculinity shield is effective, but heavy to bear. Skepta deliberately allows it to slip, offering insight into black male vulnerability, that lesser-explored aspect of black masculinity. For the best part of a decade, Skepta's career has been bobbing against the currents of his own ambitions, with all kinds of dalliances into motivational pop-rap, dance and, let's not forget, pornography soundtrack muzak. With 'Castles', Grime asks us to take it seriously – and its moments of profundity confirm that maybe we should.

1. Unlike Yungen's second bar from 'You Don't Know Me Like That', in which he bitterly informs us that he got kicked out of school in, like, Year 10, asks us to tell Miss Peacock he has a deal with Sony, and reminds us to also tell her that she's an idiot. Incidentally, Miss Peacock gets a second shout out in the first verse of 'Pepper Riddim', in which Yungen explains that rapping is more fun than uni, confirms that he did indeed get kicked out of school, boasts that he is making more dough than every kid in his year, and instructs Miss Peacock to go suck her mum.

'ill Manors'
Plan B (2012)

Grime is inherently political. At its core, it is the sound of disaffection and disenfranchisement, a marginalised youth screaming their discontent back at a society that has failed to accommodate them. It's no accident that Grime is by and large the preserve of black boys in urban contexts, because historically, black boys in urban contexts do not always prosper, falling prey to urban decay and dropping out of formal education.

This discontent is where Grime draws much of its noisy energy from, an anger that nudges into the realm of protest music. At times this is explicit, with MCs making direct reference to capital-P Politics. Dizzee Rascal probably wins the award for some of the earliest examples of explicit politicising in his 2003 debut *Boy in da Corner*, in which his anti-establishment rage was captured in a handful of quotables, including: Being a problem for Anthony Blair ('Hold Ya Mouf'); chucking grenades at Scotland Yard ('Seems 2 Be'); not obeying no policeman who ain't got a gun ('2 Far') and asking how Queen Elizabeth can control him when he lives street and she lives neat ('2 Far').

Other notable political quotables include Cas, who puts both middle fingers up, like, fuck the Tory party ('All Hallows'); Skepta, who still wants you to tell Boris he's lucky he made it rapping ('Castles'); Jme, who thinks the government must think we're dim ('Blind') and Jammz, who spends most of 'It's a London Thing' lamenting gentrification in the capital.

In 2011, London saw an outspread of rioting and social disorder, spanning two nights in August. The riots were sparked by the death of Mark Duggan, a 29-year-old Tottenham resident who was fatally shot by armed police during an arrest attempt on August 4th, acting under the Metropolitan Police's Operation Trident (established in 1998 to tackle gun crime in London's black communities). The Metropolitan Police maintains that Duggan was in possession of a live firearm at the time. Protests following the incident of his death escalated into rioting, vandalism, arson and looting, social disorder that was soon echoed in other UK cities. A four-month public inquest spanning 2013-14 concluded that Duggan was lawfully killed. However, controversy continues over the exact circumstances of Duggan's death, including an investigation from the Independent Police Complaints Commission, questioning whether Duggan was actually carrying a weapon when he was killed. It may or may not be worth noting that Mark Duggan has an affiliation to the Grime scene, having featured in the 2009 video to 'Look Out' by Skepta and Giggs. He was also listed in the RIP section at the beginning of Hattie Collins' 2016 Grime history book, *This is Grime*.

The tension between marginalised youth and governmental authority is well documented in Grime. Suspicion of and antagonism towards the police is almost a tenet of the culture, stemming far back into the historical relationship between police and urban, predominantly black communities. In 1981, confrontation between police and protesters in Brixton led to violence and rioting among the predominantly Afro-Caribbean community. Similar tensions flared up in 1985, also in Brixton, after the fatal shooting of the mother of a suspected firearms offender. Ten years later, the death of a suspected armed burglar in police custody instigated five hours of rioting in Brixton. I can remember this one; I was part of the crowd who were ushered by police into the big Pizza Hut on the corner of Coldharbour Lane (now a KFC). In all of these cases the one constant factor is the incendiary tension between police and black communities.

Ben Drew (aka Plan B) is not a black man. Ben Drew is white. This is only worth mentioning because it singles him out as a minority figure in a scene dominated by young black men. He is, however, definitely working-class, or at the very least, defiantly working-class, wearing his Working-Class Persona like a very high vis donkey jacket. This is important, because this is what 'ill Manors' is all about. As he so succinctly argues, there's no such thing as broken Britain, we're just bloody broke in Britain.

Released in 2012, the song is the title track on a concept album of the same name, which tells various tales of crime and social decay through a selection of protagonists. It also sits alongside a film of the same name, directed and written by Plan B. In all of this, the song 'ill Manors' operates as a rabble-rousing slice of agitprop, taking shots at the government for:

Deceiving the public
Neglecting schools
Demonising the working-class
Failing to invest in urban communities
Failing to keep the streets safe
Closing community centres
Financial exploitation of road users
In that order.

It's very difficult to keep up with the evolution of Ben Drew. First he's a chubby guitar strumming rapper, then he goes all UK soul troubadour in a suit, then he ditches Strickland Banks, lights up and slims down into the director-writer-actor auteur. With 'ill Manors', he's firmly in role as the sneering social provocateur. The song starts with the perfectly poised provocation about going on a safari through the city, inviting the listener to step into the front line of a class war. The video takes it further, with Plan B acting as some kind of macabre, urban ringmaster, goading the viewer with images of frenetic cut-up of staged happy slaps, cartoon exclamations and actual footage of the 2011 riots.

Depending on how you look it, the 2011 riots can be taken as: a) mindless social disorder from opportunist criminals, b) violent social protest, or c) violent social disorder on the back of genuine protest. 'ill Manors' encourages us to take option b), seeking to unite 'us' (anyone who isn't a "little rich boy") against 'them' ("little rich boys"). The video reinforces this, with a rainbow palette of skin tones, ages and genders united in disenfranchisement and shared anger against the system. In an important sense, this singles 'ill Manors' out as quite a rare thing - a socially inclusive instance of agitprop-pop.

My ambivalence over the song is that in striving to be

inclusive, it actually loses heart. It's not cathartic or healing. There's no sense of Plan B getting years of discontent off his chest. His anger is too general, too stylised, and way too tied up in the 'ill Manors' franchise. His motivation seems confused. He's not the chav he claims to be representing. His irony seems forced. All of which might explain the fact that 'ill Manors' has not survived as a definitive post-riot text, despite appearing to have all the necessary ingredients.

'All Hallows'
CASisDEAD (2013)

I'm going to front load this with a huge statement: that each of the nine things that make Cas a remarkable, compelling Grime artist is tainted by the one very big thing that has prevented him from reaching popular acclaim – his psychosis. I love Cas, I really do, but an examination of his work throws forward deep-seated problems surrounding drug abuse, violence against women and, ultimately, self-destruction. Cas is Grime's most enigmatic personality but he remains shackled to obscurity by his own macabre imagination. Welcome to Cas, formerly Castro Saint, also known as Casisdead: an embodiment of Grime's darkest side.

That said, here's what Cas is.

1. Cas is Obsessed With Talking About Food

This is great, because he's not really talking about food. He's talking about drugs. Because in *The Number 23*[1], his 2013 'debut' (actually a collection of tracks and remixes from preceding years – Cas has been around for ages), he's always talking about drugs. His lyrics exist almost entirely within the murky realm of drug sales, consumption and production. His work is relentlessly drug-obsessed. It details the minutiae of dealing drugs and using drugs and selling drugs and making drugs and describing drugs to such an extent that it all becomes magnified to cartoon proportions. And his metaphor of choice is food. If you weren't paying close enough attention, a lot of *The Number 23* might sound like a middle-class shopping list. It's an exercise in cookery semantics, with drug reference upon drug reference encoded in lines about bags of pesto, Wensleydale cheese, ovens of bread, dough, Cravendale milk, kitchens, whipping, cooking, baking, serving suggestions and food preparation in general. Not to mention the fact that he is...

2. Always Comparing Himself to Celebrity Chefs

When he talks about whipping it up like Heston (Blumenthal), cooking it better than Nigella (Lawson) or being generally wicked in the kitchen like chef (Gordon) Ramsay, Cas takes the very unacceptable world of sub-social drug economics and forces it into the very acceptable world of middle-class cookery. By comparing his adeptness at concocting drugs to the kitchen skills of well-known celebrity chefs, he warps mainstream values.[2] The juxtaposition is subversive and provocative, more or less stating that drugs are as much a part of British society as the recipes, faces and personas of famous chefs. Which makes sense, considering that he is...

3. Very British Indeed

Cas leads with an uncompromised Britishness. His vernacular is strewn with all manner of UK-specific phrases and references points, not least the frequent "slags" and "cunts" adlibs that frequently punctuate his verses – explosive reminders that you're listening to the voice of fuck you Britain.[3] And, like all Brits, there's an inherent tension to being British that Cas also explores. He seems proud of his British identity, dropping whimsical references to squash drinks in 'All Hallows' and boasting about his car's "GB sticker" in 'City Slicker', but he also seems to be in a state of near-constant frustration with the realities of being marginalised in Britain. The police are "pigs" and the government isn't to be trusted. He also makes clear his racial conflation, as evidenced in the opening bars of 'Cheese Slice', in which he tells us that he's African, but more than a fraction Anglo-Saxon (which is why his hair has to have Dax[4] in). In this sense, there's a degree of social study to Cas' lyrics that stands proud of all the colourful, crowd-baiting theatrics. Which leads us on to the fact that he is...

4. Politically Inclined

Because he says things about coming from a country where coke's no joke, before asking why you think the Queen named her son Charlie, which is, of course, a joke.

Got to love this. In two lines, Cas successfully distorts the very foundations of British establishment in a perverse suggestion that cocaine is as inherent to British culture as the monarchy. Not only is that hilarious, but it's also pointedly political, offering sharp rebuttal to the notion that Great Britain is Great because of the establishment. With a wry sneer and switchblade wit, he forces us to look at the underbelly of British society from a fresh, warped perspective. And then you get those final lines about the Tories being as far right wing as a Nani, citing this as justification for starting riots like supporters who just lost the derby.

When he wants to, Cas can get explicitly political, here aligning himself with left-wing sensibilities against the grain of the current Tory government. To end 'All Hallows' on this note, with a reference to the 2011 London riots, makes clear that Cas identifies ideological problems in the establishment that are responsible for anti-social behaviours among the populous. It's subtle, and it promotes a working-class sensibility via the football semantics[5]. Very liberal.

5. Cas Wears a Mask

And this where the psychosis starts to kick into gear. In marketing terms, the whole masked anti-hero thing is genius[6]. Cas' gaunt, grimy, reaper-esque hockey mask suggests a murky backstory that tips him into urban legend territory. Like all masked figures of folklore, the deliberate facelessness alludes to some level of trauma. It also offers the allure of the masked freedom-fighter. When he says that, ahem, hoes are, ahem, on his dick because he looks like Banksy, it's a combination of shock tactics misogyny with the suggestion that he is as elusive as he is alluring. Banksy, the street artist turned high art doyen is the epitome of success from the shadows. Cas acknowledges that he occupies a similar cultural ground – the subversive social commentator with explosive Guy Fawkes intentions and deliberate notoriety. Which all leads us on to the fact that...

6. Cas is Extremely Playful, Maybe to a Fault

I mean, he walks around in a mask. He's more or less a walking cartoon. The whole thing is surreal and theatrical: a faceless MC who lives in a drug-addled world of cartoon violence and puerile, adolescent humour. Not to mention the fact that he's witty. If I was the kind of person who writes 'lol', I would say that there are frequent lol moments in Cas' back catalogue. His punchlines do the job, coupled with a self-deprecation that warms us to his otherwise spiky persona. That said, he frequently nudges into less than palatable territories. In 'All Hallows' he riffs on the disturbing topic of date-raping young women in graveyards, before telling us that he's joking, and then cheekily warning that Nigella Lawson might not be safe before telling himself to "behave". It's an extremely warped, thunderously dark sense of humour that leaves a bitter aftertaste. Playful yes, but alienating also. Possibly because...

7. Cas is Full of Issues

All the most compelling artists have issues. Problems. Insecurities and neuroses they pour into their work, or can't prevent from informing their output. Cas has a few. His disillusionment with the scene he's part of, for a start, having started out as Castro Saint before going AWOL for half a decade and coming back with 'T.R.O.N' in 2013. He alludes to his struggle for success in the first verse of 'All Hallows', explaining that his brand of dark, macabre rap might be unpalatable for mass consumption, daydreaming about going mainstream but ultimately being too extreme for MTV Base, therefore resorting to Ecstasy to raise his self-esteem.

That final line introduces another major source of insecurity – drugs. For all the bragging and pantomime villainy and implied celebration of life as a successful street dealer (encapsulated perfectly in 'Cheese Slice'), Cas presents us with a tortured soul. 'Drugs Don't Work' is this concept's zenith, detailing the lows and lows of a life of drug abuse with zero sarcasm. It's a tone of sober reflection that bubbles to the surface in many of his songs, sometimes laced with humour, sometimes without.

Conceptually, Cas is all about creating death (through drugs, murder, celebrity chef references, etc), which means that he damns himself, which kind of might explain the tortured wringing of his entire aesthetic. The whole Dead Team/Cas 'is dead'/imreallydead.com conceit glimpses at something darker in the psyche behind the mask. It might all be theatrics, and of course Cas revels in his mentally ill persona, but you wonder if he hasn't actually been damaged in some way by a life in the shadowy margins of sub-fame, drug abuse and other things he would rather not talk about. His apparent inability to avoid imagining violence against women is a major problem, a compulsion that keeps him firmly on the wrong side of acceptable. The video to 'Charlotte' brings an extended metaphor of chopping cocaine, represented by a woman, to gory, horrific life.

Within the context of Grime, this violent misogyny is atypical and as shocking as it would be in any other context. Cas dabbles in slippery Horrorcore tropes that are an ill fit to Grime's hyperactive energy, confirming his position as an outsider within an already marginalised culture. Elsewhere in Grime, MCs readily and frequently offer up a secure image of assured masculinity, strength and aggression, and we're starting to see a Grime archetype that might prove cookie-cutter in years to come. Meanwhile, in 2013, Cas was happily accusing himself of necrophilia in clothes that were gathering moss. Little wonder that he starts 'All Hallows' by declaring himself to be a psychologist's wet dream.

While psychosis isn't an obvious lyrical playground, it remains a fertile ground for tortured explorations of self. Cas is an intense reminder of Grime's capacity to expose deep psychological ruptures in this area. I would go as far as to argue that Grime is at its most interesting when viewed from this perspective, as we shall see in the following chapter, when clashes of identity and the subsequent psychological traumas are laid bare. In hip hop, Grime's bigger, older cousin, we've already seen the full potential of psychological exploration as entertainment. Eminem has made a good career out of egging himself on to shock the mainstream, all the while exposing his most intimate mental instabilities. Like Cas, drug use is a running motif in Eminem's body of work, and also like Cas, he draws easy criticism for violent imagery in his lyrics, painted with a cartoonist's flair. Unlike Cas, however, Eminem has risen to stratospheric heights of fame and acclaim, in spite of (perhaps because of?) his uncensored shock tactics. Perhaps the ironic postscript to this is that Cas is actually far more understated a villain than he initially seems, because. . .

8. Cas is Armed With Integrity

Five years AWOL and deliberately crafting a persona might equal Marketing Gimmick, or it might equal Long Term Plan:

'All these dons who are coming up fast and in a year no-one will remember them. That's the thing that they don't understand. They're going for cheap thrills and there's a formula that seems to work in this crappy music economy that we seem to have right now but it won't last very long. I – well, we – intend to make stuff with a longer shelf-life so that even after we're gone people are still listening and they say, "Them lot were fuckin' serious, man."'

– Cas, interview with *Loud and Quiet*

And finally. . .

9. Cas is a Really Good Storyteller

And a nimble one at that. The way he dances through tones and moods of aggression, play, reflection and despair is actually unparalleled in the genre, alongside a genuine knack for storytelling and verbal picture painting[7]. His vignettes are vivid, evocative and concise. Case in point, the little four-line saga from 'All Hallows' that spins an entire dramatic thriller, complete with four distinct characters and a gallows humour plot twist: that the young woman waiting for him at home isn't answering to him because he's handsome, no, but because her parents haven't responded to the ransom note. Again, it's a nimble little punchline, clouded by dark notions of violence against women and wrapped in psychological insecurity. Distasteful, yes, compelling, absolutely.

But of course, the best story Cas tells is the one that hasn't ended yet – his career. His 2015 synth-heavy cassette-only release *Commercial 2* is a point of evolution both musically and conceptually. While Grime struggles to step out of the iron boots (or iron Air Maxes) of the early Noughties, Cas continues to make bold steps in various directions. And judging from his recent movements (not least his dazzling feature on '501' with Giggs in which, among other moments of genius, he calls himself a c-word in comparison to notorious French president Jacques Chirac), one of them is definitely forward.

---

1. I thought about listing 23 separate reasons to go alongside the title of Cas' album, but no. Anyway, the point of this footnote is that I have just spent about 15 good minutes trying to figure out why his album is called *The Number 23*. The best I can come up with is that it's something to do with 23 being a commonly cited prime number that has supposed links to weird goings-on, sinister historical events and fundamental aspects of humanity/ inhumanity. For example: The numbers of the date of the Titanic sinking add up to 23. The pattern of DNA has irregular connections at every 23rd interval. The Earth tilts at a 23-degree axis. Two divided by three equals 0.666 recurring. *Et cetera*. The mysterious spooky sinisterness of the enigmatic 23 appeals to Cas' macabre persona. I think.

2. He takes this obsession to extremes in his 2015 ode to Nigella Lawson, entitled, wait for it, 'Nigella', including a hook that repeats her name no less than six times. Then in 2016, he teamed up with Giggs under

the moniker 'Heston', aligning himself to the fiendishly experimental celebrity chef Heston Blumenthal.

3. The opening to 'Been Runnin' is a verbal slap in the face of the US rap aesthetic, with Cas sarcastically listing his way through a string of US hip hop tropes before announcing, "Fuck that." Irony upon irony though, when you realise that his 'All Hallows' collaborator, producer Skywlkr, is in fact American.

4. Unless you have hair like mine, you wouldn't have any reason to know what Dax is or why you use it.

5. This was very nearly the tenth thing I like about Cas: his frequent references to football. It's proper working-class stuff, done deliberately, I think, to make sure we know that Cas is of the people.

6. The only other rapper to wear a mask who features heavily on my iPod is MF DOOM. MF DOOM comparisons are lazy, but there are some subtle similarities – shadowy provenance, theatrical persona, rumour-baiting backstory, creates a mythology around himself, sense of humour, anti-scene anti-social aesthetic, dressing like a tramp, being a sick lyricist, etc.

7. It's no wonder that he has drawn acclaim from much of the Grime fraternity, not least of all Dizzee Rascal, who called him 'pristine', 'sick' and 'incredible' in a huge radio interview with US hip hop DJ Sway. Worth noting that Cas was the first name he went to when asked who he rates in the scene, which, in the context of a huge US radio interview, is capital-N Noteworthy.

'The Cypher'
Ghetts
feat. Ghetto and J. Clarke (2013)

The biggest challenge I've faced in the writing of this book is figuring out which Ghetts track to include in Grime's Grand Narrative. The problem is that there is no single track that encompasses Ghetts as an artist and there is no single track that slots Ghetts neatly into Grime's grand narrative. Ghetts just isn't that simple, because nothing about Ghetts will ever be simple. It's impossible to find the one moment that summarises Justin Clarke's influence upon the culture because his life is an ever-evolving lens through which we can recognise the culture for what it is. It's his journey through the genre that helps us to understand Grime. His evolution is as compelling as his art.

There's a *Risky Roadz* video from 2006 that captures a snapshot of Ghetts when he was at his most Ghetto, in every sense of the word: pre-dental work, post a spell in prison. It's a blistering, mesmeric display of lyricism; unflinchingly confrontational and surgical in its delivery of verbal javelins. Here, we see Ghetto as hungry and as focused as any MC you will ever see, lashing out with consecutive, eternally devastating quotables. I won't even try to pick any gems because almost every bar is undeniable, crafted and honed and complex and intricate but delivered with a breezy finesse that puts you in the presence of a maestro at work. A violent, rebellious, militant maestro who wants your head on a plate, but a maestro nonetheless.

This, more than anything, is the true appeal of Ghetto at this point in Grime. 2006 was one year after the release of '2000 and Life', his 24-track long debut mixtape that caused instant waves with its explosive lyrical aggression. But Ghetts was always more than the archetypal angry MC. His intelligence as a lyricist always shares centre stage with the raw energy that fuels his lyricism, delivering the impact of an uppercut with the precision of a scalpel. Combined with his insistent wordplay and refusal to dumb down on figurative techniques, you're left with one the most consistently exciting and creative lyricists in the country, ever. Seriously.

And he's jazzy with it. Ghetts has one of the most syncopated, shifting flows you will hear, experimenting with patterns and pauses and playing with prosody as par for the course. Whether it's slowing down, speeding up, dropping into a conversational whisper or punctuating a lyric with an explosive onomatopoeic adlib, his vocal variations are quite simply masterful, sometimes sounding like a crew of MCs on the same track, which happens to be the central conceit of the song I'm discussing in this chapter.

2013's 'The Cypher' is an explicit example of the struggles faced by an artist in their evolutionary journey. Every artist, in any medium, must undergo change, perhaps transformation, as they develop, building on what has come before and breaking former moulds as they strive in new directions. 'The Cypher' represents a zenith of these tensions in Grime, featuring a trinity of personas who are all one and the same MC. Ghetto: the belligerent, incendiary battle MC who we first met in *2000 and Life*, fresh off road and thirsty for the kill. Ghetts: the lyrical craftsman, full of soundboy bravado and metaphorical violence but wed to the booth, a smoother-edged Ghetto, industry-ready and first met in 2010's *Calm Before the Storm*. And finally, J. Clarke: The thinker, the father, restrained and introspective, more likely to muse on love and life than threaten to steamroll his way through the competition, first seen in 2007's *Ghetto Gospel*.

It's an easy mistake to dismiss 'The Cypher' as an artist struggling to reconcile his personas, and even easier to dismiss it as a gimmick. Yes, Ghetts may be wrestling with the notions of self that make up his identity but, due to his insight and lyrical intelligence, it becomes a moment of reconciliation that is ultimately empowering. Ghetts never seems to fall victim to tortured wranglings between id (Ghetto), ego (Ghetts) and super id (J. Clarke)[1]. Whenever you listen to any one of his projects, spanning over a decade, you get the impression that Grime is in good shape and all the more healthy for its internal conflicts. In this, the title of this track is telling. A cypher is competitive collaboration in full flow, a state of being that creates focus, energy and accountability. Just like any communal, public forum of creativity, Ghetts puts his struggle for excellence on full display and channels it into his music, feeding off the insecurity that would otherwise derail him, ready and willing to tread water in uncertain seas.

To explain the wider significance of this confrontation with identity, I can do no better than quote the spoken introduction to 'The Cypher' SBTV music video:

"You see, when you're growing up, I think the most important thing to you is finding an identity that resonates with your peers and in the best case scenario elevates you above them. Where I'm from, we hate the identities we are given because there is nothing inspirational about them, so we create alter-egos. You call them street names or aliases, but for us it's about refining who you are and who you want to be."

-J. Clarke

This is a fundamental truth for any marginalised peoples: Taking ownership of one's identity is the only assured route to self-empowerment; a rejection of societal expectations ("the identities we are given") that hinges self-worth upon peer validation. In this sense, Grime might be understood as the UK's first instance of a culture of self-empowerment among the turn-of-the-century, black, adolescent working-class. The boys in da corner who moulded Grime in '02 have matured into leaders and thinkers and earners and culture makers a decade and a half later, crafting a scene that is as competitive as it is creative. In 2013, Ghetts/Ghetto/J. Clarke embraced the thorns of his contradictions and bounced his energy off the wall of self-criticism, turning frustration into insight whilst perfectly mirroring Grime's journey out of adolescence.

As I said at the start of this chapter, the overall journey supersedes the individual moment. Like Grime the genre, Ghetts the individual has struggled to find a place in the mainstream. Most debates surrounding Ghetts revolve around his status as an overlooked veteran or underrated shining star. His chart presence has always wavered and while the numbers are consistent, they've never been stellar[2]. His debut album, *Rebel With a Cause*, came nine years after his *2000 and Life* mixtape debut. He's even tried the pop-crossover key into the industry, jumping on a track with X Factor fourth-placed finalist Cher Lloyd in 2011 alongside Dot Rotten and Mic Righteous, in a song that, apart from the Cher Lloyd parts, is actually a pretty solid example of Grime MCing.

"Grime is a culture, it's history defined and changed by the people who create it. This is the journey of one person. He is Grime. Grime is him."
-Introduction to 'The Cypher' music video, SBTV

2016 represents a point of cyclical maturation for Ghetts, which might reflect Grime's wider evolution into a new future, rooted in its past. His 2016 reprisal of the *Risky Roadz* freestyle is a reconciliation of the three Cypher identities, a slick, knowing and passionately lyrical display of Ghetts' current position as Grime's chief disciple. It is not a nine-minute long lyrical onslaught like the original *Risky Roadz* but you can almost hear the envelope being pushed in his 2016 flow. Honestly, I would rank it as a piece of performance art, each gesture, each gesticulation adding a special energy to his animated delivery. And it ends with Ghetts watching himself back on video and admiring his own talent, before reciting a few Ghetto bars from 'The Cypher' and tweeting them to his fanbase. It's a neat knot.

In this respect, Ghetts remains an artist for Grime artists to look up to. His dedication to the craft has placed him in a position of authority and high stature, all on his own terms, while his mainstream appeal has found a place to flourish in the guise of roadman party starter. And while the scene pauses to look over its shoulder before striding forward, Ghetts has already shown us how to look inwards for the biggest insights of all.

---

1. If you were in any doubt that Grime is a proper subject for a proper book, you can now relax. Not many genres of music feature an explicit example of Freud's structural model of the psyche, encapsulated by one artist in one song.

2. But as he says in 'These Words': there's passion in his voice, you can hear him pour his heart out/ And he don't give a fuck if he never makes a 'Pass Out'.

'Don't Waste My Time'
Krept and Konan (2013)

'The South got something to say, that's all I got to say.'
-Andre 3000, 1995 Source Awards

When OutKast picked up their award for Best New Artist at the 1995 Source Awards amid boos from the assembled East and West Coast industry rivals, I doubt even they could have predicted just how much the South would have to say about Hip hop in the decades to come. OutKast are among of clutch of Southern US hip hop acts who pioneered the evolution of mainstream hip hop from East Coast boom-bap and the sun-touched gangsterism of the West into something else entirely. Within ten years of Andre 3000 making his beautifully concise manifesto, the South had emerged as a dominant force in hip hop.

One of the loudest things the South had to say was that

many people are trapped in a life of selling drugs for a living. The '90s had seen outfits such as Three 6 Mafia and UGK (who would one day collaborate with no less than Dizzee Rascal in his song 'H Town') develop a concentrated 'trap' (i.e selling drugs in an environment that forces you to sell drugs) aesthetic into their music, combining hard realism about the drug-dealing lifestyle with bass-driven instrumentation to devastating effect. It wasn't long until 808 drums, malevolent synths and taut strings was the go-to audio cocktail for rappers with drug-dealing personas, selling an image of bleak success and cinematic criminality. Trap was born.

By the mid 2000s, Trap was mainstream, with hip hop A-listers across the spectrum employing Trap conventions to retain an industry edge. And by the time you got to 2013, pop acts such as Beyoncé, Lady Gaga and Katy Perry had all released music with Trappy influences. It was an inevitability that Trap would pond-hop to the UK as a successful US export. Sonically, there is something addictively crisp and detached about Trap that makes it a mouthwatering prospect for anyone trying to cast themselves as cool and aloof. Meanwhile, the drug-dealing subtext that runs beneath Trap aligns it perfectly with the kind of callous criminality that street music so often demands.

At this point, if you could find and play the instrumental

to 'Otis' by Kanye West and Jay Z, that would be great. Not because Otis is in any way a Trap instrumental (it really isn't), but because it was the first instrumental I heard Krept and Konan rhyme on. Actually, full disclosure, the very first time I heard Krept and Konan was when a Year 10 student walked into my room shaking his head, almost teary eyed, staring at various spots in the middle distance with something close to confused awe on his face.

'Joseph, what's up?' I ask.
'Sir.' He replies. 'They said one sick eight like twenty-four sevens. How do you even think that?'
'How does who think that?'
'Krept and Konan.'
'Who?'

The line Joseph was referring to came from Krept's verse in the 'Otis' remix, which helped push Krept and Konan to prominence in 2011. It's a great line, a fiendishly cryptic pun that plays with the concept of having a 'sick' eight bars of lyrics at all times, ie: '24/7', whilst deploying a part homophone on the number 1-6-8, which just happens to be the sum total of 24 multiplied by 7. This summarises the wit, energy and lyrical playfulness that Krept and Konan emerged into the scene with back in 2011. 'Otis' is a masterclass in double entendre, overflowing with puns and double meanings showcased as a kind of competitive spat between two friends. The video is similarly playful, a low-budget, handheld affair replete with slapstick, visual gags, masks on sticks, and straight to the camera grins. It's an early moment in the career of two MCs who would go on to establish themselves as one of the most successful rags to riches stories in Grime.

Skip forward two years and you get 'Don't Waste My Time', which is a different song entirely.

Yes, it contains vestiges of the wordplay that put young Joseph in a daze back in 2011, but its overall energy is in a different district altogether. It's dark and relatively humourless, detailing the heartless hedonism of the hard-hearted, rejecting love and welcoming transactional sex, staring steely-eyed at rivals and goading the authorities. It's Trap. Nocturnal and moody, pulsing on a lava-slow heartbeat, replacing exuberance with intent. And it invites Krept and Konan to project their most street personas without sinking into the murky seriousness of autobiography and trauma.

The influence of Trap on Grime goes way beyond style and sound. Conceptually, it encourages the roadman aesthetic that Grime has always contained, but never relied on. 'Don't Waste My Time' is a potent example of Trap's influence on the culture, part of a trend that has since taken hold in UK road rap with a legacy that includes collectives such as the Section Boyz and 67, as well as solo acts such as Abracadabra (who rose to prominence in 2016 with the gravelly hypnotics of 'Robbery' featuring, naturally, Krept and Konan).

Commercially, 'Don't Waste My Time' was a huge point of success for Krept and Konan, garnering international attention and helping confirm their position as top flight, charting artists, not to mention paving the way for hip hopping club hits. Krept and Konan made it clear that Grime was not the limit of their artistic realm, establishing themselves as acceptably cold Trapstars.

With Trap we're technically not even talking about Grime any more, but ultimately it's a major footnote in the proliferation of MC culture, beyond Grime's fizzly origins into darker, colder territories altogether. Trap has proven a snug fit for the UK rap scene, having been accepted without question or hesitation. Compared to the current state of UK hip hop (dominated by po-faced 'heads' and nodding moodiness), Trap is a confident, square-shouldered arena for UK rappers to preen their feathers in. The Grime/Trap overlap is bigger than ever, while Grime and hip hop struggle to meet in the middle.

'German Whip'
Meridian Dan (2014)

The way the Internet tells it, the release of 'German Whip' in 2014 signalled a resurgence of Grime in the mainstream consciousness. You could go further and say it was the beginning of a Grime Renaissance, or you could strip it back and say it was the start of a renewed interest in Grime from the mainstream. The obvious question is why? Why would a low-key release from a lesser known affiliate of Boy Better Know suddenly infiltrate the mainstream with such intensity? Why would it gain so much attention as to warrant a second official video (by Vevo) after the first official video topped seven million views?

One simple answer is, that it is simple. It's a simple song with simple aims. It's a song about driving an expensive car and looking well hard while you do it. Listening to 'German Whip', you get the impression that there is no ulterior motive, no hidden agenda, no sense of the song trying to be anything other than what it is: a celebration of how cool it is to act like a hard man and drive a big expensive car. The surprise success of the song attests to this – no-one really thought it was intended to be a breakout hit at all.

The simplicity of 'German Whip' gives it an honesty that might explain some of its appeal. For a song that makes more than a few threats of physical violence, it's seriously lovable. It's the audio equivalent of a playful shove. It makes you smile, and brings you closer while pretending to push you away. It's an underdog anthem, a concept made visually explicit in the original video, which sees Meridian Dan breaking down in a clapped-out Ford Ka before enjoying a drizzly dream sequence in which he is driving around in some kind of Mercedes.

And it's silly. Dan himself deadpans through the song with a kind of meathead likeability, chanting/grimacing his way through addictively ridiculous assertions about punching up big men and not chasing frisbees. He also gets an eternal badman salute for introducing the "who told you" flow into our lives. Then there's that hook, which really is a wondrous thing. Robotic, relentless and mad enough to contradict itself (Dan confirms that he looks like a baller before almost immediately asking if he looks like a baller = Win). It's like getting your own Terminator and reprogramming it to be your best friend, knowing full well that it's hard-wired to kill you.[1]

That all said, the knucklehead charm of 'German Whip' does not fully explain its huge impact. By 2014, Grime was over a decade old. As a genre of music, if not artform, it should probably have begun to evolve, to grow in interesting and challenging new directions and infuriate itself with the need for change, just like any other adolescent. But this wasn't happening. For over a decade Grime had suffered from commercial aspirations and insecurity over its validation in the mainstream. Crossover attempts had become a watermark for the culture and the scene's biggest success stories weren't putting out capital G Grime classics. When Meridian Dan came along, he offered Grime fans a slice of nostalgia, and (as we'll see in 'And Dat'), people love a slice of nostalgia. Simon Hiscocks (head of Grime music label, Oil Gang) outlines a telling perspective in a *Noisey* interview with Josh Hall:

'When I first got into grime... people would just do their best bars - the bars to get a rewind, their rave bars. I always really enjoyed those tunes, but then the lyrics got more and more complicated. It just wasn't really my thing.'

There's a problem here. The implication is that Grime

should not or cannot be complex and commercially viable at the same time. In an important sense, the mainstream champions Grime as an anti-intellectual genre, as though it loses integrity by veering away from crowd-pleasing 'rewind bars'. As if Grime can't be deeply reflective, insightful, lyrically inventive and nuanced, as well as ideologically provocative and challenging. As if the best bars are only the ones that get a rewind in a rave context. Speaking to *The Guardian* in 2010, Jammer spoke of Grime's potential to evolve, arguing:

'...the more melodic thing will come back. Now the mainstream is catching up with us, we've got more opportunities to make different styles of Grime.'

But this vision hasn't quite come to fruition. Grime's popularity is based in a confirmation of what it did rather than what it could do. Its resurgence is more retrospective than forward-thinking, more about the roots than the flowers.

To hail 'German Whip' as a renaissance point for an adolescent culture (with roots far older than that) is reductive. I have no problem with the song itself, or Meridian Dan as an artist, but there is something worrying going on if the mainstream can only back Grime when Grime is simple and basic and harmlessly aggressive. The mainstream response to 'German Whip' reflects the age of consumerism in which everything (including cultural ideologies) is expected to be digestible, easy and consumable. Before Grime became a thing, it was difficult, challenging and confrontational, defying conventions and provocative in its very existence. The mainstream had to adapt before it could understand and accept, which might explain why the doors to mainstream acceptance closed so early.

In terms of power politics, the success of 'German Whip' as leading Grime's Unexpected Comeback represents a return to an understandable 'other'. It confirms what was already known and accepted of the culture, in turn confirming the dominant view of urban youth. Meridian Dan is a blank canvas MC, completely inoffensive. In this persona, there's no re-cognition necessary, no challenging of preconceptions. The mainstream will only ever accept what it can understand and it jumped on 'German Whip' because it can understand it. Two years later, we're seeing a lot more Grime in the spotlight. But the Dangerous Black Boy stereotype has become a commercially viable archetype. I'm a hopeless dreamer, but hopefully (like hip hop in the '90s, when experimentation became trendy) Grime will one day confound the mainstream and break out of the confines of its given narrative.

'I've got better songs than "German Whip" up my sleeves; I've got a lot more things to say, and I can't just try and replicate that.'

-Meridian Dan interviewed in *Complex*, 2014

The postscript to all this comes in the form of Dan's post-'German Whip' output. He really has got better songs, proving to be much more than the one-hit wonderer lazy historians might take him as. His Cockney-soaked pedigree underdog persona is getting thoroughly honed into shape, with an energy drawn from the rejection of acceptance. This might explain why Meridian Dan sounds so pissed off in his hero lap singles of 2015-16. Actually, he always sounds a bit pissed off. Like he's just dented his bumper, or dropped his last Rolo. Or looked up and realised there's nothing to dry his hands with. And despite the fame and recognition that 2014's 'German Whip' afforded him, he has every good reason to be a bit pissed off, for reasons very neatly explained in the opening verse of 'Hot For Me Now'. He's a big MC, if anyone's asking. All these years now man a been grafting.

Then he asks a question full of pain and provocation: If you're hot for me now, where were you then?

This not only forms the hook for the whole song but is also a very pertinent question for new fans. In a nutshell: he's been hard at work establishing himself as a Grime MC, with minimal success, thus finding himself sidelined. Then a surprise hit song wanders along and suddenly he's flavour of the month. And the flavour is bitter, or sour grape flavour perhaps.

'Hot For Me Now' is super-provocative, because even just listening to it is an admission of guilt. Every time Dan asks where you were, in his accusatory Cockney growl, you're forced to admit that you weren't around in the early part of his career. In this way, the song reflects the mainstream's relationship with Grime in general. Grime has been sidelined by the popular consciousness for the most part of its relatively brief existence, yet is garnering all kinds of recent attention. This begs the question of non-Day One Grime devotees: if you're hot for me now, seriously, where were you then?

Meridian Dan is one of many Grime artists who can get away with this, the key criteria for asking people where they were before you were famous a) being famous Now and b) not being famous Then. Forget rags to riches and fame and fortune; the true Grimestar narrative is that of longevity. Grime stalwarts can wear their stripes with pride, safe in the knowledge that they stuck with it, committing to the scene through the wilderness years. As we move towards the clarity of the 2020s[2], the blurry vision that Grime artists had back in the Noughties is being realised in commercial and critical success. It's fair to say 'German Whip' marks a line in the sand for Grime's re-emergence from chrysalis, but more importantly, it helped raise a curtain towards the spotlight that the entire scene could walk through, after over a decade in the shadows.

---

1. This will make a lot more sense if you've seen *Terminator 2: Judgment Day*.

2. Deliberate pun.

'Shutdown'
Skepta (2015)

In 2016, I wrote an essay called Beyond Rags and Riches: The Reductive Power of Known Narratives. In the essay, I said intelligent things about the dangers of a Rags to Riches understanding of black success, focusing in part on an *Evening Standard Magazine* article about Grime duo Krept and Konan. I suggested that the Rags to Riches narrative is superficially celebratory, but is really 'mainstream endorsement couched in the politics of disempowerment'. Like I said, intelligent.

In 2015, Skepta released a song called 'Shutdown'. The chorus of this song contains three very important lines about sitting in the front row at Fashion Week, wearing a black tracksuit, and subsequently shutting everything down, just by being there.

These words paint a picture of Grime's arrival in not only

the mainstream, but in society's cultural elite. A fashion show is a perfect metonym for society's upper echelon. It's a place of stylish refinement, artistic cool, pretentious edge. When Skepta proclaims that he now has a place in the front row of a Fashion Week show, it's a bold declaration of status.

And he's doing it in a black tracksuit. Not high-end couture, not the Gucci and LV he used to wear (but threw in the bin because it made him look like a mess, and dressing like a mess nah that's not he), but in a black tracksuit – the roadman uniform of choice. With 'Shutdown', he positions himself as a Grime delegate, bopping casually and confidently into the palace.

I say 'palace' deliberately, because this is ostensibly a Rags to Riches narrative. Grime is an underdog culture, born of a marginalised social demographic and characterised by conflict. The '05 excitement around Grime had waned by the late Noughties, the scene struggling to assert itself in mainstream consciousness. Skip to 2016 and Grime seems to be enjoying a Cinderella moment; a recognition of its true worth, with mainstream acceptance and an invitation to the ball. MCs are no longer looking for that elusive crossover hit, dabbling in this genre and that genre in a bid to legitimise their bars. You don't have to rustle up a 'Pass Out' as a golden ticket to the mainstream. Grime is legitimate on its own terms. Tracksuits have been allowed in[1]. (As an interesting aside, Skepta once referred to the tracksuited look as a "get this money dress code", affiliating it with urban culture in major northern UK cities. The down to earth aesthetic created by "all black, windbreakers and tracksuits... Hats down low and curved peaks so man can't see man..." acts as a counterpoint to a US/hip hop influence so common in London. The so-called 'Tracksuit Mafia' is a UK phenomenon.)

Nowhere else is this more explicit than in Kanye West's performance of 'All Day' at the 2015 BRIT Awards, during which an all-black-everything-dressed Kanye is accompanied by about 40 British MCs, decked out in all-black tracksuits. And there's a couple of flamethrowers. Among said MCs were a who's-who of Grime front-liners, including Boy Better Know mainstays Jammer, Skepta, Frisco and Shorty, as well as Krept, Konan, Novelist[2], Stormzy and Fekky. Obviously, there's an element of cultural profiteering going on here beneath Kanye's supposed benevolence. Like all megastars, he has a vampire thirst for relevance and Grime offers up an edgy appeal that he couldn't fabricate. To promote his own credibility, he invited the most credible scene he could find, in all its tracksuited, theatrical glory.

In a sense, 'Shutdown' shares the same energy as Kanye West/Jay Z's 'Niggas in Paris'. 'Niggas in Paris' announced the arrival of an Afro-American, hip hop-born cultural elite. Skepta makes a similar statement when he says he can shut down Paris, New York and London, suggesting that Grime has finally (and defiantly) breached its local limitations. Arguably, 'Shutdown' reconciles the paranoia that has historically typified Grime with the confidence it has garnered through years of grind. Kanye proved that the mere presence of Grime can dominate a major industry award ceremony, 14 years after the So Solid Crew did the same with UK Garage. It's a tidy coincidence that a brief interlude (describing a bunch of young men all dressed in black dancing aggressively on stage), spoken by a decidedly white, female voice in the middle of 'Shutdown', almost perfectly describes Kanye's BRIT Awards performance. And legend has it that Skepta was called upon to provide the stage full of "young men all dressed in black". Neat.

An easy pitfall here is to mistake image for identity. Like artists of any genre, Grime MCs are often preoccupied with their image. This is what Kanye capitalised on in the 'All Day' performance, taking the silhouette of a black-tracksuited roadman and presenting it as the authentic image of a culture.

Skepta, I think, is preoccupied with identity in a far more compelling way. The lyrical content of 'Shutdown' is hugely concerned with matters of authenticity. In the first verse he states how this ain't a culture, it's his religion, making his identity as a Grime disciple absolutely clear. The song's production values echo this, eschewing Trappy, 808 sparseness for a much more Eski-esque sound, harking back to the early Noughties. This might help explain the song's hugely positive mainstream reception; that it is so easy on the ear and upbeat.

For those of you who want to act like a G for the camera, and you know exactly who you are, verse two is a line-by-line interrogation of realness, starting with street credibility, moving on to religious intent[3], skirting dietary honesty, returning to belief systems, and finally rounding up on the irrelevance of fashion. At the heart of all this is a difficult debate over realness and black identity, ie: what is real in the world of black culture, and who gets to claim it? Jamaican aspects of Black British culture have evolved from a specifically black, urban context into youth culture at large. The patois we hear so frequently in Grime is part of modern youth vernacular, not even tied to the streets any more. In my eight years of teaching in London, I have seen young people of all backgrounds freely using Jamaican dialects that, in my youth, were the preserve of genuine Jamaicans. Recent years have seen the steady proliferation of Jamaican culture across mainstream Britain, due in part to the ongoing popularisation of black British music. Grime's role in this is distinct, as the blackness of Grime culture (stemming back to the Windrush diaspora) emanates into youth culture as a whole. In 'Shutdown', Skepta adjudicates on realness, simultaneously positioning himself as the most real. And let's not forget that Skepta has spent a good chunk of his career dabbling in crossover alchemy, via various poppy efforts and one not-so-poppy experiment in porno-visuality. 'Shutdown', in this context, might represent a return to roots moment: defiant, brash and grounded in the kind of confidence that can only come from experience.

Perhaps then, Skepta is an MC in search of authenticity. And ironically, it is this assertion of identity that gives 'Shutdown' so much of its popular appeal. Like many of the songs highlighted in this book, 'Shutdown' is the approachable 'other' – taking an alluring subculture and serving it up it to a waiting audience hungry for a taste of the real. Arguably, 20-teen Skepta is in the process of actualising a Grime persona that will laminate Grime's pass into the mainstream. His sitting at the front like Rosa Parks line is telling. Grime is finding its own place in popular culture, irrespective of any predefined rules, and young black men are the arbitrators. There aren't many avenues in society where this is the case.

The general assumption is that Grime is currently enjoying a Rags to Riches resurgence, but perhaps it's really on a quest for authenticity beyond music industry acceptance. 'Shutdown', as a back-to-basics Grime anthem for the masses, just might be a step forward on that journey.

---

1. The significance of the black tracksuit is becoming ingrained in Grime's consciousness. In his eye-squintingly militant lyrical assault 'Wickedest Skengman 4' (2015), Stormzy brags about going on Jools Holland in a tracksuit, alluding to his (and Grime's) dismissal of protocol. Later, he assures everyone that he isn't going to stab you just because he's wearing a tracksuit, which is a very cool flip of expectations in that it acknowledges the stylised image of the roadman while promoting the very real identity of the MC. Stormzy is an intelligent lyricist.

2. 'I liked the fact that I was onstage with people like myself in my tracksuit, that was sick.' - Novelist, quoted in *The Guardian*, March 2015

3. This is huge. Since its conception in the 1930s, Rastafari survives as the spiritual root of Jamaican theism. Grime, linked in lineage to Jamaican heritage, offers a huge nod of respect to Rastafari culture. Skepta makes it clear that black authenticity as he sees it relies upon acknowledging and respecting these beliefs, pouring scorn on those who claim to follow but do so only superficially. By name-checking Haile Selassie (the spiritual figurehead of Rastafari) and stating his rejection of "isms and schisms" (Rastafari actively rejects social-isms in favour of higher spiritual beliefs), Skepta proves that he has done his homework fully, which further confirms his own authenticity. I can't think of many songs that made it onto the Radio 1 playlist that so openly extol the teachings and belief structures of Rastafari culture.

'Netflix and Pills'
Nolay (2015)

Full disclosure: I hadn't actually listened to this song before reading about it. But after scrutinising a Hattie Collins interview with Nolay in which she breaks down the lyrics, and subsequently reading and re-reading said lyrics alongside the interview transcript, it was impossible not to devote a chapter to one of the most raw, open and honest Grime tracks to emerge since the 2014 resurgence.

'Netflix and Pills' is an unflinchingly autobiographical exploration of trauma. The lyrics walk steadily through a pageant of trials and tragedies, through which Nolay has not only survived, but found definition of self. Carrying crack for her father. Indulging in substance abuse. Facing depression in the family. Addiction. Multiple suicides from loved ones. Being raped as a teenager. *Et cetera, et cetera.* It's a study of vulnerability that arrived in the year that Grime's mainstream acceptance threatened its oversimplification as testosterone music by tough black boys.

'People don't always want to hear about how invincible you are. Sometimes they want to hear that you're flawed and that you have problems like everyone else. I find art in honesty.' -Nolay, interviewed by Hattie Collins for *i-D* magazine, 2015

In a society defined by crude masculinity, women are automatically vulnerable. Grime exemplifies this as much as any other product of a broadly patriarchal society in which women are routinely objectified, treated as trophies and defined according to their sexuality. Nolay tackles this head on in the flat explanation that she was raped at the age of 14, before stating, in equally plain terms, that life is a bitch, and has been for centuries.

And she's absolutely right. The scant female presence in Grime is problematic; evidence of the genre having been constricted by misogyny. Grime, like any other male-dominated field, suffers from the pressure to promote a very stereotypical masculinity, ie: invincibility, invulnerability, emotional distance and machismo. It's little surprise that it's a woman, already existing in a state of deep social vulnerability, who would present us with a song that explicitly defies Grime's hardman conventions. If you were to act on her call for shallow MCs to show what's underneath, it wouldn't take long to reveal the insecurity and vulnerability in most MCs' back catalogue for the simple reason that we're all vulnerable. Take the 2015 roster from this book for three nearby examples:

'Shutdown' – Skepta's vulnerability over his identity and striving for empowerment in the mainstream.

'Endz' – Novelist seeking to qualify deep ambivalences over his social context.

'Wickedskengman 4' – Where Stormzy lashes out and dismantles all the preconceptions and expectations levelled at him from each corner of his cultural globe.

In all these cases the integrity of the song is rooted in introspection. Nolay, with all her demons on show, is an extreme example of the vulnerability that sits beneath the surface of Grime's bravado, making 'Netflix and Pills' an important example of modern, emotionally nuanced Grime. Tough, yes, but by no means unfeeling.

'Dem Boy Paigon'
J Hus (2015)

Whoever you think the biggest underdog in Grime is, you're wrong. Because the answer is J Hus. Why? Because you've no idea how uncool it was to be African when I was growing up.

Being an African teenager in '90s London was like being the uncool version of black. West Indians were cool, with the accent, the swagger, the rudeboy genetics and the exhilarating street music. I know personally of a handful of second generation West Africans who just straight up changed their names at school, ditching traditional names for Westernised aliases like 'Junior', so desperate to distance themselves from the Africanness that (seemed to) lack so much street cred. In popular culture, the awkward African was an established stereotype. Case in point, Matthew in *Desmond's* (the Channel 4 sitcom about a barber shop in Peckham), a figure that poked fun at how uncool it was to be black and African in a black British context. As a black British artefact, Grime has tangible links to an African heritage, not least of all due to the fact that so many of the scene's stars are second generation, British born. But just like those boys who refused to pronounce their surnames in the school register, it's been cloaked in a generic black Britishness that is assumed West Indian.

The Adenuga brothers are two prominent examples of this common phenomenon. Nigerian in heritage, born of the West African diaspora, but having adopted certain aspects of soundclash culture that are intrinsically West Indian (specifically Jamaican), up to and including the patois-laden dialect. Grime magnifies a social trend that goes way back to the '80s, whereby young black Britons of all heritages adopted Jamaican culture. Hence why Jamie Adenuga knows what 'awoh' means[1] and hence why Joseph Adenuga can say 'bludclaart'[2] with impunity.

'When I was a youth, to be called "African" was a diss. At school, the African kids used to lie and say they were Jamaican. So when I first came in the game and I'm saying lyrics like, "I make Nigerians proud of their tribal scars/ My bars make you push up your chest like bras", that was a big deal for me.'
-Skepta, *FADER* magazine

It's a big deal that Skepta's Mercury Prize-winning album *Konnichiwa* contains overt references to his Nigerian heritage. It's a big deal that Dizzee Rascal launched into his 'Bluku Bluku' verse by declaring himself the "E3 African". It's a big deal that Sway maintained a decidedly Ghanaian alter-ego throughout his debut album. It's a big deal that Chip has jumped on the Afrobeat Afroboat with Burna Boy. As an English boy with an African (Gambian) accent, a fact that might single him out as unusual in Grime's London-focused scene, J Hus is also a big deal. But far from cringing away from it, he leans in, full tilt, turning an Afro aesthetic into a virtue, a quirk into a watermark. 'Dem Boy Paigon' is an important fusion of grimy road rap and Afrobeat pop, defiantly idiosyncratic and therefore inimitable. It helps, of course, that the rise of Afrobeat as a premier genre of international black music dovetailed so neatly with his early career moves, acclimatising our ears to African rhythms. But this does not one bit detract from the ballsiness J Hus demonstrated in taking Grime and (to use an awful reality singing contest cliche) making it his own.

'Dem Boy Paigon' is a neat reminder that Grime is linked to a complicated black British heritage. Hus casually drops references to '90s RnB (ie: TLC's 'No Scrubs') as well as Beenie Man's most commercially successful moment in 'Zim Zimma'. This kind of musical stew is in the black British

20th century melting pot. More importantly, it represents a point of reconciliation for black British identities, deservedly pushing J Hus to prominence in a scene that hadn't yet produced a visibly, audibly, essentially African star.

With the broad brushstrokes that blackness tends to get painted with, one might be forgiven for thinking that Grime comes from one place, which it kind of does (London), but kind of doesn't (all those places that aren't London). It's the African diaspora meets the West Indian diaspora meets the mixed heritage second and third generation, characterised by Jamaican cultural norms. What J Hus did is remind the YouTube generation that black British could be black African too. Evolution.

---

1. It means 'know your place'. Or more like, 'yeah, you know you know your place so stay quiet.'

2. An expletive that translates to something rather impolite that I'm too British to detail in this footnote.

'Endz'
Novelist (2015)

'People say it's a resurgence. I think that's bullshit – it's always been a part of my life. It's not like grime left and then came back: in the ends and for me, it never went anywhere.'
-Novelist, *Time Out*, 2015

There's a whole generation out there who have never not known Grime. For anyone born in the late '90s onwards, Grime has always existed. And if you take the Novelist quote above at face value, Grime isn't just on the radar, it IS the radar. For this demographic, Grime's back-to-basics Renaissance moment dovetails perfectly with their emergence into adolescence/adulthood. Which must be terribly exciting. Every generation has its soundtrack and for teenagers in 2016, that soundtrack pulses at 140bpm. (Sometimes.[1])

Image-wise, Grime has successfully turned anti-glamour into a desirable commodity. The coolest look out is roadman chic: tracksuit (preferably black), hat, hood, minimal jewellery. Instantly recognisable, effortlessly reproducible, irresistibly authentic. For '90s babies looking to establish themselves in the Grime constellation, the stars are finally in alignment. Case in point, the video for 'Endz', in which Novelist, set to a backdrop of urban high rise, sits about in a tracksuit, surrounded by other hooded youths sitting/ standing about in tracksuits, sometimes eating chicken and chips, sometimes riding bikes or mopeds, sometimes walking dogs, sometimes tagging walls, at one point kicking a skateboard. 'Endz', in its lo-fi glory, celebrates the mundane to the point of turning it into a virtue. Like so many recent Grime videos, it puts the scene in its realest context; the streets, kicking moneyed glamour and club-lit ballerism to the curb.

Even though Novelist spells it with a 'z', which is the retro-futuristic street way of spelling things that normally end in 's', 'Endz' is nothing new. MCs have been crafting odes and laments to their environments for as long as a scene has existed, finding fertile ground for philosophical musings in the frustrations and joys of harsh life, hustle life, thug life, street life. The Grime MC falls neatly into the archetypal street journalist. Novelist captures the ambivalence neatly:

'It means everything and nothing at the same time. It's fucked up: bare mad shit happens – good and bad things. Two of my boys got murdered last month. I've been stabbed myself, had altercations. But the energy of the whole thing gives you so much to say and live for.'

-Novelist, *Time Out*, 2015

Lyrically, 'Endz' isn't up to much[2]. Compared to Kano's song of the exact same title, featured on his 2016 album *Made in the Manor*, it's lightweight. Kano's 'Endz' is nuanced, rich and swollen with bitter bravado. Novelist's 'Endz' is a bit lukewarm, vaguely misogynistic and conceptually limited. But I'm not criticising him for it, because he was, in 2015, afflicted with that condition that encourages and explains erratic behaviour: Youth.

At 19 years of age, Novelist is the latest newcomer to be hailed as the future of Grime, but at the moment, Grime's future is fixated on the past. It's no accident that so much new Grime is sounding like, looking like, echoing what has come before. The 'Endz' video is a Channel U throwback from an artist who wasn't there first time around. In this respect, 'Endz' represents true adolescence; trying out adulthood with earnest intent, but clumsy execution. The song is an attempt at 'real' Grime in accordance to the rules that Grime has established thus far, and, like a little kid trying to hang out with big brother's mates, it comes off as charming.

And, at times, charmingly overexcited. Case in point: The Square's 'Lewisham McDeez' (frontlined by Novelist), a song that turns hanging out at your local McDonald's into an event of anthemic proportions. It's pure teenage energy in the vein of 'Next Hype', complete with cartoon violence and random bars of aggression. But unlike Tempa T's 2009 classic, it's completely toothless[3]. The whole thing sounds and looks like a group of kids mucking about, with about as much substance as a playground cussing match, not to mention a selection of eye-rollingly simple similes[4]. In light of the very real and very serious ramifications of London's Postcode War rivalries, this must be taken as a positive development – that the latest generation are happy to rep their ends (in this case, Lewisham) with no particularly violent intent.

After years of being sidelined, Grime is now in danger of being over-hyped. The likes of Novelist may well be the future of Grime, but they need what their forebears have already had: time. Time to evolve and grow. Time to gain new perspectives on the environment they were born into. Time to widen horizons. To find other ways of authenticating themselves beyond rags and riches and street credibility.

In an important sense 'Endz' represents the final echo of

Grime's DIY heyday, offering a nostalgia that is dangerously easy to confuse with relevance. The scene has deep roots and an audible heritage[5] and in this regard, the 20-teen Grime 'resurgence' is something of a backwards glance. One hopes that what will follow might be a giant leap forward, bringing new ends into view.

---

1. Bpms don't tend to stand still. In the fickle game of what's hot and what's not. Jungle took it all the way to 180, and Grime was a solid 140, but the Trappy road rap that seeped into 2016 notched it right down to between 70 and 110. So can it be accurate to call Grime the pulse of a generation? Let the debate commence.

2. This does not mean Novelist isn't an outrageously talented MC. Watch what he does to the mic after Frisco in Channel 4's *Pirate Mentality* set (2016) and you'll see what I mean.

3. A note on hair. Tempa T is one of two prominent Grime MCs to sport a high top, also known as a 'box', the other being D Double E. Kojo 'Novelist' Kankam also has a box, but when he was campaigning to be young Mayor of Lewisham in 2012, he had a low fro. Jermain Jackman, 2014 winner of BBC's *The Voice*, also has political aspirations, going on record as wanting to be the first singing Prime Minister. This complicates things hugely because he also has a box but is not a Grime MC. I have no idea if Tempa T is interested in politics but a painting exists of D Double E depicted as a military officer (hold tight Reuben Dangoor), which is kind of political. In conclusion, there appears to be no connection between choice of hairstyle

and political/musical persuasion, which makes most of this footnote less than relevant but super interesting.

4. The Grime simile is a tricky thing. My theory is that the impact of a simile is inversely proportionate to the age of the MC. So basically kids sound like kids when they use them, but olders sound like Yoda. So when Streema spits you man are all chicken, "like KFC", I make this face :[compared to when Skepta spits he hates man, "like a nun", and I write a 500-worder on the intersection between playful belligerence and self-loathing through which he explores the self-destructive violence of young black males.

5. The first record Novelist bought was 'Serious' by Jme and you can hear his influence in the no-nonsense couplets of 'Take Time', Novelist's skankworthy 2015 collaboration with Mumdance. As Nov says in the *Time Out* interview I've been referring to throughout this essay: 'It reminded me of myself. That's why I liked it. I just thought, "Whoa, this guy reminds me of me. He's sick." I was in.'

'Wickedskengman 4'
Stormzy (2015)

I've checked. So far, to date, I've typed the word 'Stormzy' 28 times in the writing of this book, and I haven't yet devoted a chapter to him.[1] This means that Stormzy has infiltrated the analysis of 30 songs that are ostensibly nothing to do with him, which in turn means that he is a subliminally important MC.

The gods seem to agree with me. He's the second British unsigned artist to score a top 10 single[2]. He won the inaugural Best Grime Act award at the 2014 MOBOs. He went on to win Best Male Act at the MOBOs in the following year, in addition to a Black Entertainment Television (BET) award for Best International Act. He interviewed David Beckham at the launch of Manchester United's 2016/17 away kit. He heralded Paul Pogba's record £100m move to Manchester United with an Adidas-sponsored social media music video.

He out-charted the 2015 X-Factor winner's single with a festive remix of 'Shut Up'[3], which he performed dressed as Father Christmas on BBC 1Xtra. He dived tweet-first into big-P Politics by endorsing Jeremy Corbyn and calling Zac Goldsmith "a fucking arsehole"[4]. He's cemented the best endorsement/endorsee deal with Adidas since Run-D.M.C. He went on Jools Holland in a tracksuit. And he's somehow managed to get away with calling himself 'Stiff Chocolate' on more than one occasion without getting laughed off social media for all time. His debut album, *Gang Signs and Prayer*, went straght to number one. Stormzy is having a great two thousand and teen.

But the fact that Stormzy is a celebrity has nothing to do with why he made it into the pages of *Hold Tight*[5].

Three Actual Reasons Why Stormzy Made It Into The Pages of *Hold Tight*

1. He represents the full maturation and fully realised potential of the Millennial baby in Grime culture.

'I used to hate American rap. A lot of people say they grew up on Mobb Deep, Tupac and Biggie. I ain't got a clue about none of that. I wouldn't be able to tell you a single song. I just know Lethal B and Kano Vs Wiley. I think sometimes they

don't realise that, the Grime scene. I was talking to Wiley the other day, saying, "you lot are our Tupac and our Biggie[6]."'
-Stormzy, *Noisey*, 2014

Stormzy was 10 years old when *Boy in da Corner* was released. This is nothing too remarkable in itself, as lots of people were born in 1993 (and some were even born afterwards). Compared to MCs who came up as artists in Grime's formative years, he's young, ish, and he plays up to this, ish, without leaning on it too much. And he's still got bare grown men scared of him, a firm reminder of the ironic fact that Stormzy does not consider himself to be a grown man despite being a big man. . . with a beard. What you get with Stormzy is a '90s baby who has come of age within a distinct Grime context, and it's powerful to hear. He sounds like undiluted Grime feedback. Actually, he sounds like undiluted Grime feedback being PA'd back into itself, which is completely arresting. It's the reason behind his appeal – that he's authentic, direct and unadulterated (pun intended).

2. He placed soundclash culture at the forefront of the Grime resurgence at the exact moment when Grime required a return to core values.

And by 'forefront' I mean our iPad, laptop and mobile

phone screens. The irresistible power of 'Wickedskengman 4' comes from its unfiltered live energy, beamed directly into our lives via social media. It's not quite raw clash footage, but it's not quite a pre-planned, sculpted music video either. It's a hybrid, hitting the sweet spot between the two with energy and polish alike. This is exactly what Grime needed to reassert its relevance in youth consciousness – all the excitement and energy of early Sidewinder and Eskimo raves, all the raw lyricism of clashes in Jammer's basement, all the illicit appeal of pirate radio sets, opened up and made accessible to anyone with a smartphone, which, of course, is everyone.

3. He embodies the rise of the 21st century social media star.

The existence of Stormzy as an unsigned Grime superstar is definitive proof of the fact that the Internet has changed everything in music and youth culture. Fifteen years ago, an up-and-coming underground artist would have to put in dues on (probably) pirate radio, white label vinyl and live performances. Ten years ago it was mixtape hype and mainstream-baiting video efforts. Plus live performances. Now it's YouTube virals and social media. Live performances optional. Stormzy has breached local boundaries with broadband efficiency. He's the Grime hero of the hashtag generation, with a following that has grown out of itself, feeding into its own hype. The video to 'Wickedskengman 4' stands as testament to this, a kind of recorded live performance featuring a flock of fans, some of whom look very much like people who first encountered Stormzy on the YouTube screens they are now occupying. 'Wickedskengman 1' looks like a bunch of boys on the estate. 'Wickedskengman 4' looks like a community event. You can see his fame crystallising in real time. The undisguisable bewilderment on his face as he surveys the crowd of fans out to support him. The selfies that punctuate his set up, confirming his celeb status. In part 4, you see his fame being thrown back at him and packaged up in a video that will ultimately garner even more fame. It's all very chicken and egg. Some stats[7]:

'Wickedskengman 1' (Feb 2014): 470,028 views
'Wickedskengman 2' (Feb 2014): 643,144 views
'Wickedskengman 3' (May 2014): 1,502,961 views
'Wickedskengman 4' (Sep 2015): 5,755,818 views

Stormzy's rise in popularity is exponential, and there might be 4.2 million people who have seen part 4 who haven't bothered to do the research on parts 1 to 3, even though this research would largely involve clicking a link on a side bar. It turns out the song 'Where Do You Know Me From?' is asking a very pertinent question, and it's a question that Stormzy is all too willing to answer. His bars are not only unwaveringly biographical, but also unflinchingly assertive. He advocates for himself with something beyond confidence, tipping into the realm of certainty. A lot of MCs wrestle with their identities and histories through their music. With Stormzy, you get an MC who is building an identity and history with his music. A subtle but important distinction.

There are five reload moments in 'Wickedskengman 4'. The first is at 3:36, after he says he's ugly, word to J Hus, before telling us that this Rap ting is sick, regardless. This highlights the fact that success can be achieved despite being ugly, which is a neat metaphor for Rap's relationship with the mainstream and also a metaphor for Grime in general. The next reload moment is at 4.20, when he asks you to bring out your BET Award, if you have one, before reminding you that you don't and politely telling you to shut your mouth. This is a huge celebration of Stormzy's personal achievements in black music and, by extension, the wider successes of Grime as a legitimate branch of black music and black culture.

Reload three is at 4:41, when he calmly explains that some of his worst days are some of your best days before saying he will punch a Grime MC off his segway, which is a wonderfully aggressive attack on any MC who thinks their life is ok because they haven't yet realised the threat that Stormzy poses to their very existence. Reload number four comes at 5:21, when Stormzy explains that he is hated by Rap boys because he does Grime, whilst Grime boys also hate him because he does Rap. Meanwhile, good youts hate him because he's too bad, while bad youts hate him because he doesn't trap (ie: sell drugs). Then he says that fake youts hate him because, like me, he's too real, but the real youts hate him because he doesn't act. Then he pauses, says, "well" and "um" and then calmly invites everyone to go suck their mum.

Which completely dismantles all the preconceptions and expectations levelled at him from every corner of his cultural globe, and might also be the most devastating punchline ever captured in 720p. Then he says his name's Michael, by which point there has been a complete meltdown of affirmation from the assembled crowd, including a very proud and paternal-looking Krept (no Konan), hovering just behind Stormzy's left shoulder. If you pause the video at exactly 5:41, you'll see a face of absolute calm, peace and joy. Exuberant, but devoid of all tension. Michael has arrived, on his own terms, repping his area (Thornton Heath, Croydon, South London) and his culture (rapping over 'Serious' by Jme[8]), but he is ultimately repping himself. It's a rare and quite beautiful moment to be captured on video in the germination of a career, the kind of moment that would be lost in the glossy post-production of a 'real' music video. Skip forward to 5:53, and he starts telling you how he's this, how he's that, how he's blick, how he's black[9], how his hairline's going way back, but he'll still fuck your girl. Go and retweet that.

Cue reload moment five. It's a sublime flip of insecurities and self-denigration (being too dark, having a receding hairline, generally being 'ugly'[10]...) into a moment of absolute self-empowerment, irresponsibly aggressive and shamelessly disrespectful, which perfectly mirrors the state of Grime in 2016. Since 2002, Grime has been devalued, mistrusted, criticised, feared and deemed too dangerous, too 'black', too ugly for the mainstream, but ultimately it's capable of winning.

***

'Wickedskengman 4' represents a special moment in Michael Omari's career, which in turn represents a special moment in the history of Grime. It's a moment of obfuscation between the lines of mainstream and underground, proving that Grime had enough raw appeal in 2015 to propel itself out of the shadows, beyond the limelight, well into the stars.

Stormzy has made it by actually making it, rather than trying to make it, which is a needlessly complicated way of saying that his DIY, digital web 2.0 success has been on his own terms. Grime is in great shape, with a heritage that it understands and a glittering potential that is absolutely within reach. Hold tight Stormzy, who embodies this fact in spirit, as well as in deed.

---

1. Note: I didn't write this book in chronological order, even though it's published that way. I wrote it in a random order of whatever song I felt like thinking about at the time, starting, in case you were interested, with 'Incredible' by M-Beat featuring General Levy.

2. The first is a YouTuber by the name of Alex Day, who I hadn't heard of until the typing of this sentence.

3. Louisa Johnson was her name. 'Forever Young' was her song. Number 9 was its top chart position. Stormzy got 8. Shut up!

4. *The Guardian*, May 2016.

5. *Hold Tight* is the name of the book you're reading. It comes from a common shout-out used by DJs on pirate radio, meaning something like 'and a special hello to…' before you insert a name. It also makes me think of funfair ride operators who would say things like 'hold tight', and 'scream if you wanna go faster'.

6. At the end of 'New Banger', Kano hits us with the idea that Wiley is our Quincy (as in Jones) while Dylan (as in Mills, as in Dizzee Rascal) is our Michael (as in Jackson). It's a romantic notion that hints at a Grime mythology, complete with cultural legends.

7. Correct as of 29th June 2016, 9:54 am, GMT.

8. Stormzy has made a thing out of turning golden age Grime instrumentals into latter day hits, the most potent example being 'Shut Up', in which he floats over 'Functions on the Low' by XTC, which you may remember from a previous chapter.

9. I remember at school, being dark-skinned was almost the ultimate insult, a worrying throwback to caste politics that put light-skinned people further up the social ladder. For darker-skinned (usually African) boys, it was an easy diss, inviting defensiveness and resilience in equal measure.

10. Worth noting that J Hus has turned self-empowerment through self-denigration into something of an artform, having cast himself as "Mr Ugly", an ugly man who can make beautiful money. It's all in 'Friendly'.

'Coward'
Chip (2015)

Should I talk about Chip? I kind of have to, don't I? I mean,
I can't leave him out. Can I? If I don't talk about him,
people are gonna say, 'What about Chip?' I'd have written
a book about Grime that doesn't feature one of 2016's most
prominent artists. Yep. He definitely needs a chapter. It'd be
rude not to. Right?

Chipmunk is a rare example of a life lived in Grime, up
close and personal. His autobiography is tied to Grime
in a way that singles him out as a true child of Grime. He
entered the scene as a child prodigy, more or less discovered
by Wiley while he was still at school, establishing an early
footing as a credible Grime MC. His YouTube footprint goes
back to 2007 via a notoriously impressive freestyle session
on Tim Westwood's BBC show, alongside a teenage Ice Kid
and Wiley in full godfather mode. This video, above all else,

proves what everyone has always known about Chipmunk and what remains true to this day – that he can spit bars. His confidence and lyrical dexterity is unquestionable, laying the foundation for credibility and authenticity in Grime's early years.

But the thing about starting so young and being so successful is that all of your growing up happens publicly. All of your mistakes and triumphs and gear changes and false starts and moments of cringe. All of it is under the microscope, open to both scrutiny and criticism. This is the precise reason that so many child stars tend to go Bieber at some point and end up having a mugshot taken and/or requiring rehabilitation of some description in their mid-20s.

Chipmunk is no exception. His early movements in Grime's underground soon gave way to major label movements of a far slicker variety. After signing to Columbia he officially went Pop and, in many ways, went pop! at the same time. The chart hits came, but they weren't in the Grimeosphere. Eleven top-10 hits in total and a number two-peaking album, *I Am Chipmunk*, in 2009. All of this took place to the backdrop of Grime's struggle through its wilderness years, during which it remained on the periphery of mainstream acceptance.

Far from fighting the fight for the culture that birthed him, Chipmunk went in an altogether more poppy direction entirely. The culmination of this is the song 'Oopsy Daisy' – a pop hip hop ballad that was the third single from *I Am Chipmunk*. It debuted at number one in the charts and remains Chipmunk's most successful single to date. The phrase "Oopsy Daisy" remains the least grimy thing an MC can say in public.

It's easy to vilify Chipmunk for these moves, but we have to remember that was maturing in real time, on a very public stage. He was 18 when he signed to Columbia. When I was 18, I was wearing Hawaiian shirts, writing *South Park* parodies, and riding around on an import Micro Scooter (I paid £125 for mine before they were available in the UK, when only rich businessmen in Europe had them, yes). The point is that it's easy to criticise the inexperience of youth, but unlike the rest of us, Chipmunk didn't have the privilege of privacy. We watched as he set his sights on the US, forged collaborations with the likes of Chris Brown and T.I., shortened his name to Chip and all the while distanced himself from that thing we call Grime.

Late 2014 saw Chip(munk's) return to Grime, and since then, he has been energetically reaffirming his credibility as a Grime MC. This explains everything about post-2014 Chipmunk: relentless lyrical output, militant bars, fierce affiliation to his Tottenham roots, fierce affiliation to the underground, fierce independence via his own Cash Motto label, and lyrical beef with whoever wants it, whenever they ask for it. Chipmunk 2016 is officially post-pop, post-major label, and he wants everyone to know it.

In the context of Grime, Chipmunk has come through the fires of his own past. The demon he's fighting is the struggle for legitimacy that he has created for himself. You can hear the trauma in his lyrics, the anger and defensiveness that comes from having been accused of being anything less than real. From this perspective, 'Coward' is a perfect moment of confrontation between inner and outer demons, which makes it a fascinating study in Grime vs Pop vs Itself. The song is a direct diss aimed at Patrick 'Tinie Tempah' Okogwu, in response to a Tinie Tempah Fire in the Booth 2014 freestyle in which he took aim at commercially unsuccessful rappers and dropped a reference to 'Pizza Boy', a 2012 track from Chip's *London Boy* mixtape. A year later, Chipmunk retaliated in his own Fire in the Booth slot. This set in motion a series of events that would spiral into the most sprawling and entertaining tit for tat in music history, drawing responses, directs, and indirects from a whole line up of MCs including Saskilla, Bugzy Malone, Big Narstie, Yungen and Devilman. The Internet casually exploded and in 2015, it really did became Chip vs the world, with Chip laying beefy foundations for a full-blown Grime comeback.

In 'Coward', Chip kicks Tinie where it hurts – right in

the credibility. He says profoundly accusatory things about Tinie Tempah's authenticity, mocking him for not making meaningful music. He questions his ability to get a reload. He pours scorn on his wealth. He highlights the fact that Tinie wrote that he was inspired by Chip in his autobiography. He accuses him of exploiting the urban underground. And along the way, he calls him "lost" and "corny".

The irony is obvious. As the product of a career in Pop originally birthed from Grime, Chipmunk is guilty of most of the accusations he throws at Tinie Tempah. When he says he's got the game "all awkward", there are revealing subtexts at play. Yes, he's got people in the game feeling awkward because he keeps throwing diss tracks around, but his position within the game is also awkward as a result of his pop past. You could go further and argue that Chip really has got the game locked, inasfar as having proven his skills as a first-rate MC, but he's gone about it in an awkward manner. We can see similar tensions in Tinie Tempah's discography, often straddling the very different worlds of chart-ready dance pop hits and underground mixtape collaborations.

Weirdly, 'Coward' is almost like Grime having a counselling session with itself. Chip's choice of Ruff Sqwad's 'Together' is a suitably reverent nod to Grime's heritage, using a bittersweet, deeply nostalgic instrumental that gives a pained poignancy to his assault. Unlike other songs in his 2015 Year of Beef, 'Coward' is about more than soundclash bravado and kill-or-be-killed machismo. It's about the fraught relationship between success and failure, authenticity and appearance, past, present and future. He says he doesn't give a fuck but he clearly does, because in 2015 everything was on the line – his reputation, his position in Grime and his future.

***

On Guilt in Grime

Chipmunk's plight in Grime throws the concept of black guilt into sharp relief. Like working-class guilt, black guilt stems from the implicit notion that black integrity is linked to struggle and disenfranchisement: that to be successfully black means to have suffered the ills of a socially marginalised existence. The black CV automatically includes struggle and strife not as a badge of honour, but as a stamp of authenticity, for the simple reason that blackness is characterised by struggle – being subjugated, being oppressed, being mistrusted, being denied opportunity.

Blackness, as a concept, is inherently oppositional, existing as the 'other' to a white, Western norm that has been established via colonialism and transatlantic slavery. As a result, being successfully and believably 'black' means being in opposition: to dominant society, to the mainstream, to 'whiteness' in general. To avoid this, by acting not black, can feel like embracing whiteness, which in turn feels like rejecting a black heritage that is framed by 'otherness'. For any black person under pressure to locate their integrity in racial identity, the guilt can quickly set in.

Grime thrives as a counter-narrative to whiteness and therefore exists in an oppositional realm. As a culture, it actively rewards antagonism by heralding aggression and various anti-social attitudes. For the Grime MC, pressures to conform to these oppositional norms are huge. Grime artists are virtually under obligation to perpetuate oppositional attitudes in a bid to assert themselves and acknowledge a black identity. This, more than anything else, explains why the mainstream is viewed with such suspicion and derision from Grime purists, and why those artists who court the mainstream are so quickly accused of selling out. Tinie Tempah, Grime's least oppositional representative, wrestles with this openly. His 2015 mixtape *Junk Food* is titled as such because it is full of irresponsibly bad things that satisfy vices. Perversely, good Grime is under responsibility to be bad, an irony that helps explain Chipmunk's lurch towards Grime after freeing himself from the tangles of Pop. It's not simply that he had lost his way and was seeking a prodigal son return home; he might have felt guilty that he ever left in the first place.

***

If nothing else, Chipmunk's 2015 proved that conflict is most compelling when equal meets equal. Like I said a few hundred words ago, Chipmunk and Tinie Tempah are flip sides of the same coin; respectable success stories who courted industry fame in the early embers of their careers. Neither is particularly tough but both rely on some level of street credibility to sustain their relevance. In a 2015 interview with Charlie Sloth, Big Narstie said that 'going for Tinie was a cheap shot', but in one sense, the exact opposite is true. 'Coward' was Chipmunk's attempt to not only criticise Tinie Tempah's authenticity, but to also destroy the very essence of his own past that would otherwise prevent him from embracing a new future. This, perhaps, is about as high stakes as it gets. Deep.

'And Dat'
Bonkaz
feat. Stormzy (2016)

If Grime is a Millennial baby, conceived somewhere around the turn of the century, then it's now approaching the end of its teens. By which I mean that Grime is growing up. If it was a person, Grime would be getting its driving licence and taking its first holidays abroad with friends. It would be making questionable fashion and haircut choices. And it would be starting to feel the early pangs of nostalgia, remembering its infancy with the fond distance of maturity.

'And Dat' is not the first Grime track to look back on the past with fondness. MCs routinely look to the past, dropping back-when references in pursuit of 'OG' status[1]. What makes 'And Dat' noteworthy is its nostalgic approach to Grime itself. Give it a surface listen, you'd be forgiven for thinking that 'And Dat' shapes a general nostalgia; Bonkaz and Stormzy simply talking about all the fun things they encountered as kids in London (knives, guns, nicking pizza delivery mopeds, sexual encounters in the park, you know, the usual). Then there's the string of 'I remember that' memorables that offer a little nostalgia hit at a time; logging on to MSN and Bebo, eating yum yums from Greggs, lending me a pound, texting on that awful Nokia teardrop-shaped phone (difficult to do, as Bonkaz politely explains), and so on.

Look past all that, and 'And Dat' is far more Grime-centric. The hook sets the tone, with Bonkaz listing Grime influences he came up with. Instant namechecks go to the Brixton-based Roadside Gs and their Sticky Business DVDs, as well as Peckham's SN1 collective. Later, it all very gets misty-eyed over D Double E, Roll Deep, Danny Weed's classic 'Creeper' instrumental, and there's a whole-bar homage to Dizzee Rascal, before Bonkaz brings N Double A and Krept and Konan into the mix in the third verse.

None of this is accidental. Grime may not have matured into the muted realms of responsible adulthood, but it is a genre that now has the capacity to reminisce. New faces are defining themselves by old standards, in turn cementing the recent past as a golden age. In this, 'And Dat' stands as an example of emerging artists explicitly acknowledging their cultural godfathers.[2]

Beyond 2016

'New faces are defining themselves by old standards.'
-Jeffrey Boakye, *Hold Tight: Black Masculinity, Millennials, and the Meaning of Grime*

It feels like the cork has finally popped on Grime's fizzling ascent to prominence. A whole generation of MCs are striding to the front with '03 swagger, churning out bangers that adhere religiously to the Grime blueprint. But far from sounding hackneyed or derivative, they're sounding live, urgent and vital. The premature experimentations of irrelevancies like 'Grindie'[3] and chart-baiting lurches towards electro-pop have been jettisoned in favour of pure, uncut Grime – aggressive couplets and exposed wire production over 140bpms. This, more than anything else, explains the rise of the Grime anthem in 2016; a celebration of the energy that originally made Grime so arresting over a decade previous – agitated, brash and unapologetically direct.

Perhaps it's unsurprising that so many regional (by which I mean non-London) voices are emerging in this new wave. Perhaps the movement of big names in the scene away from Grime's purest sound has created a space for them. Perhaps Grime has embedded itself enough in UK culture for non-Londonness to be permissible. Perhaps regional Grime recognises a route to self-empowerment via a nostalgic throwback. Or maybe (and I think this is the one) mainstream arrogance has slipped enough to finally recognise non-London scenes that have been, until now, sidelined. And to be honest, there's a whole book to be written about these artists alone:

Devilman (the most animated MC from Birmingham to clash Skepta, forever telling him not to talk shit); Blizzard (Manchester's hyperactive wordsmith); Tremz (Liverpudlian trapping with a truly phlegm-inducing scouse lilt); Bugzy Malone (turning Chipmunk-baiting into a sport all the way from Manchester); R.I.O. (also putting Manny on the map); Kamakaze (Leicester's own); Eyez (a major talent from the streets of Derby who will cuss your mum and make you laugh in the same sentence); Lady Leshurr (getting Americans on YouTube to question whether or not a Brummie accent is Jamaican or not); Jaykae (another deeply convincing Brum Town Grime export); Mez (Nottingham hype). And of course, the social media ripples turning into waves turning into tsunamis coming from Blackpool's burgeoning Grime scene, led by Afghan Dan and characterised by somewhat naïve MCs sending for each other with as much aggression as possible. Subsequently, we've seen a very unlikely social media star emerge in the shape of the cherub-faced, foulmouthed Little T, playing at macho aggression just a little too convincingly.

As we approach the end of Grime's journey towards maturity, London's boundaries will become less of a defining factor, giving way to a UK aesthetic that transcends the capital. Why? Because poverty, disenfranchisement, marginalisation and hunger exist in urban contexts everywhere, meaning that anywhere can be a breeding ground for Grime.

---

1. Original Gangsta - a mark of respect and authority.

2. Other notable examples include, in no particular order:

Fekky's 'Dizzee Rascal' flip on 'Still Sittin' Here'.
Section Boyz's homage to 'Oi!'.
Chipmunk and Stormzy's flow-jack of Wiley's 2004 'Destruction' verse (see *Lord of the Mics* vol 1) on 'Hear Dis'.
Chipmunk channelling D Double's 'Birds in the Sky' on the 'School of Grime' hook.
Skepta bringing Megaman out of retirement on 'We Begin Things'.
Ghetts keeping Megaman out of retirement in 'You Dun Know Already'.
Ghetts giving Megaman and his post-retirement party centre stage in the 'You Dun Know Already' remix.
Tinchy Stryder's Dizzee Rascal 'Jus 'A Rascal' lyrical homage in 'ESG'.
Another Dizzee moment on the "switch your girl" opening verse on

'Pengaleng', channelling 'I Luv U'.

Yet another Dizzee moment in 'Man', with Skepta ending his hook with the fact that he only socialises with the crew and the gang, a la 'Cut 'Em Off'.

Another little Dizzee moment on 'Tarantula', where Ghetts ends the third verse with an energetic burst of 'Stop Dat' bars.

3. 'Grindie' was actually really a proper thing, with a Wikipedia page and everything. It's a sub-genre of Grime infused with Indie that lasted about five seconds back in 2006. The less said about it the better.

'10 Missed Calls'
Dread D & Jammz (2016)

'10 Missed Calls' is a completely inoffensive song. It's about not wanting to pick up your phone when people are calling you. It uses the soundclash energy of Grime as a vessel for observational comedy. It's brilliant. It's like if Michael McIntyre was a Grime artist. It's almost like a spoof Grime song, except that it features a proper MC and was put together by a legendary producer[1]. It contains a line about Jammz being so conservative on the phone that the mandem call him the iPhone Tory, which might just be the best pun on the word 'Conservative' that we, the British people, might ever hope to hear. See, when you remove metaphorical threats of bodily violence from a Grime lyric, you're left with energy and anger that can be focused on any number of targets, up to and including people who won't stop calling you on your mobile. I can't work out if this is the ultimate democratisation of Grime's soundclash aggression, or a terrifying indictment of its conceptual limitations.

One way of looking at it is that Grime is finally growing up. And watching it lurch beyond adolescence into maturity is fascinating. '10 Missed Calls' represents a decorum and almost polite self-awareness that Grime is beginning to express. It's responsibly angry, doing away with the chicken and egg violence that made Grime so controversial and risqué in the mid-Noughties, but possibly nudging the genre into tepid waters. It's evidence that Grime's mainstream success is attainable by smoothing the edges that made it so arresting in the first place. But in terms of respectability politics, '10 Missed Calls' could be problematic, if you read its total and complete lack of controversy as a limiting of its blackness, its 'otherness'. For a Grime song to be so devoid of antagonism could mean that Grime 2016 is losing its bite, and if this is the case, then '10 Missed Calls' can be taken as early warning of a culture's dilution.

Maybe Grime just isn't as scary as it used to be. It remains energetic and aggressive and furious and competitive (and fun), but it's found a degree of mainstream acceptance that means it doesn't need to be on the offensive any more. Jammz has been chipping his way into the scene since before the 2000s hit double figures, but his first big hit didn't rely on street-hardened Trap tales or screwface shows of violence.

He did it with a big instrumental and an everyman song concept.

---

1. Dread D has been doing the super club thing for a few years now under the name T. Williams, but he started out as a member of the Black Ops Crew, spearheaded by fellow Grime legend Jon E Cash. Dread D's latest resurgence is yet another example of Grime coming full circle in 2016.

'Queen's Speech 4'
Lady Leshurr (2016)

I went on a real journey with this one.

I first got wind of 'Queen's Speech 4' via a few 'have you seen this???' mentions on Twitter, and I must admit it was love at first click. The slick, one-take video and infectious bubblegum bravado sucked me right in, an instant victim to the kind of YouTube promotional campaign that is becoming a marketing staple in the mid 2010s. Lady Leshurr was funny (in every sense of the word), fresh and vibrant, spinning lolworthy punchlines over the most minimalist of Grime-pop instrumentals.

Then I got to school and every girl in Key Stage 3[1] was doing a really bad Lady Leshurr impression and telling me about brushing my teeth. So I flipped 180 degrees and decided that Lady Leshurr was the worst possible example of mindless music for the masses, and spent whole lessons talking about "real" female MCs and telling kids to watch Lauryn Hill videos for homework[2].

Then, months later, I realised that I wasn't actually skipping Lady Leshurr when she came up on any of my Spotify Grime playlists and I was forced to re-evaluate my feelings towards her as representation of The Current State of Grime. Then I started writing this book and realised that the 'Queen's Speech' series might represent something of a moment in Grime. Like I say, a journey.

'Queen's Speech 4' won't win any awards for being profound. The first bar sets the tone and says it all, stapling a simile about contemporary temporary social media to an ironically simple simile about going over your head the same way a snapback does. This is the realm in which Leshurr seems to live; unapologetic pop-culture references for the youth of today, sprinkled with playground bravado.

Thing is, it's all rather quite addictive, and actually quite effective. It's impossible not to smile when you catch the puns in her hashtag flow, even when (especially when?) they are inane.

As she says, it's banter, a sentiment of enduring appeal in this current era of jokey irreverence and post-laddism that has, to an extent, permeated adolescence in general. You could argue that the broader significance of Leshurr's Queen's Speech campaign is that it summarises the potency of Grime to satisfy the snacky appetites of the Internet generation. 'Queen's Speech 4' offers up laughs and retweetables with zero thought required, challenging nothing in particular and fighting for no noble causes. Just a string of pop culture reference points glued together with battle rap Pritt-Stick. In this, Lady Leshurr has made an anthem for the Millennials without being serious, or male, or from London[3], proving that Grime can quite easily flout its given criteria.

Now, this is the exact point in a write-up of Lady Leshurr where you might expect a huge diversion into capital F Feminism in capital-G Grime, complete with a potted history of female MCs in the UK and an exploration of sexism and misogyny in youth culture and society at large. I might have to hop that pothole though. Yes, there is an automatic level of female empowerment in the very existence of a confident female MC (operating in a decidedly male context), but Lady Leshurr just doesn't seem to be fighting that particular battle. Compared to the steel-jawed militancy of Shystie's 'I Luv U' Dizzee Rascal response, or the flag-waving militancy of Shystie's 'Woman's World', or the cautionary tales embedded in Ms Dynamite's 2-Step flow, or the confrontational realism of Nolay's 'Netflix and Pills', 'Queen's Speech 4' is pretty tame.

However:

'I'm all about female empowerment – I'm a representative in it so I'm never gonna put a female down. I'm never gonna be in beef over silliness.'
-Lady Leshurr, *Noisey*, 2015

The twist in the tale is in what I saw at school, in the behaviour of all those chirrupy girls from years 7, 8 and 9. In Lady L, they found license to be extrovert and confident within a strictly female context. Lady Leshurr, in this respect, might actually be one of the most important examples of the ongoing democratisation of Grime, widening the circled arms it throws around young people to include the modern teenage everygirl, skirting subversion but ultimately empowering, regardless.

---

1. Key Stage 3 = years 7, 8 and 9 at secondary school = little kids dabbling at being teenagers.

2. True story.

3. 0121 - the dialling code for Birmingham. I have no idea who the first UK

MC was to start shouting out dialling codes to rep their city, but it is an admittedly genius way of watermarking your persona in a scene dominated by London. Other notable 0121 Grime shoutouts include, of course, 'She Wants a Man From Brum' by Safone, a kind of Birmingham promotional video set to 140bpm. As a side note, I might go on record as saying that Birmingham has emerged as Grime's official second city.

'Thiago Silva'
AJ Tracey & Santan Dave
(2016)

I'm doing everything I can to avoid launching into a passive-aggressive attack on Drake and everything he represents. Drake, the talented rapper with the nasal flow. Drake, with his promises of violence alongside heartfelt whimpers of longing. Drake, with his overly spaced-out tattoos and wrong-side-of-creepy Aaliyah obsession. Drake, with his eyebrows. Drake, with his meme-inducing face and gif-generating dance moves. Drake, the man who actually SANG about being hyped enough to catch a body like that, despite also having RAPPED about being scared that every girl he cares for will find a better man and end up happier in the long run. Drake, who appears to have zero understanding that the kind of person who cries over imaginary romances cannot also be the kind of person who kills other people. Drake, the sing star rap star pop star who has exes that used to call him on his cell phone. Drake, with his cell phone. Drake, who really does call himself Champagne Papi. Drake, the Ross Geller of hip hop. Drake, who for some insane reason actually got a Boy Better Know tattoo grafted on his actual skin. Actually, it's not that insane a reason at all. Because he's Drake, the Canadian superstar who, like most superstars, is doing everything he can to stay relevant. And it's working.

It's working because in 2016, Drake successfully cemented an affiliation to the UK Grime scene that had been brewing for a while. In 2011 he channelled Sneakbo in the how you mean, how you mean chorus to 'Cameras', before bringing him out on tour and going as far as tweeting about him to millions of people with access to the Internet. The subsequent Grimechecks came thick and fast, including but not limited to: shoutouts to Wiley; Skepta references in his own lyrics; Instagram nods to *Top Boy*; *Lord of the Mics* reposts on the 'gram and winceful attempts at Jamaican patois.[1]

The thing about Drake which makes him so easy to poke fun at is that he's a classic try-hard overcompensator, which brings out the bully and the troll lurking within ordinary fans of music. He goes so far to prove that he is not the soft, sensitive soul that he is, that he ends up with a delightfully confused persona that makes teenage girls adore him, and invites everyone else to embrace the teenage girl within (which subsequently makes them either angry, or confused). Drake tries so hard to prove that he is down with whatever scene/attitude/style he sees as credible that he ends up throwing himself into the realms of ridicule. Like touring prominent football clubs of the English Premier League and taking photos in full Man City, Man United and Chelsea branded clothing. I would argue that the same goes for his approach to Grime.

If I was a cynic, which I am, I would raise an eyebrow at Aubrey's[2] energetic attempts to endear himself to the Grime network. The suspicion is that, with Grime, Drake is bandwagon-jumping in order to confirm his own credibility within the sphere of black music. In October 2016, Drake hunched over his keyboard and tweeted a shoutout to Giggs, AJ Tracey and Santan Dave on OVO Radio, causing a subsequent tsunami of crying emojis on Twitter the week before his huge Boy Meets World UK tour. The reason for this flood of digital tears is very simple: Drake is a huge international superstar, while AJ Tracey and Santan Dave are, well, AJ Tracey and Santan Dave, two up-and-coming London-based MCs making early waves in the scene. AJ Tracey, the new-fashioned Grime disciple intent upon casting himself as an indestructible Grime MC, all rasping bars and sparse instrumentation. Dave, the somewhat more introspective artiste, piano playing and crooning alongside autobiographical, sometimes philosophical rapping, and author of 'Wanna Know', the song that drew enough attention from Drake to garner an exclusive remix from the Canadian himself.

But if I get over myself and stop trolling for a second, there's an important subtext to all of this about the position of Grime in the popular consciousness. For the best part of a decade, Drake has been positioned square in the very centre of the pop nexus, having crafted for himself a lane of heartfelt RnB musings intersected with hip hop braggadocio. The recipe has proven both delicious and moreish, helping confirm Drake's status not only as an international superstar, but as a game-changing pop culture icon. For this calibre of celebrity to be courting Grime is hugely significant, in that it proves that the tastemakers are finally seeing Grime as worthy of serious attention.

Remarkably, 'Thiago Silva' is audio proof that neither Dave nor AJ actually need a Drake endorsement to legitimise their careers. It's a polished gem of a Grime track, detached and breezy and absolutely devoid of the anxious energy that typified Grime's early incarnations. It's got a casual confidence that skates through bravado without tripping into anger; lyrically confident, steady and controlled in its aggression. Nothing groundbreaking, but firm-footed. All from two relative newcomers who are about as old as most of my CDs, trading bars about walking into clubs, smiling and punching people in the face.[3]

What 'Thiago Silva' might represent is Grime's arrival into shiny self-confidence. It's not a throwback nostalgia trip, but it doesn't court futurism either. It's a poised slice of Grime 2016 in the year that Grime became healthy and robust enough to spawn by-the-numbers hits able to attract the attention of international superstars. I have no idea if that final point is strong enough to justify the words I spent on Drake earlier on, but I couldn't publish a book about music without letting the world know how I feel. Let's move on.

---

1. Very few North American musicians can get away with a Jamaican accent. The closest we got was A Tribe Called Quest's Phife Dawg (RIP), whose attempts were never less than endearing. Clipse get points for their allusion to Nardo Ranks' 'Burrup' in 'Mr. Me Too'. Busta Rhymes always had a bit of the islands brewing in his flow. Wyclef and Lauryn Hill definitely have a Caribbean lilt going on. KRS-One also holds his own in 'Bridge is Over', and... the list might end there. Interestingly enough, it seems that popular African-American music in general has become increasingly West Indian since 2014, with the micro Dancehall hook trend that Kanye brought to the fore in *Yeezus*, not to mention the Ragga aesthetics of recent Beyoncé efforts.

2. Aubrey is Drake's real first name. I'm doing that thing that passive-aggressive trolls do where you dismiss someone's stage name in scorn of their persona. The implication is that Aubrey is not a particularly masculine

name, which is not a problem in itself, but it jars with the hyper-masculine persona that he so often projects. Either way, yes, I think I am a troll.

3. The line about man looking up down left right and straight into a bang in the teeth is honestly one of my 2016 highlights.

'Gunfingers'
P Money feat. Jme & Wiley
(2016)

We've all been there. You're four hours into the rave/family picnic/work Christmas party (delete as appropriate), when you suddenly realise you've left your gun in the car. You frantically start patting your pockets in the vain hope of finding a spare when the DJ throws on that perfect mix of 'Rhythm 'n' Gash' with 'Breakfast at Tiffany's'. Panicked, you ask around if you can borrow someone else's gat, but Shirley's is jammed and Brian's is out of ammo. Everyone keeps chatting. You wave frantically, desperately trying to alert the DJ to your presence. He's a genius. He must be told. Too late. The reload window closes.

As the mix continues, you stare wistfully into the strobe lights/pasta salad/Christmas tree baubles (delete as appropriate) and muse over the missed opportunity to show your appreciation. If only you had remembered your gun.

Or if there was some other way. A word. A word beginning with 'b' maybe. A word beginning with 'b' that you could shout out when the DJ dropped that perfect tune. Ah well. You'll carry two guns next time.

***

The words 'booyaka' and 'brraap' are evidence of the fact that guns serve a very useful and essentially celebratory purpose in certain cultural contexts. Both words start with b and, like the word 'bang', both words are onomatopoeic. They mimic the sound of a gunshot, without having to actually fire a shot out of a gun.[1] The general idea is that a song can be so incendiary, that lyrics can be so devastating, that when heard, the only logical response would be to let fly a round of ammunition from a loaded gun. This is why 'Incredible' by M-Beat and General Levy features the word 'booyaka' as a hook, and why Sacha Baron Cohen used it as a catchphrase in his Ali G guise.

There's a level of respect afforded to the archetypal gunman in Dancehall culture. In the '90s, Dancehall MCs[2] turned gunplay into a virtue, drawing credibility from the outlaw status linked to owning, using and chatting about guns. We've already seen how Cutty Ranks fused the concepts of gun violence and soundclash bravado in 1991's

'Retreat', during an era in which the gun became embedded in lyrical norms. Ninjaman probably takes the trophy for the most trigger-happy discography, with titles including 'Gunman', 'Permit to Bury', 'Target Practice' and, my personal favourite, 'Bring Them All to Jesus'. No wonder that he is often referred to as 'Gun Gorgon', an accolade that flips the mark of respect 'Dan Gorgan' into a gun-centric context. It's also little coincidence that so many Dancehall MCs adopted names derived from high-ranking military titles, up to and including 'General' and 'Captain'.

Grime maintains this fascination with gun violence. The references are constant, far more than I can list in the space of one sentence, or paragraph, or book, as MCs seek out the badman status offered by being a firearm aficionado. From Kano telling us that the only pop you'll hear from him is "pop pop pop" then he's out, to Megaman carrying two gats easy, to Skepta warning us about what the kick-back did to his wrist, to Fekky screaming 'bu-bu-bang', to Stormzy's crafting a persona as Wickedskengman[3], or the fact that Giggs talks about the handgun – a lot, Grime and guns have been lyrically interlocked at a granular level. Instrumental Grime often draws from a ballistic audio palette, including gunshots, shells dropping onto the ground, explosive snares and the click clack insertion of cartridges.

In Grime, explosive violence is not simply a focus for

lyrical content. It also acts as a sonic backdrop and doubles down as a distinct style of delivery as well. Grime has rapid, often repetitive lyrical phrasings that are easily reminiscent of gunfire, ricocheting through abrasive syncopations on a bullet's trajectory, like a constant flow of lyrical explosions. MCs punch syllables into the music with a rat-a-tat precision, using an aggressive style to talk about aggressive things, in a bid to create energy, excitement, and a vague sense of threat. Grime's dialectic relationship with violence is a complicated maze, but its structure enables an MC to play in the labyrinth. Arguably, violence has been normalised into Grime, so much so that it has become the grid upon which artists express their creativity. This ultimately makes violence in Grime not only acceptable, but enjoyable. 'Gunfingers' is conceptualised on this footing, a mid-tempo, simmering raver that invites head-nodding and cool enjoyment.

In her 1994 essay 'Lyrical Gun: Metaphor and Role Play in Jamaican Dancehall Culture', Carolyn Cooper talks at length about the spirit of 'badmanism' at play in Dancehall masculinity. She refers to the 'ghetto gunman' as an archetype that socially marginalised men might lean towards in a bid to empower themselves, positioning themselves as outlaws in the face of social expectation. The gun becomes part of a theatrical posing, a prop in badman cosplay. The argument is that there is a level of wish fulfilment that comes with this MC-as-gunman persona. We can see this running throughout Grime, a genre of music characterised by masculine aggression, encapsulated in the image of the badman. She goes on to cite Shabba Ranks, who makes reference to a "lyrical gun" in the song 'Gun Pon Me', a metaphorical gun for people "to have fun". 'Gunfingers' is tidy example of this kind of lyrical and aural gunplay, using a double snare to replicate the sound of a gunshot.

But.

Guns are real, crime is scary, and gun crime is a terrifying urban reality. There's a reason that the Metropolitan Police Service established Operation Trident in 1998 to tackle gun grime in London's black community, mainly that the majority of gun-violence victims at the time were young black men[4]. Historically, gun murders have disproportionately affected black communities, something that Trident tackled head-on. The 2012 relaunch of Trident with a renewed, more general focus on gang crime drew understandable criticism insofar as it diminished the operation's powers to address specifically gun-related fatalities, instead targeting a broad spread of criminal gang activity. Meanwhile, London saw a 22 per cent increase in gun crime incidents in the 12 months up to December 2016[5], confirming the extent of the problem to date.

When P Money[6] says you might see gunfingers when he

comes in the place, he might not be issuing a warning or trying to be scary; he might just be inviting us to celebrate in the appropriate cultural tradition. The gunfinger might allude to a gun but, crucially, it is not a gun. It signals respect and good times, as opposed to violence and crime. From this perspective, 'Gunfingers' is an acknowledgement of Grime's Dancehall roots, inviting anyone who can point two fingers of the same hand to become a badman for 2 minutes and 49 seconds, but it's also a dark echo of a violent streak that continues to ricochet through black communities.

---

1 'Bluku' is another example of gunomatopoeia, featured in the song 'Bluku Bluku!' by D Double E and repeated as an adlib by Chipmunk in the song 'New Day'. Gunomatopoeia, in case you were wondering, is a word I have invented for the purposes of this footnote.

2. Dancehall MCs are technically known as 'deejays', not to be confused with DJs (an in disc jockeys) who rock the party on two turntables.

3. 'Skeng' is patois for a knife or bladed weapon, often confused with 'leng', which means gun. A Skengman is therefore someone to be reckoned with, hence why Jme once called himself an original Skengman warrior of the earth, who will, of course, be doing his ting until the end of time.

4. According to Claudia Webbe, writing in *The Guardian*, 2013.

5. Metropolitan Police Services crime statistics.

6. P Money is Grime's people's champion. He stayed true to the scene during the lean years, spitting on Dubstep so convincingly that many hailed him as a 'Grimestep' pioneer. He's an MC's emcee, with the ultimate accolade of having had Wiley craft a whole song about him. And he's survived one of the most lyrically potent feuds in Grime history, against Ghetto, replete with all kind of wardubs and unpulled punches. As we round off on 2016, 'Gunfingers' just might be his 'Macarena', a singalong ode to Grime's heritage that we can all join in with.

'It's a London Thing' Jammz feat. Scott Garcia (2016)

It's fitting that the penultimate song of this journey should bear this title, because Grime really is a London thing. If nothing else, we can safely say that Grime is a hugely successful cultural export (speaking in consumerist terms) born of the recent histories and inherent tensions of the UK's capital.

Jammz (last seen shouting and pouting about getting too many calls on his iPhone) is a fine example of the modern Grime MC. And 'It's a London Thing' is a fine example of a modern Grime classic. Like AJ Tracey's 'The Rumble', 'London Thing' is something of an ode to the city that birthed Grime in the first place. We're invited to bubble along to a hook that flips the Scott Garcia 'It's a London Thing' original, before a first verse that shouts out all you dons in high rise accommodation. A calm start. But straight after the first chorus, Jammz kicks into gear with some very observational, very incisive social commentary. This is where the song gets interesting, when Jammz states that London is the most paradoxical place because there are so many opposite things happening in the ends.

The final song of 2016 and the first song to make explicit reference to the concept of paradox, which of course, is the perfect summary of most of what I've been trying to say for the past 50,000 words or so. Jammz sets himself up as a watcher, calloused by a whole life lived in the ends but sensitive enough to empathise and feel pain for the problems. He sees London from every vantage point and can barely make sense of the juxtapositions it throws forward, especially regarding poverty and wealth. For anyone who's spent any time living in the capital and isn't the Queen, this is a deeply relatable concern.

A few lines on and his commentary extends to the hot topic of gentrification. I've always had the suspicion that interrogating social rifts is the true meaning and purpose of lyrical, urban music, and this is exactly what Jammz offers. When he tells us that Starbucks ain't doing shit for the ends other than pushing up rent prices, you all but want to cheer the underpinning liberal sentiment. Then you hear him say that there's still bare William Hills in the ends before he declares a fuck you to "these Conservative leaders" and you realise that Jammz is a politician campaigning for local community rights in the face of a right-wing/centre-right administration. Yes Jammz. Then you take a deep breath and exhale a sigh of relief that inadvertently turns into a sigh of despondency as you slowly look around and realise what you're looking at: a landscape of grey high rises and crawling, urban existences. There's something of this downbeat energy in the bowels of 'It's a London Thing'. It has a plodding quality that diminishes into a subdued coda rather than erupting into any kind of crescendo; a reminder that, as an urban culture, Grime might reach back into a sun-touched heritage and stare forward at a glittering future, but is arguably tied to a somewhat weary present.

'It's a London Thing' is a wonderfully direct diagnosis of London's inherent tensions, conflicts and woes. It's a cerebral, mature glance at a city that offers little to the poor beyond a dream of wealth, while writhing with violence and despair. Haunting images of violence are woven into the song's bubbly 2-Step synths, describing a dystopia of nocturnal violence and innocent screams, watched on by dispassionate observers filming it all, instead of alerting the authorities. It sits in the same bracket as 'London' by William Blake, another example of London-centric anti-establishmentarianism that scrutinises societal ills from a marginalised perspective, much like Grime could be said to do. Blake wrote about 'marks of woe', Jammz calls it "Londonitis", both are describing the same thing.

In 2003, Dizzee Rascal penned mini treatises on the state of the capital in songs such as 'Seems 2 Be' and 'Sittin' Here', deeply introspective explorations of a city that's far from pretty. Thirteen years later and Jammz is doing something similar, but different. References to Homebase and Starbucks suggest class-based, social concerns, shifting focus from internal psychological traumas created by living in antagonistic environments to wider deliberations of the state of the capital at large. With Jammz, we're getting music for everyone: all of us city dwellers who share different lifestyles in the same streets. The fact remains that when we talk about London, we're never just talking about one place; we're talking about a jigsaw of universes – overlapping geographical and cultural territories. Pockets of poverty and avenues of affluence sharing the same urban infrastructure.

As sobering a place as London can be, Grime is often intoxicated by the capital, celebrating it explicitly. MCs routinely craft lyrical odes to their little patches of the city in songs such as 'Bow E3' (Wiley) and 'Lewisham Mcdeez' (The Square), while Grime videos use a whole range of locales as backdrops for badman posturing. These can be as grand as Tower Bridge ('Jus' a Rascal' – Dizzee), or the Shard ('Big For Your Boots' – Stormzy), as mundane as a bus stop ('Golden Boy' – Elf Kid) or a chicken shop ('Big For Your Boots' – Stormzy again), as culturally resonant as the Barbican ('Shutdown' – Skepta) or as implicitly provocative as high-rise council housing (any Grime video with flats in the background).

In a sense, Grime is evidence of growth without movement, a fact summarised neatly in the understated reliability of 'It's a London Thing', a song that intrigues far more than it excites. Grime is still predominantly a London thing, despite having achieved an audience and acceptance well beyond the Tube map, established and confident enough to be putting out safe-bet anthems such as this. Yes, the scene has grown in depth, scope and reach, but it remains rooted to its origins, cemented in the city that Grime will always call home.

'Can't Go Wrong'
Wiley (2017)

Put a question mark at the end of that title and you've got a thrilling end to this journey. Because whether or not Grime will go wrong or prosper into an invincible, glittering future is the big cliffhanger question. And who better than Richard Kylea 'Wiley' Cowie to offer such a resounding answer? Can Grime go wrong? Not according to this song.

I say that because 'Can't Go Wrong' is a self-fulfilling prophecy that proves, in and of itself, how convincing Grime has finally become. It takes orchestral stabs and syncopated snares into stellar territory, proving the efficacy of Grime's most recogniseable audio trademarks, while Wiley lets us know, repeatedly, that he can't go wrong. It's the perfect punctuation point to the *Hold Tight* playlist – a fifth-gear acceleration that celebrates Grime in spectacular pyrotechnics. If this book was a party (which it is), and I was the DJ (which I am), then this chapter would be the last song of the night. And at this point you would be hastily resting your drinks on the bar before putting up two gunfingers in my general direction, signalling a wheel-up.

Wiley offers a confidence to Grime borne of well-honed skill multiplied by train-track consistency. When he tells us he 'Can't Go Wrong', it's as believable as a seasoned bricklayer trowelling cement onto a sturdily constructed, but as yet unfinished wall. Each song in Wiley's extensive back catalogue is another brick in the Grime citadel, confirming the culture at large while showcasing his personal talents. He is an artist who has turned work-rate into a virtue, putting out such a high volume of consistent material that it would almost be illogical to doubt him.

And he knows what he is. He's an MC, bruv. Steps in the place and he MCs, bruv. Jumps on the stage and he MCs, bruv. Mash up the place when he MCs, bruv. 'Can't Go Wrong' is a wolf in wolf's clothing, absolutely confident in its identity and seeking nothing other than to be what it is. Gone are the days of chart-baiting crossover attempts, or vague experiments in genre-bridging. Grime has found validation on its own terms and as a result, Grime MCs are enjoying a newfound confidence. 'Can't Go Wrong', I would argue, is a tangible example of this exuberant self-esteem: truly authentic, straight from the heart and therefore impossible to fail.

'It's a close-knit scene.'

– Stormzy, interview with Capital XTRA, February 2017

A big part of the reason that Grime is going so right is that it has evolved into such a collegiate scene. This is exemplified by Wiley's collaborative approach to music. 'Can't Go Wrong' shouts out Boy Better Know in general and Skepta specifically, in celebration of the wider success of the genre beyond Wiley's personal achievements. Elsewhere in *The Godfather*, we see a total of 19 guest appearances. It's a project that thrives on shared limelight, every contribution adding to a whole that is greater than the sum of its parts.

As he says in the hook, there really is a lot going on, with features, guest spots and cross-crew collaborations having become a genre norm in recent years. The scene has always been built around crew affiliations but, up until recently, it has also been hampered by paranoia, rivalry and crab in the bucket competitiveness. Wiley's role as a unifying figure in Grime is palpable, nurturing talent and acting as a true Grime advocate via his own relentless output. When he says that his team has a lot of dons, you get the impression that he isn't just talking about Boy Better Know or Roll Deep, but the entire Grime scene collectively; a family he can claim as only a true godfather can.

Beyond 2016: The Rise of the Grime Album

The Godfather is Wiley's 11th (and supposedly final) album, but it signals new beginnings for Grime as the genre approaches maturity. Historically, Grime has been a genre of live performance, pirate radio, crowd-baiting singles and underground mixtapes. Subsequently, in the early Noughties, you could count the number of official Grime albums (not compilations) on one hand minus the thumb: *Boy in da Corner* (Dizzee Rascal's unintentional Grime masterpiece), *Home Sweet Home* (Kano's slightly confused mainstream bid) and *Treddin' on Thin Ice* (Wiley's chart-faltering debut). But as we stride further into the 21st century, the full-length Grime album is no longer such a rarity.

2016 saw an unprecedented concentration of full-length releases from an assortment of Grime mainstays. We had Jme's *Integrity* and Frisco's *System Killer* adding weight to the Boy Better Know discography, not to mention offerings from Giggs (*The Landlord*), Wretch 32 (*Growing Over Life*), Chip (*Power Up*) and P Money (*Live & Direct*). And of course the two big releases of the year, Kano's *Made in the Manor* and Skepta's *Konnichiwa*, ended up at the Mercury Awards, with Skepta scooping the prize.

Grime started with a song here and a song there, and now we have entire bodies of work being crafted with insight and foresight in equal measure. The significance of this transition into musical industry maturity cannot be overstated. Grime is growing up, complete with widened perspectives and a new sense of its own legacy. MCs who half a generation ago were happy to pay subs and get a reload on pirate radio are now settling for nothing less than fully realised works of art. It sounds awfully simple, and I've taken the long way round to saying it, but Grime MCs are now artists. Nowhere is this evolution of identity more evident than in the careers of Ghetts and P Money.

Despite a decade's worth of mixtapes, singles, features and unofficial freestyles, it wasn't until 2014 that Ghetts dropped his debut album, *Rebel With a Cause*, nine years after his first mixtape. Meanwhile, P Money waited until 2016 for his debut, *Live and Direct*, a full eight years after his first mixtape. None of this is coincidental. The Grime MC has enjoyed an incremental rise in confidence that has been manifested in projects substantial enough to hold their own in mainstream contexts, with enough velocity to break the gravitational pull of the underground.

For the Millennial generation, this all adds up to a bunch of very exciting words that all happen to begin with P: possibility, plausibility, potential and progress. Case in point: Stormzy, who launched into prominence via social media buzz and a string of independent hits, before disappearing off the radar in 2016, only to return in 2017 with the announcement of *Gang Signs and Prayer*, his debut album – barely three years after the release of his first EP. It won't be long until we're seeing Grime newcomers entering the scene with full-length albums off the bat.

Stormzy's journey is proof of how far Grime has come since its early days of DIY hype. The underground streak is still prevalent but we are now seeing Grime polished and presented for mainstream palettes, without compromising its core characteristics. And while mainstream tastes may change and fascination with the culture might wane, perhaps the only way that Grime can go wrong now is if it starts to lose the self-belief it has cultivated so far.

Appendix
Grime: Summarised

Grime: Conceptualised

Grime comes into existence, before it has a name. The sounds and styles that would become Grime have been incubated years prior in various musical branches, culminating in early electronic experimentations. Grime slants in diagonally from the sidelines of wider, more dominant cultures, a quirky cousin, offbeat and irregular, awkward and unpredictable. The concept of syncopation is key. 2-Step lays the blueprint for the jittery energy that characterises Grime both aurally and ideologically. Grime emerges as the music of confident youth empowerment. The mainstream begins to find Grime abrasive, jarring. Grime's earliest MCs establish themselves as squawky, eccentric and overexcited, incessant with adolescent energy and impatience. There's a potentially irritating quality to Grime that means that it won't immediately be embraced by the mainstream. Grime sounds suspiciously like kids mucking about because, to a large extent, it is kids mucking about, kids who have swilled about in an audio stew of black British post-diaspora cultures and come out the other end with firm-footed, kick-to-the-door confidence.

Two interlocked strands combine to form Grime's spine: soundclash culture and pirate radio. Its deep affiliation to soundclash culture gives the Grime scene a weight far beyond its original digital glitchiness. The clash grounds Grime in a competitive collaboration, embedding pugilism, bravado and machismo into something that could easily become screechy and frantic. Pirate radio is the primary channel through which a new kind of MC culture emerges, cultivated invisibly from the mainstream gaze. This illicit, subversive quality carries deep in Grime's genetic code, which will, as we will see, be a source of deep tension as the genre begins to court mainstream lanes. Society watches on, oblivious to what lies in wait.

Grime: Realised

Grime emerges as an outsider culture; the post-Millennial sibling to UK Garage (UKG), Jungle, Ragga. To untrained (unaccustomed) ears, Grime is unusual, the sound of 'them' – a generation who are making their own rules in their own game, all blipped out on computer games and restlessly roaming an urban landscape that doesn't recognise them as adults. The adolescence that typifies Grime's inception continues to characterise the culture. Tracksuits and baseball caps, a fittingly youthful uniform for the sound of modern youth. Interviews and testimony from key players in the scene attest to this, with tales of MCs forming an identity in youth clubs, bedrooms, school playgrounds and back of top deck buses, the landscape of urban adolescence if ever there was one.

Pirate radio proves to be a natural habitat for this burgeoning culture. Outfits such as Rinse, Déjà vu and Heat FM offer a community service of sorts for urbanite teens, broadcasting MCs across London. Competitive conflict and collaborative pugilism characterise the scene, as a new generation of MCs pay their subs, write their bars, and seek kudos through pirate radio appearances.

What do you call it? Wiley asks the question and Grime is proving to be a culture almost outside of itself. It doesn't really know what it is – a set of norms without definition and therefore less than tangible. The establishing of a visitable, physical scene helps, with pilgrimages to Eskimo Dance and Sidewinder helping cement the mythology. The

Grime MC crystallises as an archetype; angry, excitable, tough, unstable, reckless. But the archetype isn't necessarily an authentic representation of Grime's key demographic. The persona Grime realises is precisely that – a persona, as in stage mask. Performative and overblown, it tips into caricature, solidifying into role. A subculture is born.

Grime: Colonised

The extreme extroversion demanded by the norms of a clash-based culture mean that MCs readily don personas which are all too easy for the mainstream to accept as 100 per cent accurate facsimiles of the true self, rather than a constructed part of a more complex whole. Jme is one of the first to challenge these ideals whilst simultaneously adhering to them, aligning cartoon violence with down to earth, cut the bullshit realism. Grime's buzz is waspish, and the sting is the thing that gives it an illicit appeal, equally frightening and intriguing to a mainstream consciousness. Much like the enthusiastic field recorders and anthropologists of the mid-20th Century, journalists begin to 'discover' Grime and seek to explore it in its natural habitat.

'...at the time, Grime was nothing more than a bunch of kids in East London messing about and having fun. Kano was still sharing a bunk bed with his kid brother, Scorcher was living with his mum out in the suburbs and Chipmunk was in secondary school (I waited for him at his school gates in Tottenham before our first interview). I'm pretty sure Jammer still lives with his parents.'

-John McDonnell, *VICE*, 2012

Grime finds mainstream validation from this new interest from people who are fascinated by what, to them, is an alien, exciting and hitherto unknown entity. Commercially, the edge that Grime flashes at the world offers instant appeal. Some early commentators launch into a co-opting of the culture, both celebrating and supporting the scene. Hipsters with a fascination for the authentic locate in Grime something real, something genuine. Can Grime ever be said to have been independent? *RWD* magazine famously documents the early years in glossy prominence, eschewing grit for something closer to glamour. There is an excitement surrounding Grime from a generation of knowing 'insiders' with their fingers on the pulse of the new and relevant, wearing their new-found proximity to the culture as a badge of honour, proof of cool.

But even cooler than that, of course, is the unstoppably wry view of Grime taken by those commentators who are too irreverent to take the scene seriously. The Grimewatch,

Prancehall approach, putting one arm tenderly around the scene while viewing it with a bemused smirk at the same time. Taking the sting out of Grime by acknowledging its inherent posturing and emphasising its adolescent context.

Neither position is ideal. The cheerleading fails to interrogate while the smirk belittles. Grime, as a black British artefact, is not yet viewed as such, acknowledged on fairly narrow terms. Grime has realised what it is doing but doesn't know what it is for. Is it a youth club for a generation of black Britons? A punkish scream of discontent? A symptom of political disenfranchisement? A channel for political disenfranchisement? A celebration of the black British diaspora? A hustle? An escape? Street reportage? A lifeline away from the risks of the road? Its wider purpose is an unexplored debate, and commentators outside of the culture begin to fill in the gaps.

Grime: Demonised

Grime's connection to the streets throws it under the shadow of suspicion. Predominantly young, predominantly black, predominantly male, ostensibly working-class faces are being recognised as anti-social (if not dangerous) and thus worthy of suspicion. Form 696 epitomises the tension between Grime and the establishment, a notorious moment in risk assessment that very nearly becomes a notorious moment in racial profiling. The original form demands details of promoters and participants in live music events, controversially including ethnic groups likely to attend as well as the target audience, essentially allowing the Metropolitan Police to 'risk assess' ethnicity.

A victim of its own notoriety, Grime readily embraces its roadman image, the persona of the streets that doesn't simply commentate on but is a supposed active participant in road activity. The worth of an MC is measured in street credibility as much as musicality. Grime seeks to empower itself by framing itself as tough enough for road. The immediate outcome of Grime's demonisation is the confirmation of its outsider status. At this point in the narrative Grime is still very much at arm's length from the mainstream, mistrusted, perhaps, and misunderstood, surely, all the while anchoring its illicit appeal.

As a post-postcolonial artefact, Grime represents a very disobedient grandchild, running amok and refusing to follow the rules. The black British handbook asked immigrant Afro-Caribbean communities to empower themselves by raising a generation of doctors, lawyers, accountants, professionals. Suddenly, inherited discipline appears sidelined, maligned by a generation of black boys who noisily flout predefined expectations.

Grime: Politicised

Anger has subtle brushstrokes.

Grime becomes characterised by an in your face aggression and confrontational energy that puts it in alignment with agitprop protest music. Grime might not always say political things but it is an implicitly political artefact, countering existing power paradigms and challenging the status quo. Grime's inherent anger ranges from screams of violence to detailed treatises on pain and the trauma of marginalised experiences. It is unrepentantly anti-establishment, setting itself up in opposition to the law and promoting a self-empowerment borne of social transgression. In the context of respectability politics, Grime is non-conformist, disrespectful. As a lyrical genre, so much of Grime is a celebration of delinquency from individuals who seem to be rhyming their way into and out of trouble, offering little more than a fuck you to any critics. A question mark hangs over the extent to which societal expectations spur disenfranchised youth to live up to their reputation. A Millennial counter-culture is born.

Grime: Galvanised

Grime becomes an unstoppable force of youth culture.

Risky Roadz. *Lord of the Mics*. Channel U. The edifice in which Grime was fertilised begins to grow and proliferate, scaffolding routes to prominence that hadn't existed years before. Faces become familiar faces become famous faces, and a handful of Grime stars are starting to form their very own constellation. Access to the scene has broken free of the limitations of pirate radio and live events, spilling into DVD footage and hot sell compilations. Industry doors creak open to let a few toes in, but it is becoming feasible for an MC to make a name without major label endorsement.

The significance of social media cannot be overstated. Web forums lay a foundation of networks that don't rely on showing up at Jammer's basement. A buzz can become a thing in a matter of clicks and the consumption of Grime can flow entirely via digital channels. For a 21st Century youth culture, this is truly galvanising. It invites technological natives to assimilate the means of procuring Grime into their lives, which in turn means that they are able to assimilate the culture itself into their lives. You can own Grime on a handheld device, or the laptop in your bedroom, or your TV, without having to take the extra step towards the scene that was demanded of you in its realisation phase. And just as quickly as DVDs emerge as a key source of Grimy consumption, YouTube strides into the frame, blocking all sunlight and dominating all scene-to-seen routes. The mainstream shrinks into irrelevance.

Grime: Democratised

Grime establishes a digital relationship with its target audience. The autonomy and mastery Grime's audience has over technology in general marries up to the ownership felt over the culture. It reaches widespread appeal and democratisation. Artists enjoy ultimate control over their output, delivering direct to audience, unfiltered and unchallenged, with little other option due to locked industry doors. Culturally, this removes all notions of Grime having gatekeepers. The gates are accessible and open to all. You don't have to look like or sound like or talk like the creators of Grime to participate in the culture; you just need to have the volition to take part. As a result, and very quickly indeed, Grime establishes itself as a pervasive youth culture, the soundtrack of street credibility. Its norms and codes become the dominant codes of modern cool, stemming back to the laid-back lean of West Indian rudeboys. The proliferation of West Indian dialect is of paramount significance. A whole generation of adolescents now speak a language that ties them to a black British heritage stemming from the Windrush diaspora. Truss me.

Grime will always be a geographical and cultural product

of London, making its Londonness a defining characteristic and London, more than anywhere else in the UK, is a product of rampant multiculturalism. In London, ethnicity is inextricably linked to urban living, one of the main commonalities of non-indigenous communities who have migrated to the UK since the Second World War. Add it all up and you get an eye-openingly significant conclusion: that Grime is a point of reconciliation for otherwise disparate black identities. Blackness in the UK is not a simple thing; it's a complicated mesh of heritages and cultures loosely held together by hue. Grime offers a far richer adhesive, introducing a UK-bred set of codes of conventions that second and third generation Afro-Caribbeans of single and multi-heritage can all opt into, without compromise, without question. Black Britain has always enjoyed an implicit unity, but Grime makes this super-explicit in a Millennial context.

Grime: Bastardised

Popularity smells a lot like commercial potential. Dizzee Rascal accidentally proves that Grime can win critical favour (and fervour), raising industry eyebrows over the possibility of cashing in on an edgy subculture replete with stars in the making. But packaging Grime is a difficult task, and the product is a difficult sell. Grime struggles to successfully play the insider game. With such lucrative wins in the crosshairs, attempts are made, with varying degrees of do-not-try-this-at-home success. The major label formula (that has been tried and tested for the cookie-cutter pop production line) proves untenable for the quirky idiosyncrasies of Grime, resulting in weirdly disperate hybrids. Grime is pegged into the wrong-shaped hole as artists keep trying keys to previously ignored doors. Crossover poses a threat, asking Grime's dedicated few to launch flailing pole vaults into mainstream citadels or construct a shoddily conceived trojan horse to the same effect. Either way: unsatisfying and largely unsuccessful. Grime-pop is instantly risible, devoid of credibility in and of itself.

The subtext here is Grime's attempted transition to empowerment via wealth acquisition. Grime is tied to social disenfranchisement in a profound way, borne of the frustration of not having tied to the aspiration of wanting to have. The get-money obsession with street economies (particularly drug sales) dovetails with an entrepreneurship that has fuelled Grime from the off, from its DIY production aesthetic to its independent promotional tendencies. This fierce independence, more than anything else, gives Grime its potency, its power.

It's a confusing irony that Grime's shift towards industry legitimacy comes at the expense of its pirate-rooted illegitimacy, which actually lent it authenticity in the first place. Commercial radio becomes a new target for Grime's fledgling stars, which poses two key questions: Who is consuming Grime? And who could be consuming Grime? Up until now Grime is a self-serving community, comprised of relatively young minds seeking only to impress their peers. The community is parochial, focused initially on one part of East London and only starting to spread citywide, let alone nationwide, or worldwide. The echo chamber effect of this proves deeply empowering. A shift in focus to a more mainstream audience might feel galvanising, but it is only a superficial empowerment. The truth is that Grime's awkward steps towards the mainstream are culturally disempowering, instigating a dilution of Grime's core values, a misalignment of its fundamental energies and a blurring of its spirit, targeting an audience who have not grown with the culture and will most likely treat it casually.

Grime: Traumatised

The damage has been done. Grime has suffered the trauma of a failed product launch, recalled and discontinued, reinstated as an outsider scene of limited mainstream relevance. It has been shelved.

Grime: Recognised

Recognition = re-cognition = a new understanding of something that always was. When we say we recognise something, we are not saying that we see it for the first time; we are saying that we are seeing it as if for the first time.

Post-wilderness, Grime undergoes a process of self-recognition, seeing itself as whole and worthy and understanding itself as if first the first time. A slew of Grime anthems emerge. Grime embraces its identity. The confidence this gives to the scene was palpable. Artists who have tinkered with their identity and struggled to find a fit strip themselves back to a core essence. Nowhere is this more explicit than in the ups, downs and ups again of Skepta. When he chats about throwing Gucci and LV in the bin, he's making a huge declaration of self-recognition. The proud declaration that the 'That's Not Me' video (a lo-fi, nostalgic affair) cost mere pounds to produce is further affirmation of the self, not to mention his militant adherence to a tracksuit dress code. Skepta's career upsurge marks a huge re-cognition point for the culture, mirrored elsewhere throughout the scene.

Meanwhile the sonic quality of Grime begins to lean back into its early years. New faces emerge with a vintage hue. The Instagram effect; a Millennial preoccupation with what came before, finding authenticity in the past. Stormzy epitomises Grime's nostalgic ability to build new careers on a throwback attitude, jumping on classic Grime instrumentals and repackaging them for Millennial audiences. 'Serious' first landed in 2006. Stormzy flips it into 'Wickedskengman 4' in 2015. 'Functions on the Low' dropped in 2004. Stormzy flips it into 'Shut Up' in 2016. Novelist jumps on Jon E Cash's 'War' instrumental in the same year, helping recalibrate the past in a contemporary context. For the culture, this is a true recognition of self which translated very quickly into commercial gain. A consumer culture is born.

***

The commodification of Grime's core, grimy tenets has been a swift and startling process. The mainstream recognises Grime's true worth and offers its attentions to a scene that was previously sidelined and demonised. But why now?

In terms of power politics, the recognition of Grime plays into existing paradigms and hierarchies. Marginalised peoples tend to stay marginalised because dominant social forces don't want to lose their dominance. This explains why Grime could never have made it into the mainstream when it was trying to emerge out of its early adolescence. But more interestingly, and far more complicated, is the idea that mainstream acceptance of Grime actually reinforces existing power imbalances. The mainstream has accepted a vision of Grime that it is comfortable with, that it finds safe, that it understands. New Grime, in all its back-to-basics glory, reinforces existing notions of urban youth and existing notions of black masculinity. It isn't particularly political, and it is therefore inherently safe. It remains adolescent, concerned with the trappings of adulthood and the exhilaration of taboo. And it poses absolutely no threat to dominant ideas of blackness. If you ask the question, 'What is being recognised in Grime's resurgence?', the answer is simple: Everything that was already understood about Grime.

The narrow terms of Grime's recognition can be seen clearly in Skepta's 2016 Mercury Prize win. *Konnichiwa* is an impressive Grime album, absolutely, replete with anthems, bangers and assertions of self. But challenging? Not really. Not to the widest paradigms. Not to preconceptions of black masculinity that have been promoted and re-promoted and made fact over so many generations. The butterfly that Grime has emerged into looks suspiciously similar to the caterpillar that entered its chrysalis in the first place. And there's a herd of elephants trampling through the room. Confirmation of negative black stereotypes? The infantilisation of black masculinity? Implicit misogyny? Underlying homophobia?

Promotion of violence? Obsession with neoliberal wealth acquisition?

Grime: Stylised

In all of this there's a danger in thinking that Grime actually is what it claims to be. By which I mean that it has cultivated an iron-clad image that is all too easy to accept as authentically true. As it stands, Grime is unquestionably cool; dominated by a clutch of shelf-ready insiders who are readily exalted for their alpha status. The archetypal Grime MC is widely recognised as such, not simply confident but successfully bold, brash and aloof, unconcerned with the parameters of social decorum and dismissive of those less alpha than himself. In short, cool.

The first problem this raises pertains to the true purpose and nature of that thing we call 'cool'. Coolness, that much-sought commodity, is an attitudinal frame of mind linked to vulnerability and fear. It's a shield, a form of armour designed to distance the individual from criticism and attack. If you're cool, you have a breezy cynicism that protects you from scrutiny by elevating you above others. This is essentially why everyone wants to be cool; because it makes them feel superior to everyone else and acts as a buffer to being flawed, being human.

One argument is that being cool is a shield that Grime did not originally wear. If you squint past the blinding cool of contemporary Grime and squint into its earliest beginnings, you'll see that Grime was never really dominated by the insiders. It was never the preserve of the cool kids or the in-crowd. It was never aloof, or breezy, or above criticism, or alpha. It was quirky, populated by the outsiders, the weird kids, the awkward blip makers and rhyme writers who didn't want to be popping champagne bottles in the UKG room, and probably couldn't get in anyway because they looked too young. Early Grime is characterised by the unusual, riddled with weird personas. Unlike the humourless cool of UK Garage, Grime was animated, tweaked and gimmicky. Consider the names alone, affectionately street, replete with cheeky adjectives and smile-inducing 'eee' endings: Crazy Titch, Tinie Tempah, Footsie, Flirta D, D Double E, Wiley, Dizzee Rascal, etc. In this, Grime always boasted a level of theatricality that took it out of the club, wielding a sense of humour that made it playful and off kilter. If cool is disinterested, Grime is excitable. If cool is casual, Grime is nerdy.

I've written at length about the significance of Jme as Grime's "only true Everyman", spinning a nerdy aesthetic that counters Grime's narrative as the preserve of a hypercool, ultra elite. This is important, inasfar as Jme is one of relatively few prominent Grime stars who actively reject the allure of reductive street credibility: he represents the freedom to shun expectations and subvert mainstream prejudices. For the Grime MC, the safest persona is the one that confirms mainstream preconceptions, meaning that achieving the desired level of cool means pandering to stereotypes. It's no accident that the emerging stars of Grime's adolescence are routinely aggressive, cool, tough, and polished with machismo, compared to the spiky idiosyncrasies of Grime's infancy. Being able to manipulate computer programmes into bar-ready beats was once a Grime prerequisite (Kano, Dizzee, Wiley, Jme, Skepta, Jammer, Footsie and Rapid to name a few MCs who cut their teeth on lo-fi production). But being nerdy is no longer an option because Grime is finally mainstream. And the mainstream is ultimately rewarding its own confirmation of black male stereotypes. It might be a telling coincidence that one of Grime's biggest quirks is also one of its biggest stars. Dizzee Rascal has successfully cast himself as something of a joker alongside his tough MC persona, often eccentric but ultimately confident enough to get away with it, with a string of video concepts that look like they were brainstormed during a drunken game of charades. In a way, he's far from cool, a fact that ironically empowers him beyond cool's limitations into a different bracket entirely.

Grime arguably exists in a state of insecurity; scared of losing face by being anything other than 'real', which is potentially debilitating for the rest of Grime. Jme is an anomaly within this context, surrounded by road-ready affiliates (including his big brother) who enable him to be himself, quirks and all. If the roadman cookie cutter continues to produce commercially viable, commercially cool Grime stars, this might possibly be at the expense of genuine evolution. In Grime, we get a black British success framed by anti-social stereotypes, an edginess that titillates mainstream appeal rather than levelling expectations. Ironically, Grime's inherent eccentricity is in danger of being evolved out of the gene pool and a lack of eccentricity will always have a homogenising effect on the culture. The real issue at hand is that Grime is finding its feet as a saleable, marketable, desirable product with the Unique Selling Point of being unassailably cool. Any deviation from this USP would jeopardise its commercial value, so it stays cool, safe, unexperimental.

But in historical terms, black cool is an important evolutionary shield. Let's not forget that as recently as the mid to late 20th Century, black people were facing a world of blatant racism, National Front marches and open discrimination. Being aloof, callous and steel-jawed (ie: cool) was an obvious armour against this threat, especially for black men who were viewed with particular suspicion. In these terms, Grime's obsession with cool, whilst existing in society's margins, is more than empowerment – it is survival.

Grime: Humanised

For all of its antagonism, paranoia, anger and aggression, Grime is actually hugely inclusive. For Millennials, it serves a similar purpose to the Black electro nu-soul movement of the late '80s, inviting a generation of liberally minded partygoers to move to a shared rhythm. The fact that Grime is becoming a festival staple is no accident, offering a unifying soundtrack for Millennials of all colours. The mainstream might finally have realised that Grime is not the scary monster in the shadows. It's a kid finding its feet in the world.

***

I started this book with a eulogy to Gregory Sylvester Coleman, the drummer responsible for six seconds of drum break that changed modern music forever. His was the first of many stories that have permeated these pages, stories about the individuals who have contributed to and shaped Grime's past and present. Stories about Reggae fans in Japan who programmed 'Rock' presets that would fall into the hands of Jamaican music-makers. American DJs who tweaked four on the floor electronic rhythms into something spiky and addictive. British DJs who sped things up and slowed things down and sped things up again. Airwave pirates who broke the rules. And ultimately, young Londoners who created a niche and broadcast it at decibels into the concrete of their surroundings.

And now I'm getting vertigo. My head is spinning. For years, Grime existed only in my iPod. I wasn't at Sidewinder. I wasn't in Jammer's basement. I wasn't at Rhythm Division. I definitely wasn't dodging ASBOs with Slimzee on the top floor. But I've been carrying the scene around with me in my headphones for as long as a scene can be said to exist.

I started writing *Hold Tight* because I could smell the bubbling point of Grime's lava-like infiltration of the mainstream and I wanted to make sense of it before it evaporated away. I felt that my narrative, as a fan of music, a devotee of culture, a young black man who has grown up with genres of black music, was pertinent to this moment of mainstream acceptance.

A year later and things are bigger than I could have expected. Grime's story has bled like wax into the cool waters of popular culture, solidifying into fact, into a story.

The voice of a generation... What punk was to rock... The sound of disenfranchisement... But to so many of us who were simply fans of music from the places we grew up in, places that weren't necessarily the ashes from which only phoenixes could rise, Grime has been a soundtrack. So every time I peer into the world and see Grime shining back at me from impossible places, I feel a lurching sense of destabilisation, like my compass has shifted.

***

Hold Tight is the outsider insider perspective, in that I place myself outside the inner circle of Grime architects, but very much inside the black British heritage that Grime has grown out of. It doesn't tell the story that's been told and it won't confirm what's already been confirmed. It's the joining of dots from a simple fan of music. I've offered a commentary on Grime's narrative filtered through my years of listening, making sense of a moment in black British history, a moment that persists into the realm of post-Millennial, digital contexts. This isn't the first book about Grime and it absolutely can't be the last. And as for the end of this book? Two words will suffice: not The End, but, of course. . .

Hold Tight.

The Grime Timeline

1948

Empire Windrush brings some of the first large groups of West Indians to the UK after the Second World War, immediately cultivating a distinct culture of black Britishness, following the British Nationality Act of the same year. The Empire Windrush was previously a German cruise ship.

1955

Lambeth stages the 'No Colour Bar' Dance, inviting 180 white English people and 180 black West Indians to a social dance intended to improve relations between white Londoners and immigrant West Indians. Does Grime bridge a similar gap in the early 21st century?

1964

Radio Caroline floats on to the airwaves and actual, wet, watery waves of the North Sea, broadcasting the first pirate radio transmissions to British listeners. Pirate radio will soon become an essential source of non-mainstream music in the UK. Radio Caroline was formerly a Danish passenger ferry.

1965

The Race Relations Act is passed by Harold Wilson's Labour government, seeking to prohibit and prevent racial discrimination in Britain. Put your hand palm down in front of you. Wobble it side to side. Make this face :/ That's the general response from the Afro-Caribbean community.

1970s

The Crossways Estate council housing development scheme is completed, comprising of three 25-storey high rises in East London. These structures will one day come to be known as 'three flats', providing an iconic backdrop to Grime's East London roots. In a few decades' time, photographer David Tonge will take a brooding picture of Wiley and Dizzee Rascal posing with the three high-rises in the background.

1977

Public National Front marches meet counter protests across London. Racial volatility is becoming ingrained in modern Britain.

1981

Riots erupt in Brixton as a result of ongoing tensions between police and the black community.

1985

Riots. In Brixton. Again.

1987

Bernie Grant, Diane Abbott and Paul Boateng become the first three black MPs elected to Parliament. All Labour.

1991

Street Fighter 2 is released for arcade by Capcom. A generation of gamers never quite recover.

1991

'Zulu Skank' by Dread & Fred completely invents Grime by accident, complete with wobbly synths, oriental top line phrasings and upbeat drum sequencing.

1994

Dylan Beale reinvents Grime, by accident, via 'Tri-fusion', an end of level boss soundtrack for the 16 bit beat-em-up *Wolverine: Adamantium Rage*. Mad ting.

Rinse FM is founded by DJ Slimzee and Geeneus, pirate broadcasting UK Garage into the London airwaves.

1997

Tony Blair is elected Prime Minister of the United Kingdom, succeeding John Major and ending 18 years of Conservative government. Grime will be born into something called New Labour.

1998

The Metropolitan Police Service launches Operation Trident, seeking to tackle gun crime in London's Afro-Caribbean community.

Audi AG launches the Mk1 TT. Off the production line will emerge a blacked-out model that Megaman will one day drive about and rhyme about.

2001

Skat D's contribution to the song '21 Seconds' finally realises the full potential of the English language. You dun kno.

RWD magazine is launched, proving conclusively that the letters i, n and d are entirely unnecessary when conceptualising the word 'rewind'.

<h2 style="text-align:center">2002</h2>

More Fire Crew land on the Top of the Pops stage with an enthusiastic rendition of 'Oi!'. They share the episode with, among others, Shakira, Oasis and Will Young, none of whom have made it into the pages of *Hold Tight* until this sentence.

BBC Radio 1Xtra is launched. The transcript of the marketing meeting in which it was decided to drop the 'e' in Extra is, sadly, lost to the annals of history.

'Pulse X' offers a viable 'first ever Grime track'.

The UK government's Radiocommunications Agency carries out 209 raids on pirate radio outfits across the country; 181 are based in London.

Eskimo Dance. You weren't there, man.

VICE magazine starts featuring Grimewatch, a cooler-than-thou, couldn't-give-less-of-a-shit-than-thou aspect to the Grime mix. Undeniably funny Grime commentary from a smirky margin.

2003

Summer. Stratford. Tower block. Top floor. Déjà Vu FM hosts a live radio show featuring, among others, Crazy Titch, Wiley and Dizzee Rascal. At one point someone calls someone else something and an argument breaks out between Titch and Dizzee. Turns out Dizzee didn't take kindly to being called a "mook". The whole thing is captured on video and immortalised on the *Conflict* DVD.

Channel U hits satellite and cable, giving me and my friends something to start feeling old to during late Saturday night PlayStation/takeaway sessions. A generation of Millennials can finally start putting faces to names and voices.

Dizzee Rascal releases his debut album *Boy in da Corner*. An international community of music journalists simultaneously agree that it is one of the greatest pieces of art to come out of the 21st Century so far. Jaws are still being picked up off the floor.

2004

Rooney 'Risky Roadz' Keefe releases his first compilation

DVD. Grime is getting visual.

2005

Logan Sama launches a late-night Grime show on Kiss FM. He also establishes a sideline in commentating on international *Street Fighter* competitions.

On Valentine's Day in 2005, a video sharing website called YouTube is launched. It will one day replace radio, CDs and vinyl as the primary channel of underground music consumption. It also has lots of videos about cats.

The MOBOs launches its 'Best Grime' category.

Kano puts his full name and date of birth on record in a guest spot on 'Routine Check' by the Mitchell Brothers.

The Rinse FM radio transmitter is disconnected and DJ Slimzee is issued an ASBO banning him from rooftops in the London borough of Tower Hamlets.

Lethal B's invincible 'Pow!' wins Best Single at the 2005 MOBO Awards, while Kano wins Best Newcomer.

Footsie calls upon forbidden alien technology, the dark arts, battery acid and luck to produce the instrumental for 'Prang Man'.

2006

Jamal Edwards founds SB.TV, promoting urban music through freestyle rap footage and music videos – including a clutch of Grime frontliners – and unleashing Ed Sheeran to the world.

The London Metropolitan Police Service launches Form 696, requiring live music event promoters to give performers' details alongside a description of the style of music being performed and (controversy grenade) details of which ethnic groups are likely to attend. Grime is in the crosshairs, because of, y'know, how black and violent it is.

2007

DJ Cheeky sets up Rhythm Division on the Roman Road in Bow, East London. For the next four years this understated record shop will become a cultural hub for Grime, through which a who's-who of the scene's originators will frequently pass.

2008

Jeremy Paxman calls Dizzee Rascal 'Mr Rascal' on national television.

2009

Bye bye Channel U. U shall be missed.

Channel AKA's rebrand is launched. What it is Also Known As remains a mystery.

Five separate number ones from five separate Grime artists hit the charts.

The Metropolitan Police Service announces a revision to Form 696 stating that venues will no longer be asked to stipulate the style of music being played.

2010

Jammer releases the best Grime album cover we will ever hope to see with *Jahmanji*, featuring a picture of himself in yellow trousers standing next to a trumpeting elephant.

Rinse FM folds up the Jolly Roger and finally goes legal.

Wiley deliberately leaks 11 zip folders full of previously unreleased music for absolutely no reason other than the fact that he's Wiley, and that's the kind of thing Wiley does.

2011

Top Boy brings Ashley 'Asher D' Walters, Kane 'Kano' Robinson, Ashley 'Bashy' Thomas, Tayo 'Scorcher' Jarrett and Derek 'Sway' Safo to our small screens in a London-based gritty crime drama.

Ancient grudge breaks to new mutiny in London, after protests surrounding the killing of Mark Duggan by armed police turn to looting and social disorder. Unsettling times, referenced in three of the songs featured in this book.

Rhythm Division ends its lifespan as a record shop. End of an era. The building re-opens as a coffee shop.

Tinie Tempah guest hosts an episode of *Never Mind the Buzzcocks*.

2012

Thames Valley Police release 'An Eye For An Eye', a Grime song designed to discourage knife crime and gang violence. At the time of writing, it has 24,579 views on YouTube.

Operation Trident is relaunched as Trident Gang Crime Command.

2013

Charlie Sloth picks up where Tim Westwood left off on BBC Radio 1 and 1Xtra, shouting about rap music and pushing sound effect buttons and repping the scene as hard as possible. His 'Fire in the Booth' segment will quickly become a hallmark of skill and industry prestige in Grime and UK Rap.

Over 5,000 people sign a petition to immortalise Wiley with a statue in Tower Hamlets. That's roughly 5,000 more people than have signed a petition for a statue of me to be erected in anywhere.

2014

Jamal Edwards is appointed an MBE for his services to music, proving that Grime can get you into the Palace.

2015

Everyone's favourite human meme Drake brings out Skepta on stage during his main-stage performance at the Wireless Festival.

A who's-who of MCs join Kanye West on stage at the BRIT Awards to jump around in black tracksuits during a performance of 'All Day'.

2016

RIP Darren Platt, Channel U founder.

Hattie Collins and Olivia Rose release *This is Grime*, a fabulously glossy documentation of the Grime scene.

Skepta and Kano both get nominations for best album category at the Mercury Awards. Skepta edges it.

Frisco and Risky Roadz orchestrate a live Grime set at 391 Roman Road, the former site of Rhythm Division, and document the whole thing in *Pirate Mentality* on Channel 4.

Donald J Trump wins the 2016 US presidential election race on behalf of the Republican Party, meaning that in 2017 there will finally be a President T on both sides of the Atlantic.

2017

20th January. My 21-month-old son awakes from his nap and calmly asks to listen to 'Functions on the Low'. Meanwhile, *Hold Tight* is officially announced to press.

Appendix:
Essays in Grime

Boys to Mandem: Grime and the masculinity barrier

Grime's credibility hinges almost entirely on preconceived notions of masculinity. In fact, masculinity might be the biggest elephant in the room when we're discussing what Grime really is and what it really represents.

Masculinity, rather than a fact of being, is a concept, a social construct, an ideological positioning that assigns certain traits and attitudes to the male of a given species. Biological maleness is absolute and real. Masculinity, on the other hand, is a fiction. The problems this can cause at both individual and societal levels are huge. Masculinity not only assumes certain traits of men but also imposes major expectations upon behaviour, attitude and competencies. To be masculine means to satisfy a long list of rugged personality criteria, codes and conventions that little boys are born into, whether they like it or not. The same, of course, goes for little girls and femininity, society having evolved into a brittle sense of binary opposition with regards to gender. Girls are submissive, boys dominant. Girls passive, boys aggressive. Girls domestic, boys practical. Girls princesses, boys soldiers. Girls pink, boys blue. Girls weak, boys strong. And this last distinction is potentially the most dangerous of all.

Above all social codes, the expectation of men to be strong is the most pervasive, bleeding into all aspects of male existence. For men, weakness is not only viewed with suspicion but actively disallowed. Man up. Men aren't permitted to show signs of weakness or be anything other than dominant. Alpha male. Earn the most money, have the biggest car, tell the funniest joke, wage the biggest war, have the sharpest suit, score the winning goal, run the fastest race, win the most prestigious award, write the best book, bed the most women, drop the sickest bar, get the most reloads. Show no emotion. Don't be soft. Be the best. Weakness need not apply.

For the individual male, this causes an instant and devastating internal flux, for the simple reason that weakness (as in vulnerability) is a prerequisite for being human. Men, just like the other 50 per cent of the human population and all other plant and animal life sharing the planet, have an automatic and necessary capacity for weakness. We can feel, we can cry, we can be flawed, we can lose. But masculinity, trampling through the room, doesn't allow this. And God forbid if you are in any way 'feminine', or gay, or introverted, or quiet, or don't particularly want to be Mr Alpha. Masculinity is a harsh and unforgiving master that will seek you out and crush you. Or shame you into crushing yourself.

There's a book everyone should read called *Incognito*, written by a neuroscientist called David Eagleman. At one point, Eagleman lists a particular set of genes that, if held, increases an individual's likelihood of committing a violent crime by 882 per cent. He goes on to state that roughly half of the human population carries these genes, including 98.4 per cent of people on Death Row in the US, underlining how dangerous these genes are. Then he drops the bomb by concluding that these genes can be summarised as the Y chromosome. And carriers are categorised as 'male'.

In this understanding, Grime is just another example of reactionary masculinity in society at large. Another context for hypermasculinity to assert itself and another trap for males to step blindly into. From the age of nil, little boys are subject to an unrelenting barrage of commands, codes and conventions, spoken and unspoken, that encourage masculine behaviour. Subsequent conformity to these codes is unsurprising, with boys doing exactly the things that society asks of men in the transition to adulthood. Be bold. Take risks. Make money. Get girls. Win acclaim. Be clever. Be strong. Be strong. Be strong.

But winning masculinity is a losing game. Because to win at masculinity you have to sacrifice humanity. The masculinity game is rigged, and everyone loses. Especially boys. And when you add black to the equation, the situation becomes even more drastic.

For young black males, the masculinity game is perilously complicated by the politics of power that contextualise blackness in our modern age. Black men are fighting generations of denigration, suspicion and disempowerment stemming back to the days of transatlantic slavery. Part of the attempt to rebalance the seesaw is a reactionary aggression, a pointed masculinity whereby black men seek empowerment through resistance. Black aggression can, in this context, be seen as protest, helping explain the normalised anti-establishmentarianism we see in some black subcultures. In the UK, Grime is a potent example of black masculinity intersecting with disaffection and self-empowerment, leaning into Eagleman's list of Y chromosome traits. Arguably, the least palatable aspects of Grime – its violence, its homophobia, misogyny, greed, criminality, latent homophobia and hypersexuality, are its most masculine – adolescent blackness seeking to win empowerment by conforming to society's warped ideals of strength. The same thing can be said of the hard-edged persona of Gangsta Rap, Grime's transatlantic, older cousin, not to mention its Millennial siblings Trap and Drill.

Grime offers a pugilistic context for the theatrics of masculinity to be played out on. If you buy into the notions of strength and invulnerability that fuel the masculinity myth, then Grime is an absolute runaway success story. It not only enables but encourages young black men to assert themselves using the most valuable currency available: masculinity – thus raising the status of the young black male to a position of social dominance and gendered empowerment. For the black British Millennial generation, Grime stars are violent examples of masculine success, triumphing over the adversity of their ancestors by projecting seemingly invulnerable macho personas. And because masculinity is one of the big myths we currently subscribe to, it's no surprise that Grime is finding popular endorsement.

But if you cast a more wary gaze over the situation, slightly more depressing conclusions are quickly reached. The macho posturing that typifies Grime becomes a sad pantomime, feeding stereotypes that little boys feel the need to play up to for survival in a hopelessly gendered world. Even more disheartening is the fact that Grime's caricatured masculinity plays into the hands of long-standing black stereotypes; that black men are all of those things that the dominant mainstream fears: intimidating, detached, criminal, tough, insensitive, unacademic. The irony is that these traits, long thought to be pollutants and threats to mainstream society, are becoming exalted within society's margins.

Listen to a Grime 2016 playlist and you'll hear the word 'man' come up, a lot. One single from Skepta's Mercury Prize-winning album is just straight up called 'Man'. It features the word 'man' 26 times. 'German Whip', the song often cited as spearheading Grime's 2014 resurgence, includes 38 instances of 'man'. However, go back to the earlier days of Grime and you get only four 'mans' in 'Wot Do U Call It?' by Wiley, in 2004. In the same year, 'Pow!', the song notorious for combusting into random acts of aggression in clubs, features only two instances of 'man'. You could argue that as the genre has evolved, pressures to man up have increased. Being a man is trendy and being macho is revered, something we've seen the very worst excesses of in the 'Alt-Right' phenomenon.

Personas are most dangerous when they are mistaken as being real, and this is where we find Grime in the early

21st century. If you hadn't already noticed, I have all sorts of feelings towards Grime that have led to me writing this book. I'm exhilarated by its energy and exuberance but frustrated by its adherence to blunt masculinity. I revel in the wit and the wordplay but worry about the misogyny. I love the casual indifference Grime takes towards the rules of decorum, but can't help but see the more insidious rules that govern its evolution. As a counterculture, Grime has huge potential to challenge the social and racial status quo. As a subculture it has the potential to advocate for marginalised, black social groups. And as a consumer culture it has the potential to sell a particular image of blackness to a waiting mainstream. But, as it transpires, complicating each of these contexts is the heavy pendant of masculinity that Grime seems under obligation to wear.

Beyond Rags and Riches: The Reductive Power of Known Narratives

There's something dangerous about mainstream thinking.

The mainstream, in its control of discourse, seems to function through aggression. It takes, dominates, appropriates, dictates and ultimately decides what Is and what Isn't, what Should and Shouldn't be. In this, non-dominant voices find themselves at the mercy of lines that have been pre-defined by society's rulers. And like all rulers, mainstream discourses tend to be rigid, brittle, inflexible and terrified of being bent out of shape.

Before I take the metaphor too far and lose everyone completely, I should explain the reasoning behind this essay's opening statement.

A short while ago, I was busy moving piles of paper from one room to the next (I call it 'tidying') when I stumbled across a copy of *ES Magazine*. A cursory flick through revealed a feature spread on Grime artists Krept and Konan. If you don't know, Krept and Konan are, to quote *ES Magazine*, 'Lords of Hiphop'. If you know a bit more, you'll be aware that they are a duo of South London-based Grime MCs who came up through a largely underground following and are now making chart hits straddling both sides of the Atlantic.

ES Magazine is a free publication distributed to commuters across London. There's nothing niche about it. For this particular publication to be featuring Krept and Konan was an exciting prospect for me. Grime is, among many things, the soundtrack of vibrant disaffection; kind of violent, energetic, playful and agitated all at once. Arguably, it's an urban-born protest genre, reaching into a long heritage of black British music. To feature in a magazine designed to distract Joe and Joanna Average on their way home from the office was, for me, intriguing.

Flick to the article in question and it was clear that Krept and Konan had 'arrived'. The article was a huge showcase of their newfound success, as marked by the glossy pictures of them in designer clothes, standing next to Rolls-Royces, posing with Rolexes and lounging in private jets. Beside a subheading that ran:

"Growing up surrounded by gang crime, rappers Krept and Konan found escape in South London's urban music scene. Now everyone from Kanye to Ed Sheeran is a fan and they're poised to break America. They tell Richard Godwin about doing time, being chauffeured by Drake and why they just want to make their mums proud."

– Richard Godwin, *ES Magazine*, 2015

And I didn't like it. But I kind of expected it.

The article is essentially a Rags to Riches story. More specifically, the exact same Rags to Riches story we have been presented with time and time again in the world of hip hop. Socially deprived, economically impoverished criminal element picks up mic and makes millions through rap. The end.

Superficially, this, like all Rags to Riches, is a tale to be celebrated. But we have to consider the context. The hip hop Rags to Riches is a mainstream endorsement couched in the politics of disempowerment. Hip hop is beleaguered by the Rags to Riches narrative. Think about it. A successful hip hop artist is almost expected to come from some kind of social deprivation, as though their salvation – and acceptance by the mainstream – is tied to their ability to overcome social and economic poverty. This is seriously reductive.

If the mainstream only accepts the success of the 'other' when that success is linked to a Rags to Riches narrative, then the Rags become overly important, and the Riches become overly valued. It is no accident that the *ES* article purports to understand Krept and Konan, but the reality is far more complex. Strictly speaking, they aren't even a hip hop act, but the article headline calls them 'Lords of Hiphop'. The mainstream brain has kicked into gear to understand, package and pigeonhole them as an understandable 'other'.

In 2015 I had the privilege to hear Breakin' Convention leader Jonzi D (@jonzid) speak about his life in hip hop at a HiphopEd seminar. He wove a rich, varied tapestry of art and culture, high and low, that went so much further than the Rags to Riches narrative. Jonzi D stated very clearly that the commercialisation of hip hop is not at the core of a culture that essentially requires no money to explore. So money cannot logically be an end goal. But, of course, Rags to Riches insists that a successful hip hop artist is one that can stand next to a Rolls-Royce in a gold watch.

Narratives are nothing new. And nothing new is known through them. In his exhaustive and excellent study of narratives *The Seven Basic Plots*, Christopher Booker explores the notion that there are a finite number of narratives that we (as a species) continue to find and recreate to make sense of our selves and our stories. This is not offensive in itself, but paired with social inequalities and power paradigms? Something very dangerous can occur.

Shortly after I presented some of these ideas at HiphopEd, Darren Chetty (@rapclassroom) leaned in to offer that these politics of narrative are exactly the focus of Chinua Achebe's classic novel *Things Fall Apart*. If you haven't read it, the novel details the life and times of a tragic protagonist, Okonkwo of the Nigerian Igbo tribe. And after chapter upon chapter exploring the intersection of generations and cultural skirmishes alongside the moral fluctuations of a seriously enigmatic tragic hero, it ends with a musing from the British Commissioner:

"One could almost write a whole chapter on him. Perhaps not a whole chapter but a reasonable paragraph, at any rate. There was so much else to include, and one must be firm in cutting out details. He had already chosen the title of the book, after much thought: The Pacification of the Primitive Tribes of the Lower Niger."

As I say, there's something dangerous about mainstream thinking. The Commissioner, in his representation of a colonial mindset, only understands what the thinks he knows of the Igbo. And of course he completely underestimates the richness and humanity of their entire culture. His casual reduction of an entire culture and one man's (unknown) story to something worthy of 'a paragraph' is at once depressing and terrifying.

The presentation of Krept and Konan as a simple example of Rags to Riches is similarly problematic. It ignores so much that it doesn't know, and worse still, fails to ask the kind of questions that might offer a new perspective to the mainstream brain. For example, one of the defining characteristics of Krept and Konan as artists is a propensity for punning and wordplay, almost of the Christmas cracker variety. Their lyrics are riddled with puns and double entendres, some quite clever, some worthy only of a groan. It was this that singled them out in the Grime scene in the first place. I find this to be a defining feature of not only their work, but many Grime artists in general, something decidedly British that has roots in variety theatre and stand-up comedy as much as in MC heritage and 'the Dozens' (the African-American art of insult-rhyming that predates rap and characterises belligerent MCing[1]).

But the mainstream lens isn't wide enough for this conversation. Anything beyond the established narrative is a distraction and therefore irrelevant. It doesn't matter that Krept and Konan might share some kind of postmodern lineage with punchline peddlers of old, because they are, quote: 'Rappers [who] found escape in South London's urban music scene.' End of.

Admittedly, there must be a responsibility for those 'in the know' to offer these new perspectives. But the marginalised voice is rarely given an opportunity to be heard, listened to and acknowledged. This conflict comes into sharp relief with regard to formal education.

During my presentation, I played an impromptu game of 'Cohort Bingo' with the audience. Call out as many cohorts as you can, as discussed by educators in educational institutions. They came thick and fast. EAL. Black Boys. G&T. Looked After. SEN. Radicalised. At Risk. NEET. White Working Class. Etc. Schools, by identifying these cohorts, are at risk of doing to children (and by extension whole sections of society) what the Commissioner does to Okwonko in the final paragraph of *Things Fall Apart*. As soon as we decide what someone's narrative is, we deny them the right to shape their own story. And worse still, we ignore their story as it might have existed so far. I'm finding that education is treated as one big Rags to Riches arc, with students too often treated as broken Cinderellas in need of the Prince Charming of assessment to get them to the university ball. As a result, we focus too intently on the Rags element. Can they read? Are they poor? Are they naughty? Are they clever? Do people like them get the Riches we want them to get? All of this stops us from asking more profound questions about their journey.

This cohort-heavy approach to education comes from a fascination with the other, and fascination and fear are close bedfellows. The Commissioner's motivation is to pacify 'primitive tribes' largely because colonists are always afraid of the unknown. The dark threat needs to be tamed, right? And the first step towards that taming is understanding. But this, I feel, is the most dangerous step, when 'understanding' is a construct built upon ideological foundations.

For these reasons, educationalists have a serious responsibility to challenge mainstream discourses in exactly the same way that Chinua Achebe challenged race/ colonial discourses in his novel (and how I should probably challenge *ES Magazine* by writing an essay on the British wit of Grime). Until then, we will be at the mercy of accepted narratives that shackle far more than they liberate.

1. According to Professor Mona Lisa Saloy, 'the Dozens' originates from the slave trade in New Orleans, where deformed or disfigured slaves were sold in job lots of a dozen or so. To be sold in this way, in these circumstances, was seen as the least respectable of existences and thus a sharp insult. This would eventually evolve into the art of insulting mothers, which is a universally recognised means of hurting someone's feelings. When I was growing up, saying "your mum" was justification enough for physical violence, or tears, or both.

'Black mates and white niggas': On whiteness in Grime

'Oliver's Army' is a wonderfully melodic pop-rock song written by Elvis Costello in the late 1970s. Among other things, 'Oliver's Army' contains a politically charged reference to a "white nigger". Conceptually, 'Oliver's Army' makes a bold statement about the exploitation of the working-classes in the perpetration of violence during times of social unrest. 'White nigger' is a racial slur that, in the context of this song, is used very cynically and very sarcastically to refer to a white underclass. In 20th Century Northern Ireland, the term was often levelled at Irish Catholics, who were routinely viewed as a social sub-class and were subjugated as a result. Popular modern folklore states that mid-20th century Britain saw the proliferation of signs stipulating 'No Irish, no blacks, no dogs.'

In 2011, 32 years after the release of 'Oliver's Army', Skepta made a reference "white niggas"[1] in his song 'You Know Me' from the album Blacklisted.

In this context, "white niggas" refers to white people who have an affiliation to black culture deep enough to align them with the black community. The lyric above might confirm a Millennial reconciliation of racial tensions among class lines, if Skepta, representing a black subcultural elite, is embracing the archetypal "white nigger" as black enough to chill out with. The lyric might also be confirmation of black superiority in modern urban youth culture, if we accept that Skepta (representing the fully matured, black, Millennial male) has the authority to accept white niggers into the black circle.

There is very little controversy surrounding Skepta's use of "white niggas", compared to the ongoing debate and censorship surrounding Elvis Costello's "white nigger" line. The simple reason for this is that 'Oliver's Army' has an automatically white, mainstream audience, who would be uncomfortable with the implicit accusation of racism and/or insensitivity towards the working-classes. Hence the reason that 'Oliver's Army' has been the subject of an ongoing censorship debate for over 30 years.

There are a few reasons why very little has been said

about Skepta's "white niggas", in no particular order:

1. Grime in 2017 is not as popular as pop-rock was in 1979, so is under far less scrutiny.

2. Skepta's line hints at racial unity, and for the liberal mainstream, racial unity will never be controversial or undesirable.

3. Skepta is black. Historically, black people have often been viewed as socially inferior to white people.

4. In the mainstream gaze, underprivileged white people are aligned with racial sub-classes.

In 2015, four years after the release of 'You Know Me', Skepta confirmed his vision of racial unity in the first verse from 'Man', featured in *Konnichiwa*. The repetition of "came a long way" underlines how this is first and foremost a story of socioeconomic empowerment. Skepta's white niggas/black mates shoutout is a celebration of the rise of the underclass. He's not talking about the unification of black people and white people in general; he's talking about the unification of black people and white niggas specifically.

Or is he? In the context of Grime being an increasingly

commodifiable artefact of black coolness, it is actually a great accolade for a white person to be called a "nigga". Far from upsetting the social order or threatening white privilege, Skepta's "white nigga" shoutout suggests that white people can indeed be as cool as black people, in an urban, Millennial context. It's a moment of inclusion that, consciously or not, invites whiteness to enter Grime's inner circle.

Grime's relationship with whiteness is complicated. The mainstream audience that Grime has courted since its earliest days is essentially a white audience, invited to buy into Grime. Meanwhile there is a minority of white Grime insiders who, unlike the white mainstream audience, exist in the same sociocultural sphere as Grime's black populace. You might include in this category MCs such as Devlin, Scratchy, K Koke, Little Dee, Shifty and Potter Payper, who talk the talk and seem authentically 'street' enough to get an automatic pass.

This group is typified largely by the 'crazy white boy' stereotype alluded neatly to by Bonkaz in 'Flex Level 100', in which he shouts out his white boys that are nutters. The ones with the cutters. All you got to do is look at them and they wanna fight. But they're his brothers like his brothers: he's colourblind. Like Skepta, Bonkaz circles an arm around his white 'brothers'. Unlike Skepta, he highlights their aggressiveness and propensity for violence, asking us to equate violence with realness and realness with blackness.

Then you get the likes of Charlie Sloth and Tim Westwood, industry devotees who have supported the scene from the underground up and continue to draw deep-seated respect and acknowledgment from within Grime's community.[2] Logan Sama is an interesting case study here. Much revered in the scene and often cited as being something of a Grime stalwart, he's also gone on record as saying that Grime 'isn't a black artform'[3]. His refusal to accept Grime as the black British artefact it undoubtedly is raises questions over the mainstream's relationship with black culture.

At this point, the notion of the dominant mainstream finding credibility in black subcultures becomes sharply relevant. In Grime, these tensions are relatively new and unresolved, highlighted by the mainstream's growing interest in a culture that inherently explores the frustrations of black marginalisation.

It's interesting that relatively few Grime artists tackle black/white relations in a more direct sense. One reason is that Grime has not (yet) been plagued with the kind of cultural appropriation that might provoke black artists. At this stage in its evolution, Grime is still wed to authenticity, meaning that the first big test for a Grime artist is to be 'real', meaning that white Grime participants tend to be authentically street, meaning that we haven't got a lot of middle-class white boys pretending to be roadman MCs. Yet. But if Grime goes the same way as the Blues, or Rock and Roll, or Jazz, or hip hop, we might start seeing white facsimiles of the real thing, which would absolutely provoke black criticism (much like acts such as Elvis Presley and the Rolling Stones are often criticised for appropriating Rock and Roll and subsequently turning it into a white genre).

As we leave the pioneering phase of Grime's early years and enter a new era of mass popularisation, new challenges will arise concerning ownership and authenticity. I would argue that Grime is in a good position to weather these storms because of one simple fact: being a Grime MC is hard. The craft behind acceptable Grime lyricism cannot be faked or fabricated, meaning that the best MCs, for now, will always be the ones who have been doing it for a while. It is no accident that Grime is populated by artists who have been developing their art for literally years now, while even the most recent stars have grown up spitting bars – entirely outside of the mainstream. Race is not an automatic concern here, but the important coincidence is that all those Grime stars who we accept as authentic, or 'real', just happen to be predominantly non-white, shifting the racial power balance, perhaps, against mainstream norms.

1. There's huge debate as to the differences and purposes of the words 'nigger', (-er) and 'nigga', (-a). For the sake of simplicity, I refer to 'nigga' as a colloquialism used by black people (usually from the United States) in reference to other black people.

2. Charlie Sloth won the Best DJ at the 2015 Rated Awards. Tim Westwood picked up the Legacy Award at the 2016 Rated Awards. Logan Sama has picked up more Grime awards than there are punctuation marks in this footnote.

3. Taken from a tweet dated 20th December 2015.

Hiphop Education in the UK: Making the Case for Grime

A few years back, I took my then Year 8 tutor group through a Hiphop Education curriculum, in which we explored the history of hip hop, wider cultural resonances, and various related socioeconomic issues including class, feminism, gender norms, and capitalism. The project began with a DJ workshop and culminated in a series of essays, each on a question chosen by individual students. During this time we analysed rap lyrics, watched documentary footage, had debates on key issues and even carried out primary research at a local shopping centre. They then had to take their essays and flip them into five-minute 'Ignite' speeches, which were delivered in a whole school event.

Before this process began, I knew my students had an

interest in hip hop. Even the most casual chats about music confirmed what we already know: that hip hop culture (and its various offshoots) is now the dominant youth culture. This, of course, is by no means a simple cause for celebration. The hypercapitalist direction mainstream hip hop has moved in has almost divorced it from social responsibility, as my class discussed after reading ?uestlove's excellent essay series: 'How Hip Hop Failed Black America'. And it is no accident that five of my 13 students chose to focus their essays upon issues surrounding gender and the subjugation of women in modern society. They were ready to interrogate rather than celebrate.

Which I found interesting. After the initial novelty of playing with records had waned, it became apparent that these kids (aged 12/13) very much saw the hip hop I presented to them as something historic. Their expertise and relatedness to the culture as they understand it is tied, inextricably, to the context through which they discovered it.

Sounds obvious, but it raises a (much debated) point about not just hip hop in education but cultural studies overall: to what extent should a student's experience of a culture steer their exploration of that culture's 'official' history? I felt as though I was giving my class an opportunity to deepen their understanding of a culture that pervades their exploratory adolescent years, but, to be honest, I'm not sure how much they cared.

Skip forward a few months to the end of term, and the obligatory classroom party, complete with Doritos, Haribo, party games and YouTube playlists. After minor protestations I quickly capitulated and let the kids take the helm. And weren't the results interesting.

As expected, the playlist was entirely black music, with no exception, again confirming what we already know: that black culture (and its various offshoots) is the dominant youth culture. Slightly more interesting was the provenance of music being chosen. It was about 90% (give or take) British. And almost entirely current. And of this selection, exclusively Grime.

I find this telling. My class (predominantly Muslim, about 60% UK-born, speaking a total of 11 different languages, spanning Eastern Europe, Asia and West and North Africa) are in firm agreement that the hottest music out is Grime music. With unfettered access to the latest hits via YouTube, these nascent adolescents seem to be pinning their flags to artists who speak in the language of their streets.

I recently read an excellent and inspiring piece on 'Why I Love Grime' by Musa Okwonga (@okwonga), which reminded me what excites me so much about Grime. Its energy, wit, underlying social protest and unashamed

Britishness make it a compelling incarnation of UK youth culture. Not to mention the fact that Grime has evolved from a very British heritage (Ragga, Dancehall, Jungle, Garage), harking back to the Windrush diaspora and proliferation of black Britain via the West African migration of the 1970s. So when I find myself shouting the lyrics to 'Man Don't Care' by Jme alongside three or four overexcited 12-year-olds, maybe I'm actually celebrating black UK music and black UK culture.

I teach in London, so it's not surprising that my students revere Grime, which is a cultural London success story. Their eyes light up with Grime. They love references to a world they can see on the way home from school, spoken in the same language they learn in the playgrounds of their schools. The glitz of American hip hop seems to be too glitzy, too glamorous, too foreign, too mainstream. Your Kanyes and Jay Zs are of an older generation, music for their parents maybe. And even your Drakes and Big Seans (who the kids love) seem to be a few years stale. While the neo-conscious movement, led by your Kendrick Lamars and J Coles, just doesn't seem to register at all. The average UK teenage music fan is looking for something closer to home, and what's closer to home than Grime?

Grime was never supposed to make it into the mainstream; it's the sound of disaffected youth shouting discontent in shows of lyricism that mean nothing to anyone other than themselves. And yet the culture has created a generation of icons who are part of the establishment, whether the establishment accepts it or not.

So perhaps when we discuss Hiphop Education in the UK we really need to discuss Grime as the embodiment of hip hop's basic tenets in this country. Perhaps Grime is the UK's incarnation of hip hop, as socially and politically important as any other musical movement. And perhaps we (by which I mean educators) should therefore give it the respect it's already earned from today's youth.

Keeping it real: Grime and extra-ordinary style

The intersection of democratisation and style is nothing new in pop culture. Hip hop veered away from its early tendencies towards theatricality with the onset of street wear, thanks largely to LL Cool J and Run-D.M.C. Punk invited devotees to undergo a DIY image makeover with gel and safety pins. Grunge asked you to stop washing your clothes. And so on. For as long as pop culture can be said to have existed as part of wider youth culture, it has drifted towards verisimilitude on its way to authenticity.

Grime has followed this pattern. The tracksuit has completely democratised a Grime look, offering an attainable level of 'roadman chic' for anyone within reasonable geographic access to a Sports Direct. Grime's elite look very much of the same universe as their fans, decked out in the attire of real mandem from actual ends, and it shares an image code with any other genre borne of real people; whereby authenticity is sacrosanct. Yes, there are overblown egos and outrageous levels of bravado, but never at the expense of verisimilitude.

Arguably, this downplayed image confirms the fact that Grime's biggest stage is the street. The theatricality of stadium-level pop would be out of place in Grime, despite Grime's newfound ability to fill stadiums. The genre has evolved beyond the confines of basement clashes and pirate radio, but its dependency on street credibility stifles moves towards opulence. Even the relative low key ballerism of UK Garage has been shunned by Grime, with bait designer labels having largely been binned in favour of sportswear. UK Garage was about club attire, characterised by the no hat no trainers or you're not coming in dress code. In the early Noughties, Grime threw such codes away and replaced them with a moneyed anti-glamour. Akademiks tracksuits, Avirex leather jackets, exclusive trainers, exclusive fitted caps, all with an import US aesthetic. It's telling that Skepta, finally in a position to lean into the opulence of high fashion, brags about donning a black tracksuit (brand unspecified) in the front row of a fashion show. Understated style is in, gaudy fashions, out.

That said, it's not that simple. Grime's preoccupation with wealth acquisition alongside street authenticity creates a contradiction that we see in the evolution of roadman chic. Streetwear, by association with success and wealth, is suddenly not the clothing of poverty. It's gained a status and allure of its own, an exclusivity. This stems back to the early days of hip hop, in which emerging artists of the mid '80s turned street brands into hot commodities. Think LL Cool J and Kangol, Run-D.M.C and Adidas. Being cool meant spending money on streetwear and dressing it up with flashy accessories like gold chains. Grime is in a similar place now – looking expensive and street at the same time, nodding to its heritage as a street culture whilst acknowledging its inherent aspiration. Compare this to US hip hop, which (due largely to the fashionista inclinations of Kanye West) has branched off into experimental regions of fashion and style (one potent example being the gender-bending provocations of Young Thug, alongside the high-end couture adopted by A$AP Rocky).

Historically, hip hop's image has occupied a full spectrum of looks and styles, from the flamboyant furs and leathers of post-Disco to the street-ready understatement of the early '80s, to the shiny empowerment of gold chains, to Afrocentric hippy chic, to workwear brand worship, to high-end couture, and everything in between. Grime, far more adolescent in its journey, has gone from tracksuit to tracksuit mafia.

For the majority of its existence, Grime has existed in a largely ineccentric state. Its realness has been rooted in a level of ordinariness, despite the quirkiness of Grime's early personalities. The flamboyance that might widen the narrow field of blackness that Grime operates in is absent, despite the fact that Afro-Caribbean cultures are often typified by a flamboyant stylishness designed to showcase wealth and status. The conflict between street authenticity and showy displays of wealth and self is captured in Grime's dress code. Look like the road, but splash out on the brands. Don't be too showy, but let everyone know you're here.

This is what makes modern Grime's rejection of high-end fashion (and subsequent adoption of affordable sportswear) so excitingly democratising – it suggests that, finally, the black male doesn't need to show off to empower himself. In a sense, a big shield has been dropped, because Grime's empowerment is coming from places other than image. Stormzy can rep himself and his culture as internationally successful in a simple Adidias tracksuit. Chipmunk can talk about wearing his own clothes, referring to his own line of branded casualwear. The days of warbling about Moschino or creating odes to European fashion houses are definitely over.

Acknowledgements

Before we start, hold tight every artist featured in this book. Your music has accompanied me on a journey from adolescence to adulthood, music that has excited and inspired and challenged a generation. Your music has changed things, you've changed things, and hopefully *Hold Tight* helps celebrate this fact. Salute.

First up, a special thanks to Mum, who always knew I would write a book, and Dad, who got me my first library card. If they hadn't taken the plunge and relocated from Ghana to the UK, I never would have been in the position to commentate on what it means grow up black and British.

Hold tight my excellent big sisters Phyllis and Marcia, whose record collections, cassette tapes and vicariously experienced social lives gave me early insights into black culture beyond the walls of our home in Brixton.

Next, hold tight my wife and best friend Sophie, who, on a long walk along the River Humber, helped me come up with a title for this book while Finlay dozed in his pram. Or was with me when I came up with it. Or came up with it herself, if you care to believe her version of events. Either way, thanks for letting me sit and tap into an iPad for hours on end when I probably should have been cooking. Also, hold tight Finlay, who sat patiently on my knee and listened to first draft chapters over breakfast on a Sunday. A special thanks to my in-laws, Maurice and Dorthe. I wrote most of the first draft in the warmth of their home in East Yorkshire, with space to think, delicious meals to eat, and unlimited Wi-fi to mercilessly use.

Hold tight everyone involved in UK HiphopEd, a remarkable group of individuals whose criticality and shared enthusiasm has pushed me to organise my own thoughts on music, politics and culture. A namecheck and huge debt of gratitude goes to Darren, through who I made first contact with Influx Press. His continued friendship and support has helped bring this book to fruition. And hold tight my students. You've kept me thinking and kept me sharp.

In this digital age it would be rude not to thank every single person who has tweeted, retweeted, liked, posted and favourited anything to do with *Hold Tight* on social media. Your support has been instrumental in getting this book out of my iPad and into the world. You know who you are. Big thanks.

And finally, hold tight Kit Caless, one of the first people to really 'get' *Hold Tight* and the best editor I could have hoped for. There's no way this book would be in the shape it's in without his guidance, support, critique and endless enthusiasm. Thanks Kit, thanks everyone at Influx Press, and apologies for all the footnotes. I know they were a nightmare to typeset.

Jeffrey Boakye, London 2017

About the author

Jeffrey Boakye is a writer, teacher and music enthusiast from Brixton, now living and working in East London. He has a particular interest in issues surrounding education, race and popular culture. Jeffrey has taught English in London secondary schools and 6th Form colleges since 2007. *Hold Tight* is his first book.

www.holdtightbook.com
@unseenflirt

photo by Victoria Bottomley

This book was made possible thanks to the generous support of the following people:

Kate ryan

Rachel Mann

Lou Champion

Rageshri Chetty

Desmond Jones

Matt Petzny

Eileen Donoghue

Annette Russell

Emily Reynolds

Christopher Prendergast

Tess Atkinson

John Eden

Papa Akuffo

Josh Kirkwood

Stefan Fuchs

Scott Manley Hadley

Lucy Moffatt

Aditi Gupta

Daniel Carpenter

Guy Shennan

Harry Baker

Dave Hostick

Shane Rector

Sarah Wray

Jonathan Gibbs

A.Schilz

Phil Chang

James Gooch

Darren Chetty

Jacques Testard

Max Porter

Will Ashon

Influx Press Lifetime Supporters - Thank you forever!

Barbara Richards

Bob West

Influx Press is an independent publisher in London
committed to publishing innovative and challenging fiction
and creative non-fiction from across the UK and beyond.
Formed in 2012, we have published titles ranging from
award-nominated debuts and site-specific anthologies to
squatting memoirs and radical poetry.

www.influxpress.com
@Influxpress